Paper Money
Collapse

Paper Money Collapse

The Folly of Elastic Money and the Coming Monetary Breakdown

Detlev S. Schlichter

WILEY

John Wiley & Sons, Inc.

Published by John Wiley & Sons, Inc., Hoboken, New Jersey.

Published simultaneously in Canada.

For general information on our other products and services or for technical support, please contact our Customer Care Department within the United States at (800) 762-2974, outside the United States at (317) 572-3993, or fax (317) 572-4002.

Wiley also publishes its books in a variety of electronic formats. Some content that appears in print may not be available in electronic books. For more information about Wiley products, visit our web site at www.wiley.com.

Library of Congress Cataloging-in-Publication Data:
Schlichter, Detlev S., 1964–
    Paper money collapse : the folly of elastic money and the coming monetary breakdown / Detlev S. Schlichter.
        p. cm.
    Includes index.
    ISBN 978-1-118-09575-1 (hardback); ISBN 978-1-118-12780-3 (ebk);
    ISBN 978-1-118-12781-0 (ebk); ISBN 978-1-118-12782-7 (ebk)
    1. Paper money.   2. Money supply.   3. Currency question.   4. Credit.   I. Title.
    HG353.S35 2011
    332.4'044–dc22

                                                                                            2011015865

Printed in the United States of America

10 9 8 7 6 5 4 3 2 1

To my parents.

The evils of this deluge of paper money are not to be removed until our citizens are generally and radically instructed in their cause and consequences, and silence by their authority the interested clamors and sophistry of speculating, shaving, and banking institutions. Till then, we must be content to return quo ad hoc to the savage state, to recur to barter in the exchange of our property for want of a stable common means of value, that now in use being less fixed than the beads and wampum of the Indian, and to deliver up our citizens, their property and their labor, passive victims to the swindling tricks of bankers and mountebankers.

—Thomas Jefferson to John Adams, March 1819

Contents

Foreword

D etlev Schlichter is not alone when he writes that "the individual decision maker is a driver of economics," but he is clearly in the minority.

That fact stands to reason. During our most recent fiscal upheaval in the United States, one out of every two economists with a job drew his or her paycheck from a government institution.

Your economist, your elected official, and your friendly neighborhood bureaucrat, your policy wonk, even your favorite mainstream journalist believes that you—the individual—couldn't possibly know what you are doing with your own money.

They think you're too stupid to make the right decision when faced with choices in the marketplace.

If you agree with them, then I'd respectfully advise you to stop reading this book right now. You'll only take offense at what Mr. Shlichter has to say.

If, on the other hand, you believe that you're capable of making a decision on your own . . . if you believe you can safely buy the goods and services *you* need when *you* need (or want) them, then you'll take to and welcome Detlev Schlichter right way.

"The market economy is not a superior organism that has its own goals," Detlev writes. The economy does not exist to "generate positive GDP" for the good of a nation. Nor are we servants subject to the whim of the formerly omnipotent "Masters of the Universe" who run trading desks on Wall Street.

We use money—our money—to make transactions. That's it. All else that follows in this book begins from that simple starting point.

Once you ignore the conventional method of viewing the economy . . . of measuring growth and counting the unemployed . . . a funny thing happens. "Failure" and "bankruptcy" become natural events even in a smoothly sailing economy. Viewed in the proper context, "failure" is not something to be prevented. It's a vital tool on the way to success. We all make mistakes from time to time. There's no one to blame. But there is a heck of a lot to be learned. . . .

Blasphemy, for some. A Godsend, for others. I'll assume that for the time being, you're in the latter group.

In this book, Detlev doesn't hold back any punches in exposing the flawed concept that is paper currency. I admire his rigor and his clarity as he straddles this unpleasant territory with ease. He doesn't name names. He doesn't bog us down in details. He doesn't enlist GDP charts from across the globe. He leaves the devilish details to other books boasting "financial crisis" in their title.

He's not likely to land an HBO contract for the effort, so I suggest you get started with Chapter 1.

If you're of the right mind-set, it will be a pleasant experience, I assure you. Detlev's crisp algebraic prose recalls one of the best systematic financial writers to tackle banking: Murray Rothbard, whose *Mystery of Banking* offers a succinct account of what began ailing the economy in the 20th century.

Unlike Rothbard, however, Detlev is a practitioner, not an academic.

You have to admire a man from the City who worked 19 years in high-yield income, pursuing the oft-maligned Austrian economics as a hobby at night.

Sometime in 2007, the hobby became his vocation. But his first real wakeup call came in 1998, post–ruble collapse and LTCM failure. The events themselves weren't the problem, Detlev began to see. How government-supported firms reacted *is;* they got bailed out and sought to manipulate interest rates.

A decade on . . . and "bailouts" have become the norm. Bankers expect them. And place their bets accordingly. The implied "safety net" has become the Achilles heel of the entire system.

Today, even as economists, the media, and policy makers search for causes of the financial collapse in 2008 (and dream up new regulations to "prevent it from ever happening again"), those same imbalances and misperceptions are building to yet another climax.

In this fine work Mr. Schlichter bursts through the notion that "everybody" benefits from stimulus. And he sets out to dethrone the economic God of the twentieth century: monetary policy.

Not only is the present monetary system less than optimal, but it's also unsustainable. To put it in the words of the technically literate: GIGO—garbage in, garbage out. The current monetary system can lead only to volatile and unsustainable economies. Forget all the macroeconomic theories and statistical validations for this or that political motive.

In a chapter in my own *Demise of the Dollar,* I had an eye-opening, if entertaining, experience documenting what I ultimately entitled the "Short Unhappy Episodes in Monetary History." The first "modern" experiment with paper money occurred in ninth-century China. After several hundred years, the Chinese gave up on "flying money" because it proved to be subject to political whims and gave rise to disastrous inflation in consumer prices.

And yet, even with numerous examples at our fingertips—France in 1717–1720 under John Law's scheme, in which paper money lost 90 percent of its value; Abe Lincoln's financing of the Civil War sparking inflation, which turned Americans off paper money until 1913; Peron's Argentinean coup in 1943, which ushered in paper and destroyed gold reserves; and, of course, Weimar-era hyperinflation—we have engaged in another experiment with paper money, this time on an epic scale.

The litany of crises we've endured from LTCM through the mortgage meltdown share DNA. Other books seeking to understand the precarious situation we find ourselves in miss the single root: our ongoing currency crisis. Digging deep, Detlev explains why we're in more danger today than ever before. That fact alone should place this book at the top of the pile at your bedside you've been "meaning to read."

Detlev's work could be *the* resource for a new generation of young economists.

As the next crises unfold, we'll need a hearty breed ready to pick apart the myths and turn toward clear, basic tenets of what keeps money working for us—not politicians and central bankers.

Addison Wiggin
Author of *Demise of the Dollar*,
Empire of Debt, and
Financial Reckoning Day
Executive Producer, *I.O.U.S.A.*
Publisher, Agora Financial, LLC

Acknowledgments

My first debt is to Debra Englander, my editor at John Wiley & Sons, who saw potential in my manuscript and whose support was crucial in bringing this book to publication.

Many thanks to Jennifer MacDonald, Melissa Lopez, and the rest of the team at John Wiley & Sons, who did an excellent job correcting my mistakes, suggesting improvements, and molding the overall text into publishable shape.

A group of friends read early versions of my manuscript, and I am very grateful for their constructive feedback, comments, opinions, ideas, and recommendations. They may not agree with all of my conclusions—and the responsibility for the final text remains entirely mine—yet all their contributions were extremely valuable. They are Paul Fitter, David Goldstone, Ken Leech, Bruno Noble, Andres Sanchez-Balcazar, and Dr. Holger Schmieding.

I would like to extend a special thank you to Dr. Reinhard Fuerstenberg. Reinhard was a most indispensable sounding board for

all my ideas and theories from the start. He has one of the most percep-
tive minds I ever came across, and he remains one of the few truly
independent thinkers. I am fortunate to have him as a friend.

Last but not least, I would like to thank my wife and children for
understanding and supporting my decision to leave the relative security
of a well-paying finance job for the uncertainty of being an untested
and, at the time, unpublished writer.

Paper Money
Collapse

Prologue

The Brave New World of Elastic Money

M ankind has used money for more than 2500 years. For most of history money has been a commodity and most frequently gold or silver. There are good reasons why gold and silver have held this unique position. These precious metals possess some characteristics that make them particularly useful as monetary commodities, such as homogeneity, durability, divisibility, and, last but not least, relative scarcity. The supply of these metals is essentially fixed. Gold and silver can be mined but only at considerable expense. Their supply cannot be expanded quickly and inexpensively. For most societies throughout history, the supply of money was therefore essentially inelastic.

Today we use money that is very different from what the vast majority of our ancestors used. Today, money is nowhere a commodity.

It is everywhere an irredeemable piece of paper that is not backed by anything. We live in a world of "paper money," although most money today doesn't even exist in the form of paper. It exists only as a book entry. It is electronic money or computer money. It is immaterial money. And because it is immaterial money, its supply is entirely elastic. Those who have the privilege of legally creating this money can produce unlimited quantities of it. Although human history and the growth of civilizations unfolded for the most part on the basis of inelastic money, modern societies around the world are now running their economies on perfectly elastic money.

Most people today do not appear to see a problem with this. Paper money works. We are all users of money, which today means users of paper money. Every day others in society accept our paper money (or electronic money) in exchange for goods and services. It evidently does not matter that these paper tickets, or bits on a computer hard drive, are not backed by anything of real value or anything material at all. They constitute money because others accept them as money. Indeed, the idea that we could conduct economic transactions with heavy gold or silver coins appears atavistic. Today, we pay increasingly electronically or by using our credit cards. Obviously, this constitutes progress. Nobody is surprised that money has changed so fundamentally. Compared to previous societies we are richer and economically and technically more advanced. It is no wonder that we use a different and more sophisticated monetary infrastructure.

However, this view tends to confuse innovations in payment technology with the basic construction of a monetary system. Even when money was essentially gold, people often used money substitutes for payment purposes. Private banks issued banknotes that were used by the public in lieu of physical gold because they were more convenient to handle. As long as these banknotes were backed by gold in the banks' vaults, they did not constitute paper money but were in fact commodity money. In principle, a society can use banknotes, electronic money transfers, and credit cards and still be on a strict commodity system, such as a gold standard. As long as every quantity of money is fully backed by gold or some other commodity in a vault, the supply of money is essentially inelastic and the economy on a commodity standard. The public simply uses various technological devices to transfer ownership of the gold money.

Inelastic versus Elastic

The question is not whether modern payment techniques, such as credit cards and wire transfers, constitute progress—they undoubtedly do—but whether the shift from inelastic commodity money to fully elastic immaterial money constitutes progress. Why has the world moved from inelastic to elastic money? Is this because of some overwhelming advantages? If so, what are they? Do economies function better with elastic money than with inelastic money? Can economies grow faster if the supply of money is not restricted by the scarcity of some commodity but if the supply of money can be constantly and flexibly expanded?

Probably, most people will intuitively answer the last question in the affirmative. It seems logical that a growing economy, in which constantly more goods and services are being produced and constantly more transactions occur, more of the medium of exchange is needed. A growing supply of money seems to most people to be the natural corollary of a growing economy.

As surprising as it may sound, this is not the case. A growing economy does not need a growing supply of the medium of exchange. It is indeed in the very nature of a medium of exchange that—within reasonable limits—practically any quantity of it is sufficient to accommodate any number of transactions. An economy does not need more money to produce and trade more goods and services, to increase its productivity and to generate more wealth. Only a conceptual and systematic analysis can prove this conclusively. Such an analysis will be part of this book.

But even before we conduct such an analysis it should be fairly clear that the notion that elastic money is required for a growing economy is rather unconvincing. Obviously, human societies have made great advances throughout history while using practically inelastic commodity money. The Industrial Revolution occurred in what was basically a commodity money environment. Between 1880 and 1914 most of the developed world was on what came to be called the Classical Gold

Standard. This was a time of rapidly growing international trade, of rising living standards, and stable and harmonious monetary relations between states.

Additionally, a quick look at present monetary arrangements with their fully elastic money supply reveals that a growing supply of money does not even require a corresponding growth in demand for money. Today's paper money can be created and placed with the public whether there is demand for it or not. This may affect the purchasing power of the monetary unit, but lack of demand is no obstacle to a growing supply.

Ben Bernanke, before he became chairman of the world's most powerful central bank, the U.S. Federal Reserve, expressed it with commendable clarity:

> The U.S. government has a technology, called a printing press (or, today, its electronic equivalent), that allows it to produce as many U.S. dollars as it wishes at essentially no cost. . . . We conclude that under a paper-money system, a determined government can always generate higher spending and hence positive inflation.[1]

It would be naïve to assume that today ever more money is being produced because there is growing demand from the public for it. Instead, we may reasonably ask what comes first in our economies with their perfectly elastic money: Is the constantly expanding supply of money the outcome of economic conditions, or are economic conditions the outcome of the constantly expanding supply of money?

Mr. Bernanke made the previous remarks in a speech about a specific economic scenario, namely the potential threat of deflation and how the Federal Reserve may counter such a threat. By controlling the supply of money, however, the central bank has enormous influence over the economy at any time. Central banks such as the Federal Reserve do not expand the money supply only at times of crisis. The supply of money is expanded constantly, usually in accordance with politically defined goals, such as a certain rate of economic growth, levels of unemployment, and moderate inflation. Money creation in our present financial system is not the natural outcome of the market and the spontaneous interaction of members of the public but a governmental tool for shaping the conditions of the economy. Injections of new money always change economic processes, and these money injections occur today almost continually. Sometimes the money supply is expanded faster and sometimes more slowly, but in principle, the money supply is expanded all the time. The money producers tell us that they have good reasons for this policy, but if these reasons turn out to be faulty or inadequate, the unintended consequences for society overall will be enormous.

Giving such extensive powers over the economy to political authorities would have appeared inconceivable to most previous societies. Indeed, one of the attractions of gold and silver as media of exchange throughout history was that their supply was essentially outside of political control. The fact that money today exists everywhere exclusively as a territorial monopoly of the state may tell us more about the changed attitudes of the general public toward state power than about the necessities of a modern economy.

Background on the "Reasoning"

Two of the commonly given reasons why state-controlled paper money is better than commodity money are that by controlling the money supply the central bank can provide a monetary unit of stable purchasing power as a reliable basis for economic calculation, and that the central bank can at times of crisis support the economy with extra money injections. As popular as these notions may be, both fail the test of history and theory dismally. It is simply a historic fact that commodity money has always provided a reasonably stable medium of exchange, while the entire history of state paper money has been an unmitigated disaster when judged on the basis of price level stability. Replacing inelastic commodity money with state-issued paper money has, after some time, always resulted in rising inflation. Indeed, the historical record is so unambiguous on this that any suggestion that paper money provides greater stability than commodity money borders on the ridiculous. Historically, exactly the opposite has been the case. It is equally a fact of history that at no point was paper money introduced in response to the demands of private citizens for a more stable monetary unit. History knows no incident of commodity money being replaced by a full paper money system purely on private initiative. By contrast, many states over the past 1,000 years have imposed state-issued paper money on their populations, always for the purpose of funding the government, most frequently to finance war.

It is true that commodity-money economies have a tendency to experience moderate secular deflation. In an economy in which the supply of money is essentially fixed, the production of additional goods and services must lead to lower prices over time. But this type of deflation does not pose an economic problem. Quite to the contrary, it has many advantages. The type of deflation that Mr. Bernanke, in the previous quote, promises to avoid with potentially unlimited money creation is of an entirely different nature. It is a crisis phenomenon that occurs in an economy that suffers from excessive levels of debt and inflated asset prices. Such an economy must sooner or later experience a deflationary correction. But excessive debt and asset price bubbles are inconceivable without a previous extensive credit boom, which in turn can only result from excessive money creation. Those who argue that "elastic" money is a blessing because we can counter deflation and depression overlook the overwhelming evidence that it is elastic money that is predominantly responsible for creating the dislocations in the first place that make a deflationary depression a risk.

Eminent economists explained long ago why an expanding supply of money is a source of economic disturbance. The British Classical economists of the so-called Currency School (David Ricardo, Lord Overtone, and others) demonstrated this in the middle of the nineteenth century. But it was the economists of the Austrian School of Economics, in particular Ludwig von Mises and Friedrich August von Hayek, who from 1912 to 1932 developed this insight into a complete theory of the business cycle. This theory is known today as the Austrian theory of the business cycle. Although it is probably the most compelling theory of economic fluctuations in modern times, it did not obtain a prominent place in the developing macroeconomic mainstream of the twentieth century. That mainstream was shaped by Keynesianism and later Monetarism, schools of thought that, despite their ideological differences, both embrace state-issued elastic money.

The British Currency School economists and the "Austrians" developed their theories under gold standard conditions. The elasticity of money that they were concerned with was different in certain respects from money's elasticity today. It was mainly the result of banks issuing banknotes or creating bank deposits that were not backed by physical gold, a practice that became known as fractional-reserve banking, and that was frequently encouraged by governments, mainly through their state-owned central banks. An expansion of the money supply, in this case through fractional-reserve banking, causes interest rates on the market for loans to drop and more credit to become available. This initiates an investment-led boom at first. However, overall investment activity now exceeds voluntary saving in the economy. As the Austrian economists demonstrated, the long-term consequences of an investment boom are very different depending on whether it is financed through proper saving or money printing. The mismatch between investment and saving in the latter case must ultimately transform the boom into a bust. Without the resources that only voluntary saving can make available, the new investment projects cannot be sustained. It becomes apparent that resources have been misallocated in an artificial, money-induced boom. The inevitable reallocation of resources and relative prices occurs in the following recession.

The recommendation from the British and Austrian economists was clear: If you want to avoid recessions, you must avoid artificial investment booms generated by cheap credit. Stick to a proper gold standard and restrict the practice of fractional-reserve banking! In other words, make money less elastic. Since the early part of the twentieth century, however, a very different policy has been pursued.

New Infrastructures and Policies

The U.S. Federal Reserve (Fed) is the central bank of the world's biggest economy and the provider of the world's leading paper currency. It was founded in 1913 specifically as a lender of last resort for Wall Street. Its purpose was not to restrict credit growth and the balance-sheet expansion of Wall Street banks but to encourage and support them. The Federal Reserve was instrumental in extending the credit-driven boom of the 1920s that set up the economy for the Great Depression. Many modern supporters of paper money and central banking consider the Fed's response to the crisis inadequate, as they would have liked to see a more aggressive injection of additional money. They focus their criticism on the Fed's role in crisis management but not on the Fed's role in the formation of the excesses that made a major crisis inevitable in the first place. In any case, the following decades saw further institutional changes to the monetary infrastructure designed to facilitate more money creation, to make the currency more elastic. In 1933 President Roosevelt took the United States off the gold standard domestically. A tenuous connection to gold was sustained for a few decades after World War II, but in 1971 President Nixon took the dollar off gold internationally, too. Most other currencies had already severed direct links to gold and had only maintained an indirect one through the dollar as the global reserve currency. Since 1971, the entire world has thus been on a paper money standard for the first time in history. Money can now be created out of nothing, at no cost and without limit.

When money was ultimately still gold, money-induced business cycles used to be fairly short, although still painful. The credit boom was limited by the inelasticity of bank reserves. When banks had lowered reserve ratios too much, they had to cut back on new lending, and when this occurred nobody could provide extra reserves to the banks and thereby extend the credit boom further. By the same token, nobody could soften or shorten the inevitable recession which was therefore allowed to unfold unchecked and thus cleanse the economy of the capital misallocations of the preceding boom more or less completely. All of this changed with the introduction of unlimited state paper money and lender-of-last-resort central banks. Naturally, in this new system the money supply is still expanded and interest rates are still artificially lowered to encourage extra investment. As a result, capital misallocations still accrue. Investment and saving still get out of synch, and the economy overall still becomes unbalanced. But the recessions—still needed to cleanse the economy of dislocations from the artificial booms—are now supposed to be avoided or, at a minimum, shortened through additional injections of reserve money whenever the economy rolls over. In a system of elastic money, credit cycles are being extended considerably, which means that the price distortions and resource misallocations become much bigger over time.

The inevitable consequences of the new infrastructure and policy have become ever more manifest. Since 1971 the decline in the purchasing power of pound and dollar—two of the oldest currencies in the world—has been the steepest in their long history. Debt levels have risen sharply and the financial industry has greatly expanded. As economists Carmen Reinhart and Kenneth Rogoff demonstrated in their extensive study of financial crises, the number and intensity of international banking crises has risen markedly since 1971.[2] Japan experienced an enormous money-driven housing boom in the 1980s and has still not recovered from the dislocations this created. The United States and Western Europe (with the exception of the Scandinavian countries) have, until recently, escaped major crises. This does not mean that these economies have not accumulated money-induced dislocations. In the case of the United States, in particular, it is evident that the monetary authorities simply managed to repeatedly prolong the paper credit expansion through timely rate cuts and additional money injections whenever a recession began to unfold.

The last time U.S. authorities allowed high real interest rates to cleanse the economy of the accumulated misallocations of a preceding inflationary boom was in the early 1980s. After the recession that necessarily followed, money and credit growth were, by and large, allowed to resume for the next three decades, not least because most of the monetary expansion was now channeled into financial assets and real estate. As the new money mainly lifted the prices of stocks, bonds, and increasingly houses, and as the ongoing but comparatively moderate price increases in the standard "consumption basket" were judged to be acceptable, money-fueled credit expansion was tolerated and actively supported by the central bank. Since the late 1990s the Fed has on various occasions successfully extended the credit boom: in 1998, when the collapse of the Long Term Capital Management hedge fund and the default of Russia threatened to kick off a wave of international deleveraging; toward the end of 1999, when the Fed injected substantial amounts of money prohibitively out of concern about potential computer problems related to Y2K; between 2001 and 2004, after the Enron and WorldCom corporate failures and the bursting of the NASDAQ bubble, when the Fed left interest rates at 1 percent for three years.

As one should expect, and as is now abundantly clear, the credit excesses and mispricing of assets have reached phenomenal proportions. In the 10 years to the start of the most recent crisis in 2007, bank balance sheets in the United States more than doubled, from $4.7 trillion to $10.2 trillion.[3] The Fed's M2 measure of total money supply rose over the same period from less than $4 trillion to more than $7 trillion.[4] From 1996 to 2006, total mortgage debt outstanding in the United States almost tripled, from $4.8 trillion to $13.5 trillion,[5] as house prices appreciated, in inflation-adjusted terms, three times faster as over the preceding 100 years.[6]

Why I Wrote This Book

It seems undeniable that elastic money has not brought greater stability. Regarding the stability of money's purchasing power, the historical record of paper money systems has always been exceptionally poor. But it is now becoming increasingly obvious that the global conversion to paper money has also failed to put an end to bank runs, financial crises, and economic depressions. Quite to the contrary, those crises appear to become more frequent and more severe the longer we use fully elastic money and the more the supply of immaterial money expands. Astonishingly, there is an established body of economic theory that explains with great clarity and precision why this must be the case: the Currency School of the British Classical economists and, in particular, the Austrian School of Economics. Their insights, however, remain strenuously ignored by the academic mainstream, the policy establishment, and the majority of financial market participants.

At this point a few personal notes from the author may be in order: Before I set out to write this book, I spent 19 years as an investment professional in the financial industry. This has given me extensive exposure to the intellectual frameworks and the accepted belief systems that dominate financial market debate. To make sense of what happens around us, we all need a set of theories that function as a prism through which we view, order, and try to understand the phenomena of the real world. These theories are usually not the object of inquiry themselves. They are the indispensible tools of inquiry and thus presumed to be essentially true. I found that, in financial markets, it is indeed a very limited set of theories and concepts that provide the commonly shared framework. These concepts are mainly derived from what became, in the twentieth century, the popular strands of macroeconomics, mainly Keynesianism, the Neoclassical School, and Monetarism. All of them embrace active government involvement in monetary affairs, and the willingness to challenge these doctrines is remarkably low. What increasingly amazed me over the years was the following: Although the dislocations of ongoing monetary expansion were becoming ever more palpable—the ever higher debt levels, the asset price bubbles and the widespread addiction to cheap credit—the very viability of a fully elastic paper money system itself was never seriously doubted. The idea that a system of elastic paper money is superior to a system of inelastic commodity money continues to command the status of unquestionable truth. As the dislocations and instabilities of the present system are getting bigger every year and ever harder to ignore, the mainstream still tries to explain them away by referring to unrelated external shocks, such as "excess savings" in Asia or increased international capital flows, or interprets them as the result of occasional policy mistakes, of the inappropriate handling of what is still believed to be a superior institutional framework. The question that is not being asked but should be asked is whether all the apparent problems are not due to the inherent instability of paper money. What if elastic money is always inferior to inelastic commodity money, as many eminent economists of the past asserted with apodictic certainty? This is the question I address with this book.

It is apparent that most commentators, politicians, and central bankers do not want to give up the comforting belief that the government can always fix the economy with injections of more money. They want to share Mr. Bernanke's confidence "that under a paper-money system, a determined government can always generate higher spending and hence positive inflation." This, however, may mean covering up the symptoms of the crisis and postponing it while making the underlying problems bigger. It also means that ever more money needs to be injected to buy the system time and to manufacture another round of money-induced and thus temporary growth. Ultimately, this must undermine the public's confidence in state paper money. Without this confidence, immaterial money has nothing to fall back on, nothing that gives it a backstop of real value. The endgame is not the self-sustaining growth that policy makers promise, but complete currency collapse.

We have already reached a point at which ever more extreme measures are being taken. Over the two-and-a-half years following the collapse of investment bank Lehman Brothers, the Fed expanded the part of the money supply that it controls directly—bank reserves and the monetary base—by more than $1.5 trillion, thus creating almost twice the amount of money of this type that the Fed had created in aggregate up to this point since its inception in 1913.[7] Ever larger sums of money are increasingly needed to simply keep the overstretched credit edifice from collapsing. The Fed used $1 trillion of new money to take large chunks of toxic assets that had accumulated on bank balance sheets as a result of bad lending decisions during the preceding boom onto its own balance sheet, and thereby prevent the banks from selling them into the market. The Fed declared it would use another $ 600 billion to boost the price of Treasury securities. The prices of a multitude of financial assets are thus being artificially propped up to avoid the market from revealing the lack of true private demand for them. Money printing may be costless to the Fed. Whether such a strategy is costless to society is a different question.

Is a system of elastic money superior to one of inelastic money? This was the question we started with. But as we are beginning to investigate the apparent fault lines of the elastic money system the question becomes a different one: Can a system of elastic, state-controlled paper money be made to work at all? Is the elasticity of the money supply that is the defining feature of a paper money system, not ultimately the cause of its undoing? If an expanding supply of money is always a source of disruption, if money injections always distort relative prices and disorient market participants, then every paper money system must sooner or later encounter business cycles. If the paper money producer, ultimately always the state via its central bank, counters the recession with additional money production, this must compound the underlying dislocations. The central bank can, for some time at least, engineer recoveries but only at the cost of additional misallocations of capital and mispricing of resources. Stronger growth through money injections is always transitory. The next recession will definitely be more severe than the previous one. The only lasting effect will be that the economy becomes progressively more unbalanced and ever more dependent on artificially cheap credit and ever more new money.

■ ■ ■

This process cannot last forever. What is the endgame?

In 1949, Ludwig von Mises stated:

> *There is no means of avoiding the final collapse of a boom brought about by credit expansion. The alternative is only whether the crisis should come sooner as the result of a voluntary abandonment of further credit expansion, or later as a final and total catastrophe of the currency system involved.*[8]

All paper money systems in history have failed. Either the paper money experiment was abandoned voluntarily by a return to inelastic commodity money, or involuntarily and violently, by the inflationary meltdown of the monetary unit with dramatic consequences for economy and society. No complete paper money system has survived.

China invented paper, ink, and printing and was thus the first to experiment with paper money, probably as early as around AD 1000.[9] Between the early twelfth and the late fifteenth centuries, extensive paper money systems were developed under the Southern Song Dynasty (1127–1279), the Jin Dynasty (1115–1234), the Yuan Dynasty (1271–1368), and the early period of the Ming Dynasty (1368–1644). In all cases, state paper money was issued to raise revenues for the state. After some time, all dynasties experienced inflation and, indeed, progressively rising inflation until their paper monies became worthless. This coincided with the collapse of the respective dynasties or their demise through conquest. Only the Ming Dynasty escaped this fate via a timely return to commodity money. After 1500 no paper money was used in China. It was reintroduced in the nineteenth and twentieth century as part of Westernization.

The early Chinese experience was repeated with remarkable regularity in the Western world. Failed paper money regimes include the ones in Massachusetts and other North American colonies from 1690 to 1764, France from 1716 to 1720, the North American colonies again around the time of the American War of Independence, from 1775 to 1781, France again from 1790 to 1803, and Germany from 1914 to 1923. The twentieth century was the century of state power, of totalitarian regimes, of socialism, communism, and fascism, and two world wars. It was also the century that was ideologically most opposed to commodity money and most willing to entrust control over money to a "determined government." Not surprisingly, it is the century with the most currency disasters. Economic statisticians define a hyperinflation as a monthly rise in consumer prices of 50 percent or more. On this definition, the twentieth century witnessed 29 hyperinflations.[10]

Currencies like the North American continentals, the French assignats, and the German reichsmarks have come and gone. Pound and dollar have survived and are now the oldest currencies in use, but this is because for most of their history they simply represented specific units of an underlying inelastic commodity. Whenever they were taken "off gold" or "off silver"—the pound, for example, during the Napoleonic Wars or the dollar during the American Civil War—they also experienced rising inflation. Their demise was averted only by a timely return to inflexible commodity money.

The history of paper money systems is a legacy of failure. Without exception paper money systems have, after a while, led to economic volatility, financial instability, and rising inflation. If a return to inelastic commodity money was not achieved in time, the currency collapsed, an event that was invariably accompanied by social unrest and economic hardship. But no matter how devastating the historical record, the paper money idea is always revived. It has resurfaced most spectacularly toward the end of the twentieth century.

■   ■   ■

This book investigates the feasibility of paper money systems. It aims to show conclusively that an economy cannot be stable if it uses a form of money the supply of which is flexible and, on trend, expanding. Injections of new money always distort market prices, disorient market participants, and lead to misallocations of resources. Money is never neutral. It can never just be an economic fertilizer that stimulates every kind of economic activity without altering economic structures.

The mainstream view today is that a zone of harmless money production exists. Therefore, if money creation is handled astutely by the central bank, society can reap the benefits of lower interest rates and cheap credit without suffering the disadvantages of economic instability and inflation. This book argues that this view is wrong. Every form of money injection will lead to disruptions. Additional growth as a result of money injections is always bought at the price of underlying dislocations that must disrupt the economy later. This is true even if the money injections occur at times of low or even negative inflation or at times of recession.

Elastic money is superfluous, disruptive, destabilizing, and dangerous. It must over time, result in growing imbalances and economic disintegration to which the proprietor of the money franchise—the state—will respond with ever larger money injections. When the public realizes that a progressively more unbalanced economy is only made to appear stable with the temporary fix of more money, it will withdraw its support for the state's immaterial monetary unit. A paper money system, such as ours today, is not only suboptimal; it is unsustainable. And the endgame may be closer than many think.

Such a drastic statement can, of course, not be based purely on the historical record, no matter how strongly supportive the experiences with paper money are of the case we are making here. History can only ever tell us what happened, never what must happen. Our case has to be built on theory. And here, we can construct our argument with considerable help from some of the greatest minds in economic science, from the great British Classical economists to Menger, Mises, and Hayek of the Austrian School of Economics. One social scientist will be of particular importance: Ludwig von Mises, whose seminal work on money and business cycles forms the basis of much of our theoretical argument. To a considerable degree our job will be to make Mises' contributions relevant for our present monetary infrastructure and to use his insights to expose the widespread misconceptions of today's mainstream. We will start our theoretical analysis with some basic premises that the reader, as a user of money, can easily test for himself or herself. All other insights will be arrived at through careful logical deduction. Only through such a process can we reach universally valid conclusions. This process also allows readers who have no background in economics to follow our argument.

This Book's Setup

This book is divided into five parts. Part One establishes some basic facts about the origin and purpose of money and money's unique characteristics, in particular as they relate to demand for money. We will see how changes in the demand for money are satisfied in a system with commodity money of essentially fixed supply. We will also elaborate the key procedures behind fractional-reserve banking and see that this practice did not originate from additional demand for money and that it is indeed unrelated to changes in money demand.

Part Two is in many ways the core of this book. By way of a theoretical analysis that starts with very simple models of money injections and, step by step, takes us to more complex and realistic models of money injections, we will show that money injections must always disrupt the economy. Today's mainstream view is that money injections lift "spending" and "inflation." We will see that this is basically correct, at least in the short run. But we will also see that every injection of new money must have many more sinister effects, in particular on relative prices and resource allocation. The widespread idea that controlled and moderate money injections can be harmless and even beneficial will be refuted.

Part Three addresses some common fallacies about price level stability as an indicator of monetary stability and as a goal for monetary policy. We will see that the notion that elastic paper money can be made to be stable in terms of its purchasing power is theoretically flawed and impossible to realize in practice.

Part Four provides a brief history of paper money systems. This section illustrates that paper money systems were always introduced by state authority and with the aim to finance government expenditure, most frequently to fund wars. All paper money systems have experienced rising inflation and financial instability, frequently leading to currency collapse.

Part Five deals with the approaching demise of the present paper money system. This part starts by identifying the main beneficiaries of this system and continues with an analysis of the intellectual foundations on which present arrangements and present policy rest. The belief in the feasibility and desirability of state-controlled elastic money is so widespread and deeply ingrained today that the policy response to growing money-induced imbalances will not only be inappropriate, but it also will be counterproductive and ultimately accelerate the disintegration of the present system. We will see how this process will most likely unfold. This is, by definition, the most speculative part of our analysis, although the number of possible endgames is decidedly limited.

That the present system must end, like all preceding paper money systems ended, is without question, and it looks increasingly likely that it will end badly. There are only two options. Either societies abandon the concept of unlimited money from nothing, allow the full and undoubtedly painful liquidation of previous capital misallocations and return to inflexible commodity money, as has been done many times in the past, or we will experience a catastrophe in form of a complete collapse of our monetary system as has also happened many times before. Sadly, the latter scenario appears much more likely at present. We are likely to witness ever more aggressive money injections by the central banks in order to keep interest rates and risk premiums at artificially low levels, to keep the overstretched credit edifice from collapsing and to sustain the mirage of solvency of state and banks. When the public finally grasps the full implication of this, confidence in the system will evaporate quickly. The endgame will be high inflation and total currency collapse.

A Note on Pronouns in the Text

In order to illustrate fundamental economic relationships, we will have to use certain archetypes, such as the consumer, the saver, the entrepreneur, the investor, and the money producer. This raises the issue of pronouns. I decided against alternating between "he" and "she" or "him" and "her" and against writing "he or she" or "him or her" and will simply use "he, him, himself." This is simply for ease of reading and is meant to be nonexclusive.

Part One

THE BASICS OF MONEY

Chapter 1

The Fundamentals of Money and Money Demand

Money is the medium of exchange. Money is useful only if there is exchange, and exchange is possible only if property or, more precisely, private property exists.[1] In a communist commonwealth, where every resource is owned and allocated by the state, there would be no place for money. In contrast, capitalism can be defined as "a social system based on the explicit recognition of private property and of nonaggressive, contractual exchanges between private property owners."[2] In such a system money will quickly become indispensable.

Of course, private property owners can exchange property without the help of money. But in such a barter economy people cannot realize the full benefits of trade because transactions are possible only whenever both parties want precisely what the other party has to offer. Person A will sell his good "p" to person B only if whatever B has to offer in exchange, let us say good "q," is precisely what A wants. The same is naturally true for person B. If one of the two parties has nothing to offer that the other party has use for, then the trade will not take place. Economists call this condition "double coincidence of wants," and it severely restricts the number of transactions that will occur in a barter economy. An additional impediment to trade is that many goods are indivisible. Double coincidence of wants and limited divisibility hamper not only the exchange of physical goods for other physical goods but also the exchange of services. Despite these inevitable drawbacks of a barter economy, the exchange of goods and services started most certainly on such a limited scale with people exchanging what both parties to the trade found immediately useful.

It was inevitable that over time certain goods came to be accepted in exchange not because they were themselves of direct use to the recipient but because they could easily be traded again with someone else for other goods or services. These goods could be cloth, beads, wheat, or precious metals. Whatever they were, they acquired a special place in the universe of traded goods in that they became the most marketable, and thus could help facilitate more transactions. Now person B can buy product "p" from person A, although A has no use for B's product "q." B can instead sell "q" to C, D, or E, accept the medium of exchange from them as payment, and use that to buy "p" from A. Person A will accept the medium of exchange in the knowledge that others will also accept it in exchange for goods and services.[3]

Thus, no more than rational self-interest on the part of trading individuals is required to explain the emergence of media of exchange.[4] It is in the interest of everybody who wants to participate in the free, voluntary, and mutually beneficial exchange of goods and services to use media of exchange. Indeed, it is in the interest of everybody to ultimately use only one good as medium of exchange, the most fungible good, and that good is called "money."

The Origin and Purpose of Money

Money is not the creation of the state. It is not the result of acts of legislation and its emergence did not require a society-wide agreement of any sort. Money came into existence because the individuals who wanted to trade found a medium of exchange immediately useful. And the more people began to use the same medium of exchange, the more useful it became to them.[5]

Money is a social institution that came about spontaneously. Other such institutions are the concepts of private ownership and of clearly delineated property and the rules and standards according to which property titles can be transferred. All these institutions came into being because people saw the immediate benefit from extended human cooperation, of cooperation that goes beyond the immediate family or clan. Such cooperation allows an extended division of labor that enhances the supply of goods and services for everyone who participates in it. Such wider human cooperation requires markets; it requires trade and thus private property and money. It is my impression that today many people would argue that we need a state, that is, a territorial monopolist of legalized coercion and compulsion, to provide society with money, to protect property, and to establish the laws and regulations to allow for peaceful exchange. Their assumption seems to be that without the state there would be no money, no laws, and no rules of exchange, and no respect for private property. This is, in my view, a misrepresentation of the historical record and a misunderstanding of the essential power of voluntary cooperation of self-interested individuals as explained by the science of economics.

Not only does the existence of money not require a state organization to issue it, but it is also inconceivable that money could have come into existence by any authority (or, for that matter, any private person or institution) declaring its unilaterally issued paper tickets money.[6] That money does exist in this form today is obvious. Yet, as the Austrian economist Carl Menger showed more than one hundred years ago, money could have come into existence only as a commodity.[7] For something to be used, for the very first time, as a medium of exchange, a point of reference is needed as to what its value in exchange for other goods and services is at that moment. It must have already acquired some value before it is used as money for the first time. That value can only be its use-value as a commodity, as a useful good in its own right. But once a commodity has become an established medium of exchange, its value will no longer be determined by its use-value as a commodity alone but also, and ultimately predominantly, by the demand for its services as money. But only something that has already established a market value as a commodity can make the transition to being a medium of exchange.

Which commodity was used was up to the trading public. Not any good was equally useful as money, of course. Certain goods have a superior marketability than other goods. As previously mentioned, it is no surprise that throughout the ages and through all cultures, whenever people were left to their own devices and free to choose which good should be used as money, they most always came to use precious metals, in particular gold and silver, as these two possessed the qualities that were ideal for a medium of exchange: durability, portability, recognizability, divisibility, homogeneity, and, last but not least, scarcity.[8] Indeed, the very rigidity of their supply made them attractive. The fact that nobody could produce them at will made them eligible. They could be mined, of course, but that took time and involved considerable cost. And their essentially fixed supply contrasted with the inherently flexible supply of the goods and services for which money was being exchanged, thus ensuring that exchange-relationships were not further complicated by a volatile money supply.

To the extent that a good begins to function as money, its value is no longer determined alone by any specific use-value that the money commodity may otherwise have but also by its monetary exchange-value, by its function as facilitator of trade. When gold and silver became media of exchange their market value was no longer determined solely by their original use-value as metals in industrial production or as jewelry. Now people had demand for gold and silver as monetary assets. This additional demand, and any changes in this demand, naturally affected the prices of these metals. When the demand for money went up, the prices of gold and silver went up, assuming that all else remained unchanged; and when the demand for money fell, the prices of gold and silver fell, again assuming that all else remained the same. Gold and silver acquired an additional element of value independent of their use-value, and that was their pure exchange value as media of exchange.

Once a commodity is accepted as a medium of exchange, its usefulness as a medium of exchange cannot be enhanced by additional creation of this good. The serviceability of money is not increased by a bigger supply. Other goods deliver a more satisfying service to the public if their supply is increased. More cars can transport more people; more TV sets can entertain more people; more bread can feed more people. These things are goods because they have use-value, they can directly satisfy the needs of their owners. This holds likewise for the means of production, such as tools, plants, and machinery. Although they do not satisfy the needs of consumers directly, their usefulness lies in their ability to help in the production of goods and services that will ultimately satisfy the needs of consumers.

However, to the extent that a good is used as money, its usefulness does not lie in any ability it may have to meet any needs directly but lies exclusively in its marketability, in its general acceptance as a medium of exchange. Its value to its owner lies in its exchange value, not its use-value. Money is valued because of what you can buy with it. If an individual has more money, that individual can buy more goods and services from the producers of goods and services. But if society overall has more money, meaning that society has a bigger quantity of the money substance, society is not richer. It has more of the medium with which to exchange things but it has not more things to exchange. The exchange-value, the purchasing power of every unit of the money commodity or money substance, will be different but this is unrelated to society's overall wealth, meaning the overall quantity of goods and services. It follows from this that—outside of the extreme cases of acute scarcity or abundance of the monetary asset—any amount of the good money is optimal. Any quantity of the money commodity or money substance will be sufficient to allow the money commodity to fulfill all functions of a medium of exchange.[9]

To illustrate this important point, let us revisit the community of A, B, C, D, and E that we met earlier in this chapter when demonstrating the benefits of money. Let us assume this community uses gold as a medium of exchange and the available supply of gold and the various preferences of the trading individuals result in an exchange-relationship of 1/10th of an ounce of gold for 1 unit of A's product "p" and 1 unit of B's product "q." Person A is willing to sell his product "p" to person B and accept 1/10th of an ounce of gold in return for it. Person B has acquired the gold by selling his product "q" to another member of the community. Person A can equally use the gold to buy goods and services from C, D, or E. The benefit that this community derives from using the available amount of gold as a medium of exchange is the same as if the community had a smaller or larger supply of the precious metal at its disposal. Let us assume that the supply of gold was smaller and that the exchange ratio would turn out to be 1/20th of an ounce of gold for 1 unit of "p" or "q". Or, we could imagine a third scenario, in which the community had a much larger quantity of gold and the exchange ratio would be, let us say, 1/5th of an ounce of gold for 1 unit of "p" or "q". Obviously, with different overall quantities of gold being available, not only would the exchange relationship between gold and the products "p" and "q" be different, but also would the exchange relationships between gold and any other tradable good and service.

If the amount of the medium of exchange that is available to the community is different, it follows naturally that the purchasing power of each unit of the medium of exchange is different. However, this does not—and, logically, cannot—affect the usefulness of the medium of exchange. The benefit that society derives from using gold as a medium of exchange is identical in every one of these cases. As gold functions as a medium of exchange and does not deliver use-value but only facilitates trade, the size of its available supply is entirely immaterial. Once a good is used as money, practically any amount of that good is optimal for fulfilling all the functions that a medium of exchange can fulfill. As long as the good in question has all the attributes listed here and is therefore the most fungible good and widely accepted, nothing stands in the way of it delivering all the services that a medium of exchange can ever deliver. All the benefits that society can derive from using a medium of exchange can be derived from any amount of the medium of exchange.[10,11]

The goods gold and silver fulfilled two functions, one as industrial commodities and items of jewelry, the other as media of exchange. If we consider only the former, then more gold and silver means more industrial commodities and more beautiful things that fulfill our desire for decoration and beauty. In this respect, more gold and silver means more wealth. But if we consider only gold and silver's role as media of exchange, then an increase in the supply of gold or of silver does not enhance their serviceability as money and does not enhance overall wealth. To the extent that a society uses its gold and silver exclusively as money, this society is not richer if it has more gold and silver.

Today, money is simply a piece of paper with numbers printed on it. Whether a pile of banknotes adding up to ten thousand dollars is a lot of money or not depends entirely on what you can buy with it. When there was a much smaller quantity of dollar banknotes, or book entry claims to dollar banknotes, circulating in the U.S. economy, ten thousand dollars could buy you more goods and services than today. The exchange value of money is different—its purchasing power is different—if the supply of money is different. This is true for any type of money. But this is all. The U.S. economy does not work any better or any worse if the overall supply of what is used as money, whether it is gold, silver, or specific paper tickets, is larger or smaller. This is the logical consequence of money having pure exchange-value and no direct use-value. Societies that have more goods and services are richer. Societies that have more "paper money" or book-entry money are not richer. Societies that have more commodity money are richer only to the degree that the monetary commodity can be reemployed as an industrial commodity or as an item of jewelry. To the extent that the monetary commodity is used as money, society is not richer if it has more of it at its disposal.

The Demand for Money

An important concept that leads to much confusion and misunderstanding is the concept of the demand for money. How much of the monetary asset is desired?

Demand for money is not demand for wealth. In colloquial speech it is often assumed that everybody wants more money, that the demand for money is therefore limitless. But what people mean by this is the demand for wealth, for control over goods and services, but not demand for the medium of exchange as such. Money has no direct use-value. Goods and services have use-value. Thus, nobody would want to hold all his wealth all the time in the form of money. He would at least have to exchange some of his money for food, clothes, and accommodation, thus converting some of his money-holdings into goods that have use-value. And even a person who has sufficient wealth to acquire all the consumption goods that he presently desires would probably not hold the remaining wealth entirely in the form of money but invest it in debt or equity claims or other investment goods.

The monetary asset has important disadvantages to other goods and services and claims to goods and services. It neither satisfies needs directly as consumption goods do, nor does it help produce consumption goods in the future as investment goods do. Holding the monetary asset thus involves opportunity costs. The one essential advantage that the monetary asset has over all other goods and services is its general acceptance in return for goods and services. Like no other asset, it can be exchanged for any other good or service instantly and with no or minimal transaction costs. This marketability gives its owner a flexibility that no other good can provide. The demand for money is demand for readily usable purchasing power. People have demand for money because they want to be ready to trade. The demand for money can also be called the demand for cash holdings although the term *demand for money* will be used here. It is that part of a person's overall possessions that is most readily exchangeable for goods and services on the market.

It is the uncertainty and unpredictability of life that causes people to hold the monetary asset. People hold some of their wealth in money because they want to have the flexibility to engage in exchange transactions quickly and spontaneously. The relationship between the demand for money and the number and volume of overall transactions, however, is tenuous. We can illustrate this with the following thought experiment:

If we imagine for a moment an economy in a state of equilibrium, or, as the economist Ludwig von Mises, whose work we will come across many times in the course of our investigation, put it, an "evenly rotating economy," an economy in which the same procedures and activities unfold with unvarying regularity again and again and in which therefore every transaction is completely predictable, there would be no need for anybody to hold money.[12] Everybody could precisely match the time and the size of their outlays with the time and the size of their incoming revenues. Excess income could always be fully invested. In a world of no uncertainty, there would still be transactions but no need to hold a monetary asset. Everybody simply needed an accounting unit but nobody had any actual demand for money holdings. Of course, such an economy is pure fantasy. It is entirely a theoretical construct that helps the economist mentally isolate, analyze, and describe certain procedures. It could never exist in the real world. The mental construct of the evenly rotating economy is, within limits, useful for economic science. But these models struggle to account for the demand for money, which is a phenomenon of the real world of uncertainty and unpredictability.

How much of the monetary asset anybody wants to hold is ultimately subjective but it is clear that it depends crucially on the purchasing power of the monetary unit. In our example above of a community of A, B, C, D, and E, how many ounces of gold a person will want to hold as his cash balance will be different in each scenario. If the community has relatively large quantities of gold available for use as money then the purchasing power of each unit of gold will be—all else being equal—relatively low. Let us assume that exchange relationships determined by market exchange come out at 1/5th of an ounce of gold for one unit of "p" or "q". In this scenario the same person will want to hold more gold than if the community overall had relatively small quantities of gold and the purchasing power of each unit was relatively high (for example 1/20th of an ounce of gold buys one unit of "p" or "q"). The purchasing power of each ounce of gold is different in the two scenarios. Therefore, the flexibility that each ounce of gold provides as a medium of exchange to its owner is different. As demand for money is demand for readily exercisable spending power, a person with an unchanging demand for money will hold different quantities of the monetary unit if money's purchasing power is different.

The same applies to fiat money. Nobody has demand for a specific quantity of banknotes or a specific number of coins, just as under a gold standard nobody has demand for a specific amount of gold. Demand for money is always demand for readily exercisable purchasing power. It is purchasing power that one demands, not the money substance as such, whatever it happens to be. It follows that every quantity of the monetary asset is sufficient. Different quantities of the monetary asset only mean that different exchange ratios to goods and services develop, that the monetary unit's purchasing power is a different one. And it is purchasing power that we demand when we demand money.

Naturally, every person has it in his power to adjust holdings of the monetary asset precisely according to personal preferences. Of course, a person's overall wealth sets a limit to how much of the monetary asset the person can own. Also, every person must have a bare minimum of nonmonetary goods to stay alive (food, shelter). But within these limits every person can hold exactly the amount of money he wants to hold. If a person wants to hold more money, he can sell assets or reduce money spending. If a person wants to hold less money, he can spend the money on goods and services. It would be absurd to make the claim that a person really wanted to hold less money but cannot reduce his money holdings. If nobody in the economy accepted the surplus money in exchange for goods and services, then this form of money would have ceased to function as money. After all, general acceptance is what makes money money. By the same token, no person could claim to want to hold more of his wealth in the form of money but be unable to exchange his other possessions for money. In that case, one would have to question if the person's other possessions were not worthless and if the person already held his entire wealth in the form of money. Because of the high marketability of the monetary asset, which is the precondition for its function as money, every person holds exactly the quantity of money that the person desires to hold.

But what if everybody in society wanted to increase money holdings? Would that not require somebody to come up with a plan to produce money? The answer is no.

The demand for money can always be satisfied by a change in money's price, meaning its purchasing power. If people have a higher demand for money, they will sell goods and services to raise their money holdings. This is, as we have seen, what every single individual does in order to raise money holdings. If the desire for higher money balances is widespread or, as we may assume to make the point very clear, if everybody wanted higher money holdings, everybody would start selling goods and services or reduce money-spending on goods and services. As a result, the money prices of goods and services would fall and the purchasing power of the monetary unit would rise. But the rise in money's purchasing power is precisely what will satisfy the additional demand for money. This process will last until people are again happy with the quantity of money they hold. The increased demand for money is increased demand for purchasing power in the form of money, and this demand will be fully met by a fall in money prices, meaning the rise in the purchasing power of every unit of money.

The key difference between money and all other goods and services is again that money has only exchange value and not use-value. If demand increases for any other good, somebody has to produce more of that good for this demand to be satisfied. Additional demand for TV sets and cars can be met only by producing additional TV sets and cars because only additional units of these goods can satisfy additional demand for their services. Demand for cars and TV sets is demand for the use-value that these goods provide. Money, however, does not need a producer. Every amount of money is optimal. If the public wants to hold more money, nobody has to produce more money. As money has exchange value, the extra demand for money is synonymous with extra demand for money exchange value and can be met instantly by a drop in prices, that is, a rise in the purchasing power of the monetary unit. By selling goods and services in order to raise money balances, as all people do who want to raise their individual money balances, the community collectively exerts downward pressure on prices and the resulting drop in prices is in itself sufficient to satisfy the increased demand for money. No new money needs to be produced to meet additional demand for money. Conversely, if the demand for money declines, people will "sell" money holdings for goods and services. The result will be a rise in the money prices of goods and services, meaning a drop in the purchasing power of money. This is the unique feature of a medium of exchange. Demand for and supply of money are coordinated by changes in purchasing power, not by adjustments to the physical supply of monetary units. Just like all individuals can hold, at every point in time, exactly the money purchasing power they desire simply by buying or selling goods and services, so the economic agents in aggregate can hold, at every point in time, exactly the money purchasing power they desire simply by selling or buying goods and services and thereby adjusting the purchasing power of the existing stock of money.

Here is another way of looking at this specific feature of money: It is a fact of history that fundamentally different substances have functioned as money. Nobody will deny that gold and silver functioned as money, and nobody can deny that, today, pieces of worthless paper and even electronic book-entry claims to such pieces of paper function as money. What made these substances "money" was evidently their acceptance in voluntary exchange for goods and services rather than any ability of these substances to satisfy needs directly. But if money is money only because it is generally accepted as money in exchange for goods and services that have use-value, then its value must be pure exchange-value. Once we agree on this point, all the conclusions of this chapter follow logically: Once a good is established as money, no additional quantities of this good are needed. The performance of an economy is independent of the supply of money. Within reasonable limits, any quantity of money is. optimal. Money production is redundant. Supply of and demand for money can always be brought in line by changes in money's purchasing power. Society overall and every individual in society can satisfy their demand for the monetary asset without the help of ongoing money production.

These conclusions are necessarily true. The reader can check them for himself. As a user of money the reader will know why he holds money and what determines the amount of money he wants to hold at any point in time. We all hold cash balances because we want to be ready to trade. If we did not value the flexibility, the readiness of instantly engaging in economic transactions with others, we could as well put all our wealth in consumption goods that satisfy our needs or in investment goods that generate returns and that deliver more consumption goods to us in the future. Holding cash involves opportunity costs. We hold money balances only to the extent that we value the flexibility that they give us higher than the additional things we could enjoy if we spent the money. How high we value that flexibility is subjective. It varies from person to person and for the same person will change from time to time, depending on personal circumstances. What drives the desire for flexibility does not have to concern us here. But whatever our desire for "spending flexibility" is, how this translates into demand for a specific quantity of money naturally depends on the purchasing power of the monetary unit. Demand for money is therefore demand for purchasing power in the form of money. It follows that changes in money demand can always be met by changes in money's purchasing power.

This explains why societies can function and grow with inelastic commodity money. Inelasticity of supply is no hindrance for a commodity to be used as money. Or to put it differently, there is no basis for the widespread belief that somebody has to meet the growing demand for money in a growing economy—or in an economy that may for other reasons have a growing demand for money—by creating more of the money substance. This fallacy is based on an inappropriate transfer of the laws of supply and demand from the sphere of goods that are demanded for their use-value to the sphere of money, which is demanded only for its exchange-value.

The Functions of Money

The skeptical reader may at this point still raise the following objections: First, the case is built on money's function as the medium of exchange, but standard economic textbooks also ascribe other functions to money, such as a store of value or a unit for accounting and monetary calculation. Second, the changes in money's purchasing power that result from changes in money demand could be disruptive. These changes may help satisfy the new money demand, but they could be disruptive for money's role as a basis for economic calculation. Maybe it is better to adjust the money supply in response to changes in money demand in order to avoid constant changes in money's purchasing power and prevent the price level from becoming too volatile. Third, if money production is not needed, how can we account for the growth in banking, which for a long time has included the issuance of money substitutes and fiduciary media, the latter meaning uncovered claims to money proper that are used by the public just like money, for example demand deposits. How can we account for the fact that the world has moved away from commodity money of fixed supply to paper money of perfectly flexible supply?

These are all good and valid questions. We will address each one of them in detail in the course of our investigation. At this juncture it may just be sufficient to make the following points.

All additional functions that can be assigned to money are the result of money being the accepted medium of exchange. These functions, important as they are, are derivatives of the medium-of-exchange function. Because money is the medium of exchange and every good or service is traded against money, money prices are ideal for economic calculation. As to money being a vehicle for storing wealth, it is apparent that many other assets can be used for that purpose, too. Many of these have the additional attraction of potentially generating returns over time. Money does not offer any returns. It can therefore compete with other potential storages of wealth only by offering something special, and that is its universal acceptance in exchange for goods and services, its unique marketability, the ability to be exchanged for goods and services faster and more conveniently than any other asset. That, after all, is why it is money. So we are again back to the medium-of-exchange function of the monetary asset.

Certain financial assets, in particular high-quality debt claims that are traded in very liquid markets, can sometimes become "near-monies", and their owners may thus feel a reduced need to hold money proper. But these assets are fundamentally different in that they constitute simultaneously somebody else's liability and therefore always carry an additional risk. Proper commodity money, such as gold, but also fiat money in the form of irredeemable paper tickets, is a financial asset that is not somebody else's liability at the same time. The purchasing power of this money only varies with changes in the demand for money, and, in the case of paper money, also with changes in its inherently flexible supply. We see here that the inflexibility of supply in the case of commodity money makes it a superior store of value.

There is obviously a scenario in which money does generate a return, and that is during times of deflation. As we will see in detail later, in an economy with an unchanged money supply but rising productivity, meaning a growing supply of goods and services, prices will on trend decline. This is called secular deflation and is to be expected in a commodity money system. The purchasing power of the monetary unit appreciates over time. The money that sits in my bank account or that is in my pockets will over time buy more goods and services. It is clear that this is very different in today's world of universal paper money in which the paper money producers—the central banks—usually aim for a steady depreciation in money's purchasing power, which means they aim for constant moderate inflation. In short, the store-of-value function of money is fulfilled much better in a system of inflexible commodity money than in a paper money system. A detailed discussion of these points will have to wait until we discuss advantages and disadvantages of deflation.[13]

We will also discuss the second point regarding the potential for purchasing power stability of paper money in detail in a later chapter. But it is already apparent that this argument for the introduction of elastic money is very different from the notion that a growing money demand means somebody has to produce money and that, therefore, some form of elasticity in the money supply is required. Ongoing money production is simply not needed. It is not true that society needs a money producer who can satisfy changes in money demand and that it is probably best to entrust this role to the state. Money was not invented by the state, and it is certainly not a "natural monopoly" of the state. Money has evolved organically and spontaneously from the voluntary actions of trading individuals. Once the market has identified the suitable monetary commodity, no further production of this commodity, nor any other adjustment to its supply, is needed. Those who advocate elastic paper money cannot claim that it is necessary or inevitable. They have to show that it is superior to inelastic money. Their argument will have to be that by replacing the money of the market—a commodity of relatively inelastic supply—with elastic fiat money under the control of the state, better results can be achieved for society overall. This is obviously a much weaker argument. It relies crucially on the appropriateness of the specific theories according to which money production is beneficial. We will look at these arguments in detail later.

However, our conceptual analysis of demand for money and how it differs from demand for any other good or service has already revealed a fundamental problem for any central bank trying to avoid fluctuations in money's purchasing power that may result from changes in the demand for money. The problem is the following: If the demand for any good or service rises and all else remains the same, the price of that good or service will rise in relation to all other goods and services. At the higher price, some of the demand for this good or service will now go unfulfilled. However, the higher relative price will provide an incentive to producers or potential producers of this good or service to produce more of it and, if indeed more of that good or service is then being produced, the extra demand may finally be met and the price recede again in response to the additional supply. This is the standard process for any good that has use-value. The situation is different with money, which is demanded only for its exchange-value. In the case of the monetary asset, a rising demand for money—all else being equal—will lift money's price relative to all other goods and services. The purchasing power of the monetary unit will rise. However, at the higher "price" no demand for money goes unfulfilled. As demand for money is only demand for money purchasing power, the higher purchasing power in itself has fully satisfied the additional demand for money.

Naturally, this cannot be said of any other good, which, in order to be a good at all, has to provide use-value, which can never be satisfied simply by a change in the good's price. It follows that even a money producer who claims to print money only to satisfy any additional demand for money and to stabilize money's purchasing power, faces a fundamental problem. In order to avoid a rise in money's purchasing power, the money producer has to anticipate the rise in money demand before it articulates itself on the market. This appears to be impossible given what we said previously about everybody's ability to satisfy changes in money demand instantly. The money producer would practically have to know that money demand were about to go up before the economic agents themselves knew. Whenever the demand for money rises, economic agents will act upon this change immediately. They will instantly raise their cash holdings and exercise downward pressure on the prices of goods and services. The purchasing power of money changes practically simultaneously with the demand for money. After such a rise in money's purchasing power has occurred, the money producer knows that demand for money has gone up but his role is nevertheless redundant: The purchasing power, which he set out to stabilize, has now risen anyway and the extra demand for money is fully satisfied through this rise in money's purchasing power. In the case of goods and services that have use-value, changes in market prices communicate changes in the preferences of the consumer. In the case of money, price changes (changes in money's purchasing power) also communicate shifts in preferences but, at the same time, the price changes constitute the full satisfaction of the changed preferences. Those who advocate an elastic form of money in order to absorb sudden changes in money demand and to keep money's purchasing power stable will have to explain how the money producer is supposed to anticipate changes in money demand before they affect purchasing power. We will revisit this point when we discuss the concept of price level stabilization in full in a later chapter.[14]

The third point about the rise of banking, and fractional-reserve banking in particular, is a different one. What fractional-reserve banking is and how it came about will be explained in more detail shortly. Here, a couple of short comments may suffice.

Fractional-reserve banking introduced a degree of elasticity into the money supply even at a time when money proper was still a commodity of essentially inelastic supply. Banks created so-called fiduciary media, that is, uncovered claims to commodity money.[15] These claims could come in the form of redeemable banknotes or redeemable deposits, redeemable into gold that is. As these were not backed by the banks' physical holdings of the monetary commodity and yet were still used by the population just as if they were money proper, their effect was to—de facto—expand the supply of what was used as media of exchange in the economy. Because fractional-reserve banking developed spontaneously in the market, the advocates of elastic money will point toward its existence and longstanding history of practice as proof that the market has demand for an elastic form of money. How else could the market have supported fractional-reserve banking for so long? How can fractional-reserve banking as a market phenomenon be reconciled with our statement above that ongoing money production is not needed and that a changing money demand is satisfied fully and naturally by changes in money's purchasing power alone?

In order to answer these questions, we will first draw a number of additional conclusions directly from money's unique position as a good that is solely demanded for its exchange value. We will see that whoever manages to issue a form of elastic money and have it accepted by the public as a general medium of exchange is in a very special position. In contrast to any other producer of goods and services in the economy, the money producer enjoys the unique privilege of being able to happily ignore the level of independent demand for his product and yet produce very profitably. Because of money's unique features, money production can proceed regardless of money demand.

The Unique Position of the Paper Money Producer

For the reasons that the monetary asset is different from any other good, the position of the money producer is different from the position of the producer of any other good. If commodity money is replaced with fiat money—a condition that is now universal—ongoing money production becomes possible. The good "money" can then be produced very cheaply, even at essentially no cost. At the same time it can be "sold" and distributed more easily than any other good, as the characteristic feature of money is its unique marketability. The money producer can instantly exchange it for any other good or service. This is not the case with any other good or service produced in the economy, as these have necessarily use-value and thus meet specific needs. The salability of every other good is therefore limited by the as-yet unfulfilled demand for the specific satisfaction it provides. Money's use is universal.

Moreover, essentially any quantity of money can be produced and placed with the public. If, as we have seen, any demand for money can be satisfied by a rise in the purchasing power of the monetary unit, then it must be the case that any additional supply of money can be absorbed via a drop in the purchasing power of the monetary unit. One follows logically from the other. If unwanted amounts of money are being produced and distributed (they simply have to be spent by the money producer) they will tend to raise money-prices in the economy, meaning they will lower the purchasing power of each existing monetary unit. With money demand being unchanged but with the purchasing power of every monetary unit now being lower, the public will willingly hold larger quantities of the monetary asset. As he produces ever more money, the money producer will have to live with an ever-declining purchasing power of every additional unit of money he creates (a minor nuisance given that he can produce at almost no cost), but he will never face a situation in which unsalable amounts of the monetary asset pile up in his warehouse, a situation that is indeed a risk for every other producer in the economy.

The producers of goods that have use-value, for example cars or TV sets, may also try to place extra units by lowering their price, but such a strategy faces some tight restrictions. On the one hand, there is the higher cost of production compared to the almost costless production of paper money. On the other hand, there is the fact that even at lower prices the public will not absorb unlimited amounts of additional cars and TV sets. Given that these goods offer use-value, demand for them is satiable.

Even today's mainstream consensus does not contest that an injection of new money can always be absorbed by a rise in prices. The public can essentially be made to hold any amount of money. It is certainly the case that a fast and sharp drop in money's purchasing power can lead to whatever is being used as money lose its status as a medium of exchange completely. This is what happens in the final stages of a hyperinflation that ultimately leads to a currency's collapse. But as long as an economy's form of money maintains its status as the medium of exchange, supply and demand can always be completely aligned via a simple change in purchasing power.

Because of what makes money money, the producer of money is in a unique situation: He can produce money very profitably, and although the public has no need for any additional units of his product, as any demand for money is demand for readily exercisable purchasing power and can easily be met by automatic changes in the purchasing power of the monetary unit, the money producer can place essentially any amount of his product. The privilege of ongoing money production has no basis in any need of the capitalist economy for a money producer. Nondecaying precious metals with an essentially fixed supply are ideally suited for the role of monetary asset, and they have fulfilled that role for centuries.

The Monetary Asset versus Other Goods

This is a very important point that is crucial for a full understanding of our present system of fully flexible state paper money and extensive fractional-reserve banking. Before we analyze fractional-reserve banking in more detail in the next chapter, a couple of additional conclusions can first be drawn from the fundamental difference between the monetary asset and all other goods in an economy.

As no ongoing production of money is needed, society can derive no advantage from having competing producers of the good "money." In the case of all other goods and services, which necessarily have use-value, competition among the existing or even potential competition from new producers of goods is essential for ensuring that the optimal number of goods is produced at the lowest possible cost. In the case of the medium of exchange the optimal amount already exists, and there is no advantage to be had from lowering the cost of money production. Lowering the cost means that more money can be produced with the same or even lower factor input, but more money is of no benefit to society. More of any other good or service with use-value is a benefit to society. Thus, factors that can be allocated either to money production or the production of any other good and service should always be allocated to producing nonmoney goods and services.

The verdict is the same when it comes to choice. The advantage that competition by private producers offers in terms of delivering goods and services with different specifications that cater to individual consumer preferences and tastes does not exist when it comes to the good "money."

The competition among producers today guarantees that the consumer gets not only one type of car and one type of TV set but a whole range of cars and TV sets. It is advantageous to society that the specific preferences of its individual members can be met. But this is the case only because these goods and services have use-value. The enjoyment somebody derives from his own car or TV set would not be diminished—and potentially would be enhanced—if these items were completely customized to meet individual requirements, and if everybody else in society used types of cars and TV sets with different specifications. This is not the case with money. The good "money" is only useful for anybody because others in society use the same good as "money." A customized form of money that only one person uses is no longer money. It would no longer be a medium of exchange. It would be useless. A medium of exchange logically requires that others use the same form of money, too. Widespread use is the precondition for a good to be money. Universal use would be ideal. Customized money is a logical impossibility. Indeed, the more universally accepted a good is as money the more valuable it will be as a medium of exchange.

The standard reasons for why a competitive market of private entrepreneurs is best in providing goods and services—reducing the cost of production and thus allowing an expansion of production with an unchanged or even lower factor input; producing a greater variety of products to meet specific consumer needs; technical progress—do not apply to the good "money." The very fact that money is unchanging in terms of its supply and its specifications and widely accepted in its uniformity makes it ideal as a medium of exchange, and it explains why the precious metals gold and silver have been chosen as the ultimate form of money throughout human history.

For similar reasons, proposals for "currency competition" by private money producers do not seem convincing either. One of the most famous promotions of this idea is the one by Friedrich August von Hayek, also of the Austrian School of Economics, who suggested in his book *Denationalization of Money* (1976) that the state's territorial monopoly of money printing should be revoked and the supply of paper money opened up to the competition of private money producers.[16]

Hayek was, next to Ludwig von Mises, the other outstanding representative of the second generation of Austrian School economists. His first two publications, the German-language *Geldtheorie und Konjunkturtheorie*[17] (1929) and his first English book, *Prices and Production*[18] (1931), were contributions to the Austrian business cycle theory, which had been founded by Hayek's mentor, Ludwig von Mises, with the publication of Mises' seminal book on money in 1912. For his work,

Hayek received the Nobel Prize in Economics in 1974 (Mises having died in 1973). The work of Mises and Hayek will have a great role to play in our further analysis, although we cannot agree with Hayek on this point.

Hayek proposed competition in paper money production not because he thought that this would supply society with more and cheaper paper money but because he thought a competitive market would produce "better" paper money, meaning less inflation-prone paper money. According to Hayek, paper money competition is supposed to avoid the overproduction of money that is a constant problem if money production is under the exclusive control of the state. With competing paper monies to choose from, the public would be less exposed to the inflationary policies of a single territorial monopolist. Again, it is clear that lack of additional demand for money is no obstacle to the paper money producer if he wants to create ever more money. But in a system of multiple paper monies, if the inflationary consequences became too painful, the public could at least switch to another provider. Based on our analysis thus far, we can already identify some flaws in this proposal.

It is evident that a society with multiple media of exchange would not realize the full advantages of using money at all. The coexistence of multiple monies is suboptimal as it partially defeats the very purpose of having a medium of exchange in the first place. Money is more useful to its owner the more transactions it can facilitate instantly, without, for example, having to be exchanged for something else first. The more widely accepted a medium of exchange is, the more valuable and useful it is to its owner and thus society overall. A universally accepted medium of exchange that would facilitate any transaction between anybody in the world would, of course, be the optimal currency. This is precisely the reason why, historically, communities have exhibited a tendency toward adopting the same commodity as money. Gold was the first, and has so far been the only, practically global medium of exchange.

A look at today's world-spanning patchwork of local state paper monies can illustrate this point. From a global perspective, markets are today partially segregated by the use of multiple state fiat monies, each of which enjoys regional dominance due to the state monopoly of issuance, legal tender laws, and longstanding history of local use. This monetary arrangement reintroduces an element of barter into international market exchange, an undoubtedly suboptimal arrangement.

We can illustrate this with an example: If someone earns an income in the United Kingdom in pounds but wants to spend part of it in the United States, that person has to find somebody who wants to do exactly the opposite. Only then can the person exchange some of his pounds for dollars. We meet here again a form of "double coincidence of wants" that characterized the barter economy. This would not be necessary if both countries were on an identical commodity standard, such as a true gold standard. Pounds and dollars would simply be specific units of gold, and although each country would probably mint its own gold coins or print its own gold-backed money-certificates (banknotes that are not paper money but represent commodity money), they would essentially use the same money. Thus, money could flow from one country to another, similar to the way in which it flows today from one region to another region within the same country or currency area. This is how gold money facilitated international trade under a gold standard.

The closest the world has ever come to a global form of money, which is logically the most valuable form of money for co-operation on markets and a global division of labor, was the time of the Classical Gold Standard, from 1880 to 1914. Although these arrangements were far from ideal and certainly no blueprint for the best conceivable gold standard, the Classical Gold Standard still marked a remarkable period of strong growth, expanding global trade, and harmonious monetary relations between nations, a period abruptly brought to end by the First World War.[19]

I do not think that many people today realize that the abandonment of the international gold standard and its replacement with a multitude of local paper money franchises under state control during the twentieth century constituted economic regression and not progress. In order to deal with the inefficiency of partial barter, an active market in the various state monies has developed, the 24-hour, several-trillion-dollar-a-day foreign exchange market. Today's public seems to consider this market the epitome of international free markets and uninhibited capital flows. This is a misconception. In fact, the global foreign exchange market essentially constitutes a second-best solution by money users to cope, as best as possible, with politically motivated monetary segregation. The desire by every government to issue its own paper money for its own political reasons is a powerful hindrance to global market integration and effective division of labor and human cooperation across political borders. Today's foreign exchange market is a makeshift to minimize the cost from monetary nationalism. "The high technology and the elaborate financial instruments in the foreign exchange and money markets are no more the expression of a high degree of market development than the increased sophistication of burglar alarms is evidence of a greater degree of public security" (John Laughland).[20]

Hayek's proposal to go back to multiple monies even in societies that already benefit from the use of one unified medium of exchange would deprive money users of some essential advantages of using the established form of money and for this reason the public may simply reject it. We have already seen that money could not have come into existence by anybody issuing worthless paper tickets and declaring them money. Today essentially worthless paper tickets are accepted as money mainly because of their particular history, meaning their origin from proper commodities and the established tradition of using them in exchange. People feel comfortable using these paper tickets as they know that they enjoy wide acceptance. Against these established paper monies, new paper monies issued by new paper money producers will hardly stand a chance.

Again we see a fundamental difference between money and any good or service that has specific use-value. When governments give up monopolies in postal services, airlines or TV programming, private competitors can quickly gain a foothold, not only by finding more efficient ways of delivering a similar service but often simply by catering to individual needs and providing more tailored versions of the product or service. "One size fits all" is always an inferior approach when it comes to the provision of goods and services that deliver use-value, but in the case of money, which is demanded only for its exchange-value, "one size fits all" is indeed quite appropriate. Hayek might be mistaken when he believes that the public may want to swap a widely accepted uniform medium of exchange that suffers from a steady loss of purchasing power for a multitude of less widely accepted monies that have a more stable purchasing power.

Herein lies an important advantage for the paper money producer once his money is widely accepted as a medium of exchange: The advantages of staying with the established medium of exchange are sufficiently large and the costs of switching to a new medium of exchange sufficiently meaningful that a considerable degree of ongoing decline in the monetary unit's purchasing power can be expected to be tolerated by the public. The paper money producer can create substantial amounts of new money, slowly inject them into the economy and the public will absorb this money by raising the money prices of goods and services. History shows that established media of exchange remain in use even at relatively elevated inflation rates for a long time. Of course, the public will try to protect itself as best as possible against the negative effects of the creeping loss of purchasing power. People will try to keep their cash balances fairly low or to anticipate further price rises when setting prices in the here and now. This will inevitably accelerate the decline in the purchasing power of the monetary unit and it may ultimately lead to complete currency collapse. But it is usually only in the later stages of the inflationary process that the public shuns the established money completely and switches to other media of exchange, like foreign currencies or commodities. But for as long as monetary expansion is ongoing but not excessive, the public will usually manage to adjust its economic activities to money's declining purchasing power.

This is precisely the reason why paper money standards have again become so widely accepted. They can appear to be stable and manageable for a considerable length of time. The most visible effect of elastic money is ongoing inflation, the constant deterioration in the purchasing power of the monetary unit. But as long as the inflation rate is not intolerably high, individuals and corporations have learned to live with this particular effect of an expanding money supply. If continuous moderate inflation were the only problem of expanding money, it would be difficult to see why the present system of elastic money should be unstable and unsustainable, why it could not last forever, as is indeed the consensus expectation today.

As the present economic mainstream treats inflation not only as one of many problems associated with elastic money but as the only problem, it is maybe not surprising that paper money systems enjoy again such wide acceptance. By itself, continuous moderate inflation is not an insurmountable problem. Modern macroeconomists have even elevated moderate inflation to the status of a policy objective and the consumer price index to standard-bearer of monetary stability. However, as this book shows, changes in purchasing power are not the only effects of elastic money, and not the most sinister ones. An expanding money supply will always change relative prices, the allocation of resources, and the direction of economic activity, too. Over long periods of ongoing money injections and a constant but fairly slow decline in money's purchasing power, there must occur a continuous mispricing of assets and misallocation of resources that will lead to a progressively more unbalanced economy. These dislocations will come to the surface whenever the flow of new money slows down. If the money producer then reaccelerates money injections, these misallocations can be covered up and new dislocations can be added, at least for some time. Ultimately, the superficial stability of moderate, never-ending but easily digestible inflation will make way to a much starker and more troubling choice between either a painful deflationary recession that finally cleanses the economy of the accumulated misallocations of resources, or the progressively faster injection of ever more money that helps postpone the recession but must ultimately lead to less tolerable levels of inflation. A paper money system with moderate inflation is not as stable as it may appear for a long time—even to the paper money user. As the elasticity of the money supply is the key issue at the heart of this problem, giving the public a choice between various elastic paper monies will not avert the ultimate disaster.

The fundamental question is simply, why have a system of elastic paper money or elastic paper monies in the first place? No ongoing production of money is needed, and commodity money, which can deliver all the services money can ever deliver, comes without the systematically destabilizing properties of elastic money. It is also already denationalized money outside the control of the state. Hayek's proposal therefore appears unnecessary and impractical, and it fails to fully address the inconsistencies of any system of elastic money. It seems surprising that Hayek, in his later years, advocated competitive elastic monies and even suggested they could be better than a gold standard[21] considering his close association with Ludwig von Mises and his own contributions to Mises' cycle theory half a century earlier. The implications of that theory should be that elastic paper money is always inferior to inelastic commodity money. *Denationalization of Money* thus illustrates how far Hayek had, by 1976, abandoned some essentially Misesian concepts and had—despite the unorthodox premise of his book—moved closer to the intellectual consensus of the time. Naturally, those who remained in the Misesian tradition rejected his proposals.[22]

■ ■ ■

With the unique position of the money producer explained we now turn to the question of fractional-reserve banking. We will see that the money production of fractional-reserve banks is equally not restricted by money demand. Fractional-reserve banking is an essential compo-nent of the present paper money system. It therefore demands closer inspection.

Chapter 2

The Fundamentals of Fractional-Reserve Banking

Over the 50 years up to the onset of the recent financial crisis, industrial production in the United States increased by a factor of roughly five.[1] Over the same period the amount of dollar notes and coins in circulation increased by a factor of 26.[2] The Federal Reserve's wider aggregate of money, M2, which in addition to the currency in circulation includes various forms of bank deposits that can be used fairly easily for transactions, increased by a factor of 25.[3] That this money was not needed, we can state with complete certainty. Neither was it created in response to any autonomous demand for cash by the general public. Indeed, the demand for money did not rise anywhere near as much over this period as the supply of money did. The public could be persuaded to hold these massively inflated quantities of media of exchange only by severely diminishing the purchasing power of every single dollar. Over this period every dollar lost about 86 percent of its purchasing power if measured on the basis of consumer prices. In 2007 $1 bought about 14 percent of what it bought in the late 1950s.[4]

Why was all this money produced? The short answer is, because the money producers could do so and deemed it appropriate. This may at first appear to be a facetious answer. But if the supply of paper money is not regulated by the independent demand from money users, as we have just concluded, then it must be purely the result of the activities of the money producers. In the modern financial world the money producers are the state and the banks. In this section we will focus first on the banks.

Money Supply without Money Demand

That most money today is produced by banks can easily be ascertained by a look at Federal Reserve statistics. The Fed's money supply measure M2 includes currency in circulation, demand deposits at banks, various time deposits, money market funds, and a few other items. All of these constitute what is used as money in the United States today. Of the 8.8 trillion dollars in M2, about 915 billion are dollar notes and coins and about 700 billion are money market funds (as of December 2010). The rest are demand deposits and various time or saving deposits at banks. In short, about 80 percent of what is money according to Federal Reserve definition is a balance sheet item at a bank.

The general public does often not appreciate that this is money that the banks create. Many people still believe that all money must originate with the central bank. In a way, this is not entirely incorrect. The ownership of any paper money franchise ultimately rests with the state and therefore its central bank. However, the central bank has extended a license to the banks to also create specific forms of money. Under the guidance and with the explicit support of the central bank, the private banks are allowed—and frequently encouraged—to create book-entry money or deposit-money, the type of money that exists purely as a balance sheet item at the banks.

These balance sheet positions are regarded as a form of money because the banks promise their customers to convert them upon demand instantly, or fairly instantly, into money proper. It is this promise of instant redeemability which persuades the public to consider these deposit claims as media of exchange in their own right. That such a deposit at a bank can be used to pay someone who is also a customer of the same bank is straightforward. All the bank needs to do is transfer the book entry from one account holder to another, and the deposit can thus function as a medium of exchange. But if the bank customer wants to transact with someone who is not a customer of the same bank, he needs to convert the book entry at his bank either into physical money (notes and coins) or into a deposit at another bank, that is, the bank of the person he wants to transact with. It is therefore crucial that the bank assures its customer that the book entry constitutes indeed a claim to the instant delivery of such other forms of money. The bank promises to convert the deposit claim instantly into physical money or a transfer to another bank.

As explained previously, we have demand for money because we want to be able to engage in transactions spontaneously. Money is that part of our wealth that gives us the most flexibility and that can most easily accommodate economic transactions. To the extent that the public considers the promise of the banks to redeem instantly to be credible, the public considers bank deposits to be as good as money and thus to fully meet their demand for a fungible asset, that is, money.

However, to the extent that banks engage in fractional-reserve banking they do not have sufficient reserves to meet all the claims of their depositors. Naturally, reserves are notes and coins (physical money) in the banks' vaults and deposits that the banks hold at the central bank. These deposits can be used in interbank transactions or can be exchanged for more bank notes and coins. In a 100 percent reserve banking system, every deposit at a bank would be fully covered by a deposit at the central bank or by notes and coins in the bank's vault. In this case, every deposit could indeed be instantly redeemed, just as promised by the bank. However, fractional-reserve banking means that not all bank deposits have to be covered by reserves, by notes, coins, and central bank deposits, and that the banks can decide—within limits—what percentage is to be covered by reserves. As normally only a fraction of depositors demand redemption at any given time, the banks decide to hold reserves only for a fraction of their deposits. Consequently, the banks can create uncovered deposits and thereby add to the supply of what is considered money in the economy. They become money producers.

How can banks create these deposits? They do this simply by extending extra loans, which are usually granted by crediting the account of the borrower with deposit money. Obviously, nobody takes out a loan to keep the borrowed amount in form of a deposit at the bank. But nevertheless, some of the money that a bank lends to customers in the form of uncovered deposits can still be expected to stay at the bank as deposits, for example, whenever the person who takes out a loan uses it to pay somebody who is also a customer at the same bank. But even if the loan leads to transfers to other banks and thus to an outflow of reserve money, these other banks are likely to create new deposit money in the form of loans, too, and probably at the same time. Thus, some of the money they create will lead to simul-taneous transfers in the other direction. As these transactions can be netted at the central bank, only a limited amount of reserve money is used in the process, thus allowing the banking system in aggregate to expand the money supply. On the basis of a limited pool of reserve money, the fractional-reserve banks can create additional deposit money and can therefore fund part of their loan business through money creation.[5]

In fact, even most of the currency in circulation, that is, the physical money of notes and coins that cannot be produced by the banks, has its origin in fractional-reserve banking. This is money that the banks created first in form of deposit money but that the public then decided to exchange partially for physical notes and coins. The central bank then produced the notes and coins to allow the banks to pay out the depositors. This is one of the ways in which the central bank supports— but at times also controls—the activity of fractional-reserve banks. Of course, the notes and coins could have come into being simply by the state producing them and using them to pay its employees, its contrac-tors, welfare recipients, or others who get money from the state. Historically, this has been a common avenue for states to distribute their newly created paper money. Given the present financial infrastructure, this would be an unusual process today.

Money as an Enhancer of Lending Activity

We may now rephrase our answer to the earlier question of how all this money came into existence despite the fact that there is no independent demand for more money. The answer is that this money came into being because those in charge of the paper money franchise considered it advantageous that banks should enhance their lending activities via the creation of more deposit money. They therefore encouraged and supported money production via fractional-reserve banking, for example, by lowering the cost of borrowing reserve money from the central bank or in the interbank market. The rate at which such borrowing occurs is set administratively by the central bank. Additionally, the central bank can create extra reserve money out of thin air and give it to the banks. The central bank can do this easily by buying assets from the banks, usually government bonds, and crediting the banks' account at the central bank with new reserve money. Not only is fractional-reserve banking inherently profitable for the banks, but it also expands the amount of available credit in the economy. The by-product of this process is more money, but as long as the inevitable decline in money's purchasing power is not too steep the public can adapt to it and, so the money producer must have reasoned, everybody wins.

This brief description may appear to many readers to be a bit unfair. Is it really the case that the extent of bank lending in an economy is largely the result of administrative decisions by central bankers and of the specific strategies of fractional-reserve banks rather than the spontaneous interplay of many market participants? It is often assumed that because banks are nominally private companies that they can only create money to the extent that the market has demand for it. Private banks must respond to private demand for money. But, that this is not the case, we have already established. We have seen how demand for money is satisfied and how additional supply of money can be placed regardless of any demand. The massive expansion of the money supply in recent decades was considerably in excess of any increase in money demand. Banks are not even in the business of satisfying demand for money. Banks are in the business of taking deposits and making loans. They are operating in the credit market. The demand that is relevant to their business is the demand for loans.

Banks, as far as they engage in fractional-reserve banking, do much more than other financial intermediaries, such as fund managers, that just channel savings into investment. Banks expand the supply of what is used as money in the economy. They are money producers. Not only are the banks not restricted in this practice by any given demand for money (as we have seen above), they are not even restricted by any given level of independent loan demand. To the extent that they create extra money, they can lower interest rates, which, under normal conditions, will generate additional demand for loans. It is mainly the banks' willingness to lower their reserve ratios—to lower the ratio of reserves to instantly redeemable deposit claims—that determines how much money they can lend and at what rates. It is this activity of banks and the support of this activity from the central bank that today accounts for the majority of ongoing money production. And this is the reason why we have to take a close look at the fundamentals of fractional-reserve banking for our investigation of elastic money and its economic consequences.

From this analysis we will see that fractional-reserve banking on the scale it is practiced today is not the outcome of a free and uninhibited market but possible only with ongoing political support in a system of pure paper money with a central bank that assumes a role as lender of last resort. In such a system banks get big but cease to be independent capitalist enterprises. They become extensions of the central bank and transmitters of economic policy. In such a system, credit availability is less the result of market processes, such as the bargaining between savers and borrowers on capital markets, but predominantly the result of the central bank's monetary policy. In order to fully appreciate the essential concepts of fractional-reserve banking and all its implications, we must look at how this practice came about and what was needed to sustain and grow this practice to its current importance. We will now take a look at a stylized history of fractional-reserve banking.

The Origin and Basics of
Fractional-Reserve Banking

The first bankers were goldsmiths. When money was essentially gold or silver, goldsmiths entered the field of financial services quite naturally, first by assessing the metal content of gold or silver coins, for which they were uniquely qualified, and later by also taking gold or silver money on deposit and by lending gold and silver money against interest. A charge of misappropriation has been made against these early bankers. The basis for this allegation is the assumption that those who deposited money with them were simply seeking safekeeping services. Carrying heavy gold or silver coins around is cumbersome. It is therefore fair to assume that a natural demand for deposit and safekeeping services arose and that goldsmiths were natural providers of these services. If the contract between depositor and goldsmith/banker constituted a true deposit contract, ownership of the money continued to reside with the depositor. In principle, a depositor retains property titles to the deposited goods and can demand their instant return.

Goldsmith/bankers might already have been in the business of lending gold from their own inventory, which, of course, would be unobjectionable as they had clear ownership of this gold. But to the extent that they began to use the gold that was deposited with them under safekeeping agreements for extending loans on their own account, they committed acts of embezzlement. They used other people's property for their own gain.

Let us first assume that the original agreement between goldsmith/banker and depositor was indeed a pure safekeeping arrangement and that the banker honored this arrangement. Consequently, the gold continued to be the property of the original depositor. It remained in the vaults of the goldsmith/banker, who was not entitled to use the gold for any other purposes. He was not allowed to add it as an asset to his balance sheet, and he certainly was not allowed to lend it to a third party. Most probably, the depositor received a warehouse receipt that certified his ownership of the gold. This warehouse receipt or money certificate[6] was a paper ticket but it was not paper money in the sense that we have used the term so far. Each paper ticket was—this is our assumption—100 percent backed by physical gold and therefore represented a proper claim to commodity money. There is no reason why such a paper ticket should not be accepted as money in exchange for goods and services. The paper ticket was fully backed by gold, instantly redeemable in physical gold, and therefore practically as good as gold. It was of course more convenient to use such a paper ticket than heavy coins of precious metal for transactions. Therefore, we can assume that such money certificates were soon in use as means of payment in lieu of physical gold. Importantly, the issuance of these money certificates did not change the overall amount of money in the economy. The money supply was still determined by the available supply of the money commodity, in this case gold. The money supply did not become elastic. The circulating money certificates simply constituted an innovation in payment technology. They allowed an easier transfer of ownership in money but they did not expand the money supply.

Now let us assume that the goldsmith/banker lent half of the gold in his vault to a third party. Whether the depositor knew about it or not is a question to which we will come shortly. The goldsmith/banker might have lent the gold in one of two ways: either by handing the physical gold to the borrower or, considering that warehouse receipts on deposited gold were now in circulation and accepted as media of exchange in their own right, he might have simply printed additional warehouse receipts and lent those against interest. In one big leap he had become a fractional-reserve banker. More warehouse receipts were now in circulation that came with a promise from the banker to redeem them instantly into physical gold than there was gold in the vaults of the bankers. Now the supply of what the public uses as money had indeed expanded.

It is extremely unlikely that the banker's loan customers borrowed the money in order to keep it in cash. The predominant reason for taking out a loan (and paying interest on it) is naturally to obtain other goods and services that one urgently desires. The borrower would have spent the money on goods and services. As a result the extra money led to additional transactions and the newly printed warehouse receipts ended up in the hands of other people. Multiple claims on the same quantity of deposited gold now circulated, and whoever from the enlarged group of holders of warehouse receipts was first to demand repayment in gold would have been paid out with the money that the original bank client had deposited.[7] Once reserve ratios drop sufficiently, this is indeed very likely to be somebody who never even deposited gold in the first place but only received the warehouse receipts as payment in a commercial transaction.

What if the original depositor found out about it? Would he not be upset? Would he not consider his property rights violated? He had deposited gold for safekeeping purposes and now the banker, in order to increase his loan portfolio and to make more profit, had issued additional claims on this gold, the depositor's property. The answer is, surprisingly, not that clear-cut. Of course, the depositor might have been upset that the original contract had not been honored. But if the banker laid open his business strategy and drew up a new contract with his depositor, it is not unreasonable to assume that the depositor would consent to the practice of fractional-reserve banking. Indeed this is largely what happened historically and what led to the widespread acceptance of this practice. So why would the original depositor agree to it?

We have to remember again that money is only demanded for its exchange-value, not for any use-value that the money substance may also have. In what shape or form money comes is immaterial. Money is money as long as it is accepted as money in transactions. It follows that the original depositor had no interest in the gold as a precious metal. He did not consider it to be an item of jewelry or an industrial commodity. It was a medium of exchange. He now held a piece of paper that might or might not be backed by gold but as long as it was accepted as money in transactions it served the purpose of money. Additionally, the banker may give a fraction of his income from lending the money to a third party to the original depositor; that is, he may pay him a small amount of interest on the deposited gold.

While there is a risk that the public, upon learning that the tickets are no longer fully backed by gold, may refuse to accept them in exchange for goods and services or may not accept them at face value, this is not necessarily the case. The critics of fractional-reserve banking are obviously correct when they point out that, in legal terms, the various holders of the circulating paper tickets hold a very different asset from the original 100 percent warehouse receipt. What they hold now is in fact paper money. In order to distinguish such a medium of exchange from proper commodity money, it has been called a "fiduciary medium." We can think of it almost as a derivative of the proper commodity money.

It is of course very unlikely that the bankers could have lowered the reserve ratios very drastically over a short time. In our example, the jump from 100 percent reserves to 50 percent reserves in one big move is a bit extreme. This would probably have undermined the confidence in the new medium of exchange. But if banks lowered their reserve ratios gradually and if they managed to meet the redemption requests of anybody who requested to be paid out in gold in the meantime, a considerable injection of new money, or fiduciary media, could have been achieved.

It appears that even in the early days of banking the goldsmith/bankers openly advertised this new practice and tried to attract additional depositors by paying them interest on their deposits. British financial journalist Ellis T. Powell reports that as early as 1676 a tract by the title "The Mystery of the New-Fashioned Goldsmiths or Bankers" explained that:

> *this new practice giving hopes to everybody to make Profit of their money, until the hour they spent it, and the conveniency, as they thought, to command their money when they pleased, which they could not do when lent at interest upon personal or real Security; . . . .*[8]

This quote nicely illustrates the appeal of fractional-reserve banking to the depositor. Even before the invention of this technique, the depositor could have lent his money at interest. But that meant the money was invested, and the investment could not be liquidated easily in order to enter a new transaction. The interest income on such debt claims is in part compensation for the loss of the flexibility to transact spontaneously, which the original amount of money (in the form of money) had provided. The bank deposit appears to break down this barrier between money and debt claims. Bank deposits seem to be both at the same time. This is possible only because of the bank's promise to repay instantly in money proper (gold) and, related to this, the acceptance of these uncovered claims against the bank by the general public in lieu of money proper.

From a legal perspective it is clear that the depositor does not hold money proper any longer. Ownership of the gold has certainly passed on to the banker. The fact that interest is being paid should provide a strong indication that the depositor is no longer contracting for safe-keeping services only. If the deposit were a safekeeping arrangement, why would the banker pay the depositor and not the depositor the banker? By entering an agreement under which the bank is paying the depositor interest, the depositor must accept that the bank uses the money to earn interest in the market. Money is the medium of exchange and never generates income as such. It makes no difference whether it is under the mattress of its original owner or in the vault of the bank. *Pecunia pecuniam parere non potest,* as was already understood in ancient Rome: Money cannot beget money. In order for any income to be generated, the money has to be spent, or, as is the case here, be used as a "reserve" for the banker's issuance of fiduciary media as part of his loan business. As money's only value stems from its ability to facilitate exchange, it would be absurd to expect anybody to pay a fee for tem-porarily being in possession of somebody else's money but not being allowed to exchange it for anything else. The original owner of the money thus necessarily relinquishes ownership of the money and instead receives ownership of a debt claim drawn on the bank.

Relinquishing Ownership of Your Money to the Bank

This is an aspect of banking that is often not fully appreciated even today. Whenever we pay money into a bank we exchange ownership of money for ownership of a claim against the bank. In 1848, in a ruling by the House of Lords, Lord Cottenham, the lord chancellor, expressed this with remarkable clarity:

> *Money, when paid into a bank, ceases altogether to be the money of the principal; it is then the money of the banker, who is bound to an equivalent by paying a similar sum to that deposited with him when he is asked for it. . . . The money placed in the custody of a banker is, to all intents and purposes, the money of the banker, to do with it as he pleases; he is guilty*

of no breach of trust in employing it; he is not answerable to the principal
if he puts it into jeopardy, if he engages in a hazardous speculation; he is
not bound to keep it or deal with it as the property of his principal; but he
is, of course, answerable for the amount, because he has contracted.[9]

The differences between traditional commodity money and these
new fiduciary media is now becoming apparent: When our original
depositor had physical gold money in his possession he owned an
accepted medium of exchange that was not also somebody else's liability, and the aggregate supply of which could not be expanded in the
short term. Of course, more gold could be mined, minted, and then
brought into circulation, but as this was both time consuming and
expensive, he would not have had to fear any sudden changes in the
purchasing power of his gold money stemming from any changes in
the money supply. This does not mean that the purchasing power of
his money holdings was necessarily stable. As we have seen in our
analysis of money demand, any changes in the public's demand for
money would have resulted in changes in the purchasing power of the
monetary unit.

Now that the depositor has possession of fiduciary media, either in
form of a redeemable but uncovered banknote or a redeemable but
uncovered bank deposit, he still owns an accepted medium of exchange.
This is at least our assumption. It is a requirement for fractional-reserve
banking to work. However, this money-like asset is simultaneously
somebody else's liability, namely the liability of the banker. It also can
be created fairly easily. Its supply can expand considerably, even in the
short term. If the banker is willing to lower his reserve ratio further,
he can create more fiduciary media and distribute it through his loan
business. The purchasing power of every unit of this medium of
exchange may still change in response to changes in money demand,
just as was the case with commodity money. But in addition to this
effect, the purchasing power of the monetary unit will now also change
in response to changes in its supply.

In the process of fractional-reserve banking, money users exchange
inelastic commodity money for fiduciary media of a more elastic supply.
This requires that the money users consider fiduciary media to be sufficiently close to money proper to adequately fulfill its services, which

means the fiduciary media are accepted in place of money proper in transactions or they can be instantly converted into money proper. In using this form of medium of exchange, the money users expose themselves to new risks from the supply side of money. As more media of exchange can now be produced quickly and relatively cheaply, the risk has increased that the purchasing power of each unit of money will decline. Additionally, the money users are exposed to the risk that the bankers will issue too much fiduciary media or will suffer losses from their loan business so that other money users will question their ability to redeem in gold and refuse to accept their fiduciary media. Thus, there is no free lunch here, as the quote from 1676 might at first convey. To own money and own an interest-bearing debt-claim at the same time is still impossible. In depositing money in a bank, ownership of money has been relinquished. Money has been exchanged for a claim against a bank, which—one hopes—is almost as good as money. Inevitably it comes with extra risk, and the interest income it provides can be considered compensation for this risk.

It would not be entirely incorrect to compare fractional-reserve banking with a Ponzi scheme. The depositors pool their money holdings in a bank and get paper receipts in return. They know that the banker will issue more receipts as part of his lending business so that ultimately considerably more paper tickets circulate than is money in the bank to pay out every holder of a paper ticket. However, the banker shares some of his profit from this process of money creation with his depositors, which is their incentive to participate in the scheme. Individual depositors may from time to time take money out of the scheme, but it is important that not too many do so. Should, for whatever reason, the confidence in this scheme diminish, more holders of paper tickets will ask for redemption and try to get money proper out of the scheme before the reserve is depleted. The stability of the scheme rests entirely on the confidence of every member in its sustainability.

With the onset of fractional-reserve banking, the overall money supply indeed became elastic. Commodity money and fiduciary media, or derivative money, began to circulate next to one another. They may be different assets from a legal perspective but as fiduciary media were accepted and used by the money users just like commodity money, the supply of what was used as money in the economy did indeed expand.

The essence of the process described here is still at work in every fractional-reserve banking economy in the world today. The difference between money proper and fiduciary media has, however, largely disappeared from the discussion. In a paper money economy, no form of money, not even the reserve money that modern banks cannot produce themselves and that has replaced a metallic reserve as the basis for the fractional-reserve banking process, is backed by anything of real value or anything material at all. Thus, all types of money can today be created practically without limit.

Having gone through the basics of fractional-reserve banking we can now expose some of the fallacies about this practice that are still widespread.

Misconceptions about Fractional-Reserve Banking

First, the expansion of the money supply does not occur in response to any rise in money demand. Nobody who participates in this process, and thus makes it possible, does so out of any desire for higher cash balances. This is even the case for the borrower. Only rarely will somebody take out a loan in order to simply hold a larger cash balance. People who take out loans are usually buyers of goods and services and sellers of money. They have a high marginal demand for goods and services and a low marginal demand for money. That is precisely why they take out a loan. It is only because the borrowers desire immediate control over additional goods and services and the specific satisfaction that these goods and services provide that they are willing to endure the cost of interest payments. Conversely, the person who has an increased demand for money is a seller of goods and services in order to obtain more of the medium of exchange. This person has a high marginal demand for money, a strong desire to obtain the flexibility that only the universal medium of exchange can deliver and, consequently, a low marginal demand for goods and services, which necessarily can satisfy only specific wants. To this day, public debates on monetary matters frequently confuse the demand for money with the demand for loans. Not only are the two completely different, but they also originate from opposite desires.

In the case of the depositor and the bank, it is very clear that neither participates in the process of fractional-reserve banking to obtain higher money balances. The goal of the depositor is to combine the flexibility that only ownership of money can provide with interest income that only an investment can provide. The goal of the bank is to generate additional profits from extending loans. If any of the constituencies that enable fractional-reserve banking to proceed—the depositor, the banker, and the borrower—were to develop a higher demand for money, that is, a more urgent desire to hold assets with an immediately usable spending power, they would do what we just described. They would sell assets, either consumption goods or investment goods, or curtail their ongoing outlays on acquiring consumption goods and investment goods, and build up cash holdings. If a sufficient number of people have a higher demand for money and all else remained unchanged, the purchasing power of money would have to rise. A rising demand for money does not lead to more fractional-reserve banking. As before, it leads to downward pressure on prices or an upward pressure on the purchasing power of the monetary unit. The reverse would occur if the demand for money declined. However, the effects on money's purchasing power from the demand side are now mixed with any effects from the supply side. At times of generally falling reserve-ratios and therefore accelerated money production through fractional-reserve banking, the resulting decline in money's purchasing power could partially compensate or even fully offset the rise in money's purchasing power stemming from an autonomous rise in money demand. However, both effects are entirely independent. The extent to which fractional-reserve banking is practiced is completely unrelated to the extent that the public has a higher demand for money. Demand for money does not initiate, direct, or limit the creation of money through fractional-reserve banking. To the extent that the fractional-reserve banker is willing to lower his reserve ratio and expand the creation of money and to the extent that he can maintain the acceptance of his money as media of exchange, he is a money producer and can produce regardless of demand. He benefits fully from the privilege of producing a good that is demanded only for its exchange value.

Second, the extent to which fractional-reserve banking occurs is not the result of independent loan demand from the public, and thereby regulated by it. The demand for loans is, under normal circumstances, not independent of the level of interest rates. If a bank decides to lower its reserve ratio, all it has to do is simply lower the rates on new loans to increase the demand for loans, which it can then meet by expanding the amount of uncovered deposits. Loan demand is not an independent entity to which the banks only respond passively. All else being equal, lower rates mean higher loan demand.

We conclude that the fractional-reserve banks are constrained in their money creation neither by any independent demand for money nor by any independent demand for loans. If they are willing to lower reserve ratios and thus run a higher risk of illiquidity—that is, being unable to meet redemption requests—they can increase their loan portfolio by encouraging additional borrowing through lower rates and place the additional money in the market place independent of the state of money demand. If money demand has not risen, the additional money will be absorbed via a tendency toward higher prices, that is, a lower purchasing power of the individual monetary unit. The only constraining factor is the overall level of reserves and the risk of a bank run. If too many people ask to exchange their fiduciary media for money proper, any bank will face the risk of running out of reserves. Naturally, this risk increases if the bank is perceived to be in trouble, maybe as a result of problems in its loan portfolio. Once the soundness of a bank is questioned, outflows are likely to accelerate. In a fractional-reserve banking system, and that means today practically every banking system, every bank is potentially at risk of a bank run. A paper money system and a fractional-reserve banking system are confidence-based. Once the confidence goes, the system collapses.

This is the real regulating factor of a fractional-reserve banking system, and not demand for money or demand for loans as is often assumed. As long as confidence is maintained in the soundness of the banking system, the banks can create more money and place this money with the public. They can increase borrowing and therefore overall levels of debt.

Today extensive measures have been taken and an elaborate regulatory infrastructure has been erected to reduce the risk of bank runs and to increase the confidence of the public in the soundness of the fractional-reserve banking industry. More importantly, the abandonment of a metallic standard and the adoption of a full paper money system have removed the inelasticity of bank reserves. When banks run low on reserves and face increased outflows (naturally redemptions are no longer in gold but in physical paper money or in the form of transfers to other banks), they can get new reserves from the central bank, which has a lender-of-last-resort function and, under a paper money standard, can create as much reserve money as it wishes "at essentially no cost" (Bernanke). Naturally, in such a system the public no longer distinguishes between the various banks in respect of their reserve policies. Maintaining higher reserve ratios and thereby running a lower risk of a bank run conveys no competitive advantages on any bank. Such a financial system greatly increases the potential for money creation through fractional-reserve banking.

We thus find our initial statement confirmed. Contrary to the impression one gets from reading the financial press or following most debates on monetary economics today, the explosion in money in circulation over the past 30 to 50 years did not occur in response to a rise in money demand or loan demand. It occurred predominantly because central banks and other state institutions have actively encouraged the practice of fractional-reserve banking and have thus allowed banks to create—profitably, of course—substantial amounts of new money, place them with the public at declining levels of purchasing power, and thus increase the amount of new money-induced credit. This has certainly encouraged more borrowing and therefore higher levels of indebtedness. Whether this has overall been beneficial or detrimental to the economy and financial stability, we will discuss in detail later. What is evident already, however, is that the constantly expanding supply of money is not the outcome of economic conditions, and certainly not of independent market forces, but that the economic conditions we face today are the outcome of the constantly expanding supply of money. The expansion of the money supply is the result of monetary policy, which in turn is guided by the belief that more credit through money creation is desirable. Our society does not live with an ever-expanding supply of money because its individual members need more money or demand more money but because the money producers decide to supply it. This can be because it is profitable to them or, if we are willing to be more charitable in our assessment of motives, they believe it is good for the overall economy. Whatever the reason, the supply of money is not regulated by market forces, such as the interplay of cost of production and consumer demand that operates in the markets for all other goods and services. Once paper money has been established, the production can proceed practically without cost and without regard for money demand.

The Stability of Fractional-Reserve Banking

It is evident that the practice of fractional-reserve banking involves risks to the banks. Fractional-reserve banks issue claims against themselves that they know they are unable to meet. Every fractional-reserve bank is at risk of bankruptcy if too many depositors ask for their money back. Their solvency thus depends on accurately predicting the probability that a larger than usual amount of these claims could be presented at the same time.

It is not unreasonable to assume that over time banks will learn to manage this risk, to get a handle on the frequency of redemption requests and work out some sort of stable reserve ratio. Once such a stable reserve ratio has established itself, the process of money creation will obviously have come to an end, at least if the amount of reserve money does not change again. There will then be more money in circulation, in the wider sense of the term—that is, including fiduciary media—than in a system with 100 percent reserve banking. However, this new and larger supply of money would again be fixed. In order to create again more fiduciary media, the banks would need additional reserves. Under a pure gold standard this would be possible only to the extent that more gold gets mined and is brought into circulation as money. This process is, crucially, out of the control of the banks and the central bank. Once a stable and, from the point of view of the banks, sustainable reserve ratio has established itself, the money supply is no longer determined by bank policy or the central bank's monetary policy. The process of adding money to the system would have stopped and we would be back to a system of essentially inelastic money.[10] The notion that fractional-reserve banking means ongoing issuance of ever more new money is fallacious. Money creation requires a lowering of reserve ratios, and in a free market with commodity money strict limits to the lowering of reserve ratios exist.

It is therefore not apparent why the practice of fractional-reserve banking, once it commenced, should lead naturally to a system such as the present one of unconstrained creation of money and an endlessly elastic money supply. Such a system requires one of two things. Either banks manage, on their own, to lower reserve ratios ever further and thus fully replace commodity money with fiduciary media. As we have seen, this is highly improbable as it would clearly involve too much risk for the banks. Once reserve ratios have reached a certain level, the risk of bank runs would become extremely high, at least if banks continued to be truly private firms at full risk of bankruptcy and without guarantees from the state. In any case, no historic example exits of private banks replacing a society's commodity money entirely with their own paper tickets.[11] Or, the base of reserves on which the banks conduct their fractional-reserve banking is also made to expand constantly. This is the path that has been chosen in the real world. Inflexible commodity money has everywhere been replaced with state fiat money. In a paper money system, reserve money can be created at essentially no cost by the central bank. Its supply is therefore fully at the discretion of the central bank. Its supply is fully elastic and can be made to expand constantly. We conclude that fractional-reserve banking by itself does not lead to a system of fully elastic money. Such a system requires fully elastic bank reserves and that undoubtedly necessitates action by the state and the introduction of paper money as an act of politics.

How fractional-reserve banking would have developed over time in an entirely free market with hard commodity money at its core and without any interference from the state is not easy to ascertain. Many observers will doubt that this practice would have any stability on its own accord. They will point to the early history of banking, which was invariably one of occasional bank runs and panics. Maybe there is something about fractional-reserve banking that causes it to always be unstable and unmanageable. If this is so, the reason for this must be the unpredictability of the public's use of fiduciary media. As the record shows, time and time again the public became unwilling to accept more fiduciary media and instead tried to increase its holding of commodity money. This was particularly the case at times of recession when people wanted to hold money again in the form of an asset that was not simultaneously somebody else's liability and that did not depend for its acceptance on the soundness of the issuing institutions. The growing desire on the part of the banks' clients to revert to money proper put then additional strain on the fractional-reserve banks. They were forced to raise reserve ratios—if at all possible—and reduce the supply of fiduciary media, which almost certainly exacerbated the stress in the economy. Most advocates of the present system of state paper money, elastic reserves, and lender-of-last-resort central banks will argue that because of this innate instability of fractional-reserve banking it requires the support of the state. This, however, can be justified only if the practice, despite its inherent instability, is still deemed advantageous for society overall.

This appears to be the core assumption that has been guiding banking regulation and monetary policy for the past hundred years. It constitutes the intellectual foundation for our present financial infrastructure. Money creation through fractional-reserve banking is supposed to be beneficial to society, but fractional-reserve banking is also considered fundamentally unstable and in need of controls and guidance from the state. It cannot be left to the free market. Most of today's infrastructure has therefore been designed with the risk of bank failures and bank runs in mind. The goal of lender-of-last-resort central banks and other measures taken by the state, such as deposit insurance, is not to restrict or impede fractional-reserve banking as such. To the contrary, in aggregate these measures lower the public's concern about the solvency of individual banks and consequently allow banks to run lower reserve ratios than would be possible in an uninhibited decentralized banking market.

But an alternative view about the innate instability of fractional-reserve banking exists. This is the view that fractional-reserve banking is not inherently unstable because the bankers keep making mistakes and cannot control their business risk, but that fractional-reserve banking itself adds to overall economic instability and is thus to a large degree responsible for the periodic recurrence of recessions, which leads then to the public's concerns about the stability of banks and aversion to fiduciary media. We may jump a little bit ahead at this point but we will soon see that eminent economists have long ago suspected that extending credit on the basis of money printing as opposed to true saving has sinister effects on the overall economy. Credit based on money creation has the potential to create booms and busts and thus destabilize the banks. It is this relationship to overall economic volatility that makes fractional-reserve banking so inherently risky. If this is indeed the case, the policy implications should be very different. Fractional-reserve banking should then not be encouraged and subsidized but restricted or maybe even banned.

In the following section we will look at the history of fractional-banking and its intimate relationship with the state. We will see that the practice was from the start the subject of investigation and debate for the economists. Many of them had serious doubts about its benefits for the overall economy. Fractional-reserve banking was not invented and then happily and readily embraced by the public as a means to provide cheap credit. Neither did it achieve prominence in a smooth evolutionary process of ever-wider public acceptance. In fact, its rise to its position of dominant bank business model was rocky and marked by controversy, and it ultimately required political support.

Fractional-Reserve Banks, the State, and the Economists

There can be little question that states have been involved in fractional-reserve banking almost from its beginning, sometimes with the aim to confine it, more often to encourage it. "Surprising though it may seem, banking has one characteristic in common with alcohol consumption, drug taking and prostitution. No matter the strictness with which officialdom tries to restrict and control it, banking—the operation of a deposit-taking and lending system with a reserve of well under 100 percent—is irrepressible. It always resurfaces in another place or reappears in much the same form, if with a different label," writes Tim Congdon, an advocate of fractional-reserve and central banking.[12] It may be true that fractional reserve banking cannot be eliminated. The attraction of participating in a money-creation scheme is simply too powerful, and as long as it goes well, depositors, bankers, and borrowers all seem to win. Congdon's statement may, however, be a bit unfair to those engaging in alcohol and drug consumption or prostitution, as they can claim that the consequences of their activities are borne only by the consenting adults who participate in these activities. Our further investigation will show that reasonable doubt exists whether that is the case with fractional-reserve banking. Be that as it may, the statement is surely rather one-sided because the historical record shows that official-dom itself has more often than not yielded to the temptation of joining forces with the fractional-reserve bankers and using banking and money creation as a means to fund the state.

This was often achieved by the states starting their own banks. The Bank of England, often called the mother of all central banks, was founded in 1694 by the British government as a lender of last resort from the start—a lender of last resort to the government, that is. The Crown did not enjoy a favorable standing among private creditors at the time, and the Bank was founded explicitly to extend credit to the state. From the start it was given a number of valuable legal privileges that immediately cemented its dominant status in the nascent English banking industry. Importantly, the Bank was allowed to issue bank notes against liabilities of the Crown, which meant it monetized them.[13] During the first 100 years of its existence, the Bank was already permit-ted by the government on several occasions to suspend specie payment. During these intervals, the government allowed the Bank to default on its promise to redeem in gold and still continue as an issuing bank, thus temporarily introducing irredeemable paper money to the British economy.[14]

From the beginning the history of fractional-reserve banking was one of state involvement, booms and busts, bank runs, occasional panics, and asset bubbles. It also provided from the start a topic of research and debate for the young science of economics. One of the most remarkable and colorful of the early economists was Richard Cantillon. His treatise *Essai sur la Nature du Commerce en General,*[15] posthumously published in 1755 and thus a quarter of a century before Adam Smith's *The Wealth of Nations* (1776), already dealt with, among many other things, some of the effects on the economy of an expanding money supply through banking.[16] Cantillon already showed that the new money would not simply lift all prices and certainly not lift them proportionally to the money inflow. The early recipients of new money gain at the expense of later participants. This insight—known as the Cantillon effect—tends to be underappreciated in present discussions, which often give the impression that new money reaches everybody simultaneously and directly impacts some general price "index." As Cantillon pointed out, certain prices are bound to respond more and respond faster than others to the inflow of new money. Thus, relative prices always change in response to money injections, and this must affect resource allocation and economic structures.

Furthermore, Cantillon showed how stock prices might be unduly elevated in response to money injections, a subject on which he was indeed an authority: As an Irish expatriate and successful banker in Paris in the early eighteenth century, Cantillon became a partner in the Mississippi Company, a paper money bank founded by another expatriate in Paris, the Scottish adventurer and monetary theorist John Law (1671–1729). Law had devised a plan to issue paper money that officialdom in France readily embraced, not least because the government was practically bankrupt at the time.[17] The resulting inflation generated a massive asset bubble, the famous Mississippi bubble, which, when it finally collapsed, not only left Law impoverished and discredited but the French government in an even more desolate fiscal position. Cantillon, however, had taken his profits and returned to London a wealthy man, ready to write his book.

Skepticism about paper money and fractional-reserve banking persisted among the early social scientists, in particular in France, the home of a number of exceptional economists in the eighteenth century. One of them was the "philosophe" Count Antoine Destutt de Tracy (1754–1836),[18] an articulate opponent of paper money who exerted a strong influence on U.S. presidents Thomas Jefferson and John Adams. Jefferson even edited the first English translation of de Tracy's main work, which became a standard textbook in the U.S. market at the time. The antipathy of America's second and third president toward banking and paper money was corroborated by their experience and their study of history. By the early nineteenth century, America had already experienced two paper money disasters: the paper money experiment that started in the late seventeenth century in Massachusetts[19] and the one around the American Revolution,[20] both of which ended with the respective monies being all but worthless. Additionally, France had given a vivid demonstration of the perils of elastic money with the hyperinflating assignats, the paper money of the French Revolution.

In a letter of March 1819, Jefferson wrote to Adams:

> *The evils of this deluge of paper money are not to be removed until our citizens are generally and radically instructed in their cause and consequences, and silence by their authority the interested clamors and sophistry of speculating, shaving, and banking institutions. Till then, we must be content to return quo ad hoc to the savage state, to recur to barter in the exchange of our property for want of a stable common means of value, that now in use being less fixed than the beads and wampum of the Indian, and to deliver up our citizens, their property and their labor, passive victims to the swindling tricks of bankers and mountebankers.*[21]

Indeed, if one is to look with Professor Congdon for representatives of officialdom who were skeptical or even hostile to fractional-reserve banking and its money-producing capabilities, one will indeed have to look to the United States before 1913. Apart from Jefferson and John Adams, the list of statesmen who were antibanking and anti–paper money includes Presidents George Washington, John Quincy Adams, Andrew Jackson, Martin van Buren, Henry Harrison, and James K. Polk.[22] Two attempts by the supporters of monetary expansion, notably the bankers themselves, to establish a national central bank failed.

Meanwhile, in Britain, further progress was made on the economic science of money and banking. When in 1797 the government of William Pitt put the country again on a de facto paper standard by stopping the Bank of England from redeeming notes in specie—this time in order to obtain funding from the Bank for the war against France—an intense debate, known as the bullionist controversy, began over the economic consequences of this policy.[23] During this debate the British economists of what became known as the Currency School demonstrated that an expansion of money in circulation not only tends to lift prices, but it also initiates a business cycle by setting off a credit-driven boom that will inevitably transform into a recession. Their insights played an important role in the passing of the 1844 Bank Act, also known as the Peel Act, which banned the issuance of banknotes by private banks. While intended as a restriction on fractional-reserve banking, it ultimately failed to inhibit the creation of deposit money by the banks, and it also had the spurious effect of strengthening the monopoly position of the Bank of England. Nevertheless, it constituted one of the few incidents in which academic concerns over money expansion swayed the political debate.

In the 1870s a breakthrough in economic science occurred, the so-called marginal revolution, which was spearheaded by three economists: William Stanley Jevons in Britain, Carl Menger in Vienna, and Leon Walras in Lausanne. The new methodology introduced a different approach to analyzing economic phenomena, one that places great emphasis on the subjective valuations of the acting individuals and the marginal changes that drive their behavior. Basing his work on the methodology developed by Carl Menger, Austrian economist Ludwig von Mises set out to apply the new economic approach to money and credit. The result was Mises' seminal work, *Theorie des Geldes und der Umlaufmittel* (1912, second edition 1924),[24] which should translate as "The Theory of Money and Fiduciary Media" but was translated as "The Theory of Money and Credit." This book laid the foundation of what has since been known as the Austrian Theory of the Business Cycle. Mises elaborated this theory further in his 1928 book *Geldwertstabilisierung und Konjunkturpolitik.*[25] The contributions by Mises' protégé, F. A. Hayek, were mentioned previously.

The conclusions of the Austrian cycle theory are similar to those of the British Currency School, but they are based on a more penetrating economic analysis. We will have the opportunity to look into this theory in more detail later. At this stage it may be sufficient to say that the Austrians showed how an increase in lending as a result of additional saving by individuals and an increase in lending as a result of money creation have initially very similar effects on an economy's capital structure. But the ultimate consequences are very different. "Saving gets us genuine growth; credit expansion gets us boom and bust" (Roger W. Garrison).[26]

The Desire for Elastic Money

As far reaching as the Austrian conclusions were, they ultimately had little influence on the politics of the day. The idea that cheap credit was a source of prosperity became the new zeitgeist and central to the design of the modern financial infrastructure. The credit-driven boom—irrespective of whether it was funded by proper savings or bank-credit creation—came to be viewed as desirable, the bust as the isolated, presumably unconnected disturbance. If only the correction could be done away with and the boom extended, the economy could enjoy an uninterrupted expansion, practically forever.

The ascent of this belief was probably most remarkable in the United States, where the political and banking establishment became determined to break with the longstanding antibanking and anti–paper money tradition of the country and finally establish a European-style central bank as a lender of last resort to Wall Street. The goal was not to curtail and limit fractional-reserve banking but to support it and allow it to be conducted on a larger scale. The drive for more elastic forms of money was not, as is often assumed all too readily, dictated by circumstances, such as the changing demands of a more industrialized economy. As we have seen, more money was not needed and was not demanded. Nevertheless, bankers and politicians wanted to enjoy the upswing that easy money could provide for a limited time and they wanted to get rid of the inevitable corrections, the bank runs and recessions that are the other side of the fractional-reserve banking coin. The launch of a central bank as the first step toward fully elastic state money was not dictated by economic circumstances and was certainly not backed by the latest insights of the science of economics. It was the result of politics.

Those leading the charge for a new financial architecture put the logic of the British Currency School and the "Austrians" on its head: Greater stability was now to be achieved by making money more elastic rather than less elastic. As Edward B. Vreeland, congressman from New York and coauthor of the 1908 Aldrich-Vreeland Act, which constituted an important step toward the establishment of the Federal Reserve, remarked in 1912: ". . . the elasticity of cash is important," but "the elasticity of credit is of vastly greater importance."[27] Vreeland continued: "Go to England, Austria, France, Germany—any great country abroad. Not one of them by law requires a bank to keep a dollar of reserve on hand."[28] But, according to Vreeland—and rather bizarrely by the standards of economic logic—this was supposed to make these financial systems safer: ". . . we find that not one of them has had a money panic for more than fifty years."[29]

In their influential study *A Monetary History of the United States, 1867–1960,* Milton Friedman and Anna Jacobson Schwartz, both advocates of paper money and central banking, noted that the "Federal Reserve System was created by men whose outlook on the goals of central banking was shaped by their experience of money panics during the national banking era. The basic monetary problem seemed to them to be banking crises produced by or resulting in an attempted shift by the public from deposits to currency."[30] The latter part of this sentence could read, "attempted shifts by the public out of uncovered fiduciary media issued by the banks and previously accepted by the public, into money proper." The Achilles heel of this system may then be seen, more accurately, not in a fickle public but instead a banking sector that issues uncovered claims against itself. And the solution may then be found straightforwardly in restricting this practice rather than providing a backstop for it and thereby encouraging it. Friedman and Schwartz continue: "This in turn required the existence of some form of currency that could be rapidly expanded."[31] Evidently, this was in contradiction to the very concept of a gold standard and hard money, a conflict that Friedman and Schwartz acknowledge.[32] In any case, by 1913 the Federal Reserve System had been established as a lender-of-last-resort central bank. With an apparent safety net in the form of a government-backed agency now in place, the risk of bank runs—the only real constraining factor to money creation by the banks—was greatly reduced. Fractional-reserve banking could now be conducted on a larger scale. Money had become more elastic.[33]

When the United States entered the International Gold Standard in 1879, its citizens held on average $2 in bank deposits for every $1 in physical currency. In 1929, on the eve of America's Great Depression, they held on average $12 in deposits for every dollar in physical cash.[34] Money injections on such a scale have rather sinister effects, as the "Austrians" had explained. Consequently, by the late 1920s, money-induced dislocations were so meaningful that a sharp economic correction had become inevitable. A cleansing of accumulated capital misallocations was necessary—as painful as it was. The various forms of state intervention that became popular during the 1930s' New Deal, however, greatly obstructed this process and thereby protracted the period of pain and misery unnecessarily. Instead of the quick and sharp contraction that occurs in uninhibited markets, the U.S. economy was put through a crippling and dragged-out slump.[35] In any case, the general sentiment in favor of state intervention meant that government-supported money creation was not identified as the source of the economy's malaise that it was. To the contrary, it was again viewed as the solution.

According to widespread belief, recovery was expected only from the state, and for the state to deliver growth the state had to be able to create yet more money. In 1933, Roosevelt took the dollar off gold domestically, giving the state complete control over the monetary sphere within the United States. To allow unlimited inflationism, the time-honored alternative to state paper money, gold, had to be ostra-cized. Per executive order, Roosevelt confiscated all privately held gold in the United States and banned private ownership of it. In what should have been the shining hour of the Austrian theory, as it was by the early 1930s not only practically uncontested in the realm of business cycle theory but had also proven useful for predicting and explaining an economic disaster, it was instead ignored. By 1933, the major con-tributions from Mises and Hayek on the origins of business cycles had been published and the theory had found its way into the English-speaking world.[36] Yet, it had practically no impact on policy. The political mainstream now embraced state action, mistrusted the market, and harked back to old mercantilist ideas, which found a popular restatement in the 1930s in the works of John Maynard Keynes. The insight that expanding money disrupts the economy was ignored and forgotten, the comforting belief that printing more money could always buy the government a recovery became instead the new creed. To this day, the monetary infrastructure and the dominant monetary policy framework are but the institutionalized belief that a constantly expand-ing supply of money is good for the economy. During normal times, money is to be expanded slowly and moderately to aid growth but not to ignite inflation. At times of recession or deflation, money is to be expanded forcefully in order to stimulate the economy and encourage spending. Thus, for 70 years the wrong lessons have been drawn from the Great Depression, which makes a repeat of this tragic event simply a question of time.

After the Second World War, no return to commodity money occurred and the last remnants of an international gold standard were disposed of in 1971 when Nixon closed the gold window. Under U.S. leadership, the world began to increasingly embrace social democracy as the dominant societal model, even though the term remains unpopular in the United States to this day. But whatever the name one gives this system, it is undeniable that a return to Classical Liberalism or anything similar to nineteenth century laissez-faire was not achieved and not even attempted. In the new system, the economy was nominally capitalistic in that most enterprises were privately owned. Yet, the state played an important and over time increasingly active role, to be witnessed, among other things, by constantly rising levels of taxation, regulation, and public debt. With the collapse of communism in 1989, the mixed economy, meaning the combination of mostly privately owned means of production with democratically legitimized state interventionism, became the globally dominant societal model. That the state should supply the economy with its own paper money under a regional monopoly, that the state should thus control and flexibly adjust the supply of money and constantly expand it, had become unquestioned features of this system.

The full effects of paper money expansion were not felt in the first two decades after World War II. Many countries were still rebuilding their financial infrastructure during that time, and in the United States the banking sector was saddled with numerous state-imposed regulations, including restrictions on the level of interest rates on deposits. This did not allow the banks to take full advantage of fractional-reserve banking. Ironically, the state thus created obstacles to money creation, on the one hand, but on the other hand simultaneously supported fractional-reserve banking by providing flexible and expanding reserves to the banking industry. By the 1970s, the restrictions were lifted and, even more importantly, the last link to gold was severed. As nobody could any longer demand to exchange dollars for gold, the dollar became an irredeemable piece of paper, a transition that most other currencies had already completed at this stage. The world had now entered the brave new era of fully elastic paper money systems.

Summary

We conclude that elastic money is not the natural outcome of the market or of a growing economy. Elastic money is not needed, and an ongoing expansion of the supply of the monetary asset not required nor demanded by the public. As with any other good, supply of and demand for money are constantly aligned by market forces. However, in contrast to any other good, money is demanded only for its exchange value, not for any use-value that the monetary asset might have. Therefore, the market forces that coordinate supply and demand in the case of money only need to adjust money's exchange value, that is, the purchasing power of the monetary unit. This happens naturally as a result of the constant buying and selling of money by the public in response to any changes in the demand for money relative to the demand for other goods and services. While changes in the public's demand for any other goods or services can be satisfied only by changes in the physical supply of these goods and services, changes in money demand are always and instantly met by changes in money's purchasing power. No changes in the supply of money are needed. A society that uses money does not require ongoing money production.

However, for the very same reasons, should a money producer manage to establish himself and have his irredeemable paper tickets accepted as money in the economy, then this money producer can produce and place with the public, at a profit to himself, practically any amount of money he wishes. In contrast to any other good or service, lack of demand is practically no obstacle to the production and distribution of money. Additional money will be absorbed by the economy at a lower purchasing power of the monetary unit.

An element of elasticity has always been part of the monetary infrastructure, simply through the mining of the precious metals that used to be the dominant forms of money. This elasticity has historically been of minor importance, however. Even discoveries of new gold or silver deposits, which have naturally caused an expansion of money in circulation and thereby led to inflationary distortions, never generated the type of economic disruptions that have become the hallmark of systems of elastic paper money.[37]

For the past 300 years another element of elasticity has become important, fractional-reserve banking. To the extent that banks manage to issue uncovered claims on money, such as uncovered banknotes or bank deposits, and have these uncovered claims accepted by the public in lieu of money proper, they become de facto money producers and can profitably place this new money, or fiduciary media, by extending more credit. Again, this process does not occur in response to, nor is it controlled by, any independent demand for money on the part of the public. Fractional-reserve banking is unrelated to money demand. Even to loan demand the relationship is tenuous because, if banks are willing to lower their reserve ratios, they can offer newly created deposit money at lower interest rates. Under normal economic conditions, this leads to additional borrowing.

Fractional-reserve banking is risky for the banks as it involves the issuance of uncovered claims that can be presented at any time. Not surprisingly, it has proven to be a rather unstable business. In a free market with hard money at its core, the practice of fractional-reserve banking is ultimately severely restricted by the limited availability of reserves and the risk of bankruptcy. This changed fundamentally when the state began to support fractional-reserve banking in a structural way by providing fully elastic bank reserves and a government agency as a lender of last resort. These institutional changes increased substantially the ability of banks to create credit through money production. The effects of this process have long been the subject of research and debate among social scientists.

In sharp contrast to many pioneers in the field of economics, modern-day economists tend to support the state paper money system. When commenting on the substantial expansion of money-induced credit in the years and decades preceding the recent financial crisis, Professor Congdon stated that "central banking allowed banks to reduce their ratios of cash and capital to their assets, and so lowered the cost of finance to non-banks, but . . . these benefits could be enjoyed only if the central bank had a lender-of-last-resort function."[38] Among financial market participants, it is also readily accepted that extra credit through bank money creation is universally beneficial to the economy. Yet, to assume that this is always the case clearly contradicts the findings of the British Currency School and, even more so, those of the Austrian

School of Economics. Ludwig von Mises and his followers have shown convincingly that the long-term effects of the expansion of credit are very different depending on whether credit is backed by saving or backed merely by money creation. If additional credit is extended via money production the additional investment that is being promoted has ultimately no support from the sphere of real resources. Only voluntary saving from the consumer can redirect resources from consumption to investment in accordance with the consumer's preferences. This is why saving is ultimately essential for the expansion and maintenance of the capital stock, which requires, after all, real resources, including labor, to sustain it.

In the case of money-induced credit, no resources have been freed up by the consumer from their present employment close to immediate consumption and made available for investment projects that will yield returns only in the more remote future. The consumer still demands these resources for immediate consumption purposes. Sure, money creation can temporarily lower interest rates and can generate the illusion that extra saving is available. But the resulting money-induced rise in investment will be unsustainable. Once the money flow slows, it will become clear that resources have been misallocated and a cleansing of the economy of these misallocations becomes necessary. What elastic paper money, expanding bank reserves, and lender-of-last-resort central banking can achieve is only to extend credit booms, which must mean that the accumulation of dislocations becomes ever more burdensome. To avoid the inevitable correction, ever larger amounts of money will have to be injected into the economy, a policy that must ultimately undermine the acceptance of paper money itself.

Money creation in today's financial architecture is decidedly not a market phenomenon. It is a political phenomenon. The money supply can simply be expanded to the extent to which the central bank supports the banks' money creation and thus allows them to profitably enhance their credit business. At the end of 2010, the U.S. Federal Reserve declared the supply of money in the United States to be around $8,800 billion, using the statistical definition M2 to define what constitutes money. According to this measure, the supply of money more than doubled in the preceding 12 years.[39] It would be a grave error to assume that this expansion was the result of economic conditions, of the workings of the market economy, and the spontaneous interaction of the various participants in financial markets. Cause and effect work in the other direction. The economic conditions in the U.S. economy are in fact the result of the creation of money that the Fed stimulated and supported over this period. Had the Fed decided to accommodate a slower expansion of money, less money would have been produced. Had the Fed decided to accommodate a faster expansion of money, more money would have been produced. (Although, in the latter case, the financial crisis that commenced in 2007 would then probably have started earlier, as will be shown later.) The same is true for other paper money economies.

In the present monetary system, the growth of the money supply is largely the consequence of discretionary political decisions. That these have far-reaching effects on many economic processes cannot be denied. Mainstream economists often advertise the power of money injections to stimulate economic activity during recessions. But if money injections can work as an anticrisis policy tool, even if only for a short time, this confirms precisely that they constitute discretionary and exogenous changes of economic conditions. If an expanding money supply had no impact on the use of real resources in the economy, it could not be a tool for stimulating the economy. And modern paper money systems are designed to constantly expand the supply of money, not just at times of crisis. It follows logically that the present system of ongoing money injection is a system of ongoing manipulation of the economy, of continuous intervention, of a constant discretionary change in key economic variables.

In economics debates it has become standard practice to identify two consequences of expanding money as being a boost to growth (spending) and a boost to the price level (inflation). This is what Mr. Bernanke did with the earlier quote: "The U.S. government has a technology, called a printing press. . . . We conclude that under a paper-money system, a determined government can always generate higher spending and hence positive inflation."[40] But this is a dangerous simplification of what elastic money does. Increasing the supply of money must change relative prices. Consequently, it changes the use of resources. Consequently, it changes the distribution of income and the direction of economic activity. After an expansion of the money supply an economy will not simply have a higher GDP and a higher price level. This would be the case only under the naïve assumption that the new money would simply boost all existing activities proportionally to their previous contribution to GDP. After an expansion of the money supply, the economy will have a different resource allocation, a different structure of economic activity, and a different income distribution. It is a heroic assumption indeed to maintain that the entirety of these consequences is always a "benefit to society." Many eminent economists, in particular those of the Austrian School, had their doubts.

■   ■   ■

In the next part of this book, we will investigate the full range of necessary consequences that every discretionary injection of money will entail. In order to draw decisive conclusions, we have to do this in the form of a careful systematic analysis. We will start with a very simple and indeed unrealistic model of money injections and then move, step by step, to more realistic models. This process allows us to start with basic assumptions that the reader can easily check for himself, and in moving to more complex models we can work out the essential effects of elastic money even in more complex settings. In order to follow our reasoning, no background in economics is required. Certain economic concepts that are necessary to understand the more realistic models, such as saving and interest, will be explained to the extent that they are needed.

Part Two

THE EFFECTS OF MONEY INJECTIONS

Chapter 3

Money Injections without Credit Markets

We will start our analysis of the effects of an expanding money supply with a model that is purely a mental construct. It is a simple thought experiment that was famously used by David Hume about 250 years ago in his essay "Of Interest."[1]

Even, Instant, and Transparent Money Injection

Let us assume that a money producer increases the individual cash balances of every person in society through an act of magic by exactly 10 percent overnight. If a person had $1,000 in money the evening before, that person will now have $1,100 in money holdings. A person who had $50 in money will now have $55. The overall amount of money in the economy thereby increases by 10 percent but, importantly, this happens instantaneously, with everybody affected at the same time and in exactly the same way. This is a one-off event; no additional money injections follow. We will make one additional assumption: Every person, as he wakes up and goes about his business, not only knows immediately that he magically received an additional 10 percent of cash, but he also knows that everybody else has received an additional 10 percent of their previous money holdings, too.

This is, of course, a most unrealistic example of money injections. However, we can quickly see that this fantastical scenario is the only one imaginable, in which the increased supply of money affects the price level only and does so in a way that is exactly proportional to the change in the money supply. As we adjust the model step by step to make it more realistic, other effects of money injections will become relevant. But in this initial scenario it is rational for everyone to refrain from changing any spending patterns, from changing the composition of the consumption of goods and services, and of saving and investment, and only to adjust nominal prices. It will be instantly clear to everyone that, first, society overall has not become richer. Society has now an additional 10 percent of its medium of exchange but it does not have any more goods and services to buy with this extra money. Second, nobody's relative position in terms of wealth or access to the medium of exchange has changed. Surely, the only rational thing to do is to adjust all nominal prices and nominal prices only. By lifting all prices by 10 percent, the overall effect of the increase in the money supply is fully and instantly absorbed. There are no second-round effects. This is all that has to be adjusted. As demand for money is demand for purchasing power in the form of money, the person who was content to hold $1,000 in money the previous night will, after a rise in all prices of 10 percent, be content to hold $1,100, and the person who previously was happy to hold $50 in money will now gladly hold $55.

Given that every individual can hold exactly the cash balance he desires at every point in time, we must assume that each person held exactly their desired money balance before the injection of new money. Therefore, all prices have to rise by 10 percent in order to make everybody equally content with holding the enlarged cash positions. Everybody's supply of money has increased by 10 percent via the act of magic from the money producer. Now, via the rise in all prices by 10 percent, everybody's demand for money has increased by 10 percent, too. Every person in their role as producer (entrepreneur, worker) will charge an extra 10 percent for all goods and services sold, while in their role as consumer every person will be willing to pay an extra 10 percent for all goods and services bought.

This magic injection of new money has no impact on the production of goods and services, on resource allocation, or on income distribution. None of these variables will be altered as a result of the additional money. In this model, new money will only have an impact on prices and, as it affects all prices simultaneously and to the same extent, every conceivable statistical average of prices will go up by the same extent. Only in this most unrealistic model is the change in the price level proportional to the change in the money supply.

If we look at our model economy through the prism of macroeconomic statistics, it is clear that nominal GDP went up by 10 percent; that the price level went up by 10 percent and that real GDP was unchanged. No new economic activity occurred in response to the money injection. The amount of money is entirely unrelated to the number of economic transactions, as we have already established in the previous chapters. More money as such does not mean a different economic performance. As we will see, it is the specific process of how money is injected into the economy that normally generates additional activity. This activity is always adjustment activity, that is, additional transactions by which the economy copes with a changing money supply. But if money is injected in the way just described, evenly and completely transparently—but only if it is injected in this way—it will result exclusively in nominal price changes.

If the money producer wanted to achieve the effects that today are generally associated with an expanding money stock—higher "spending" and higher inflation—he will be disappointed as he only gets inflation but no additional "spending." With even and transparent money injections he will only get price effects. In order to stimulate additional economic activity, he has to at least obscure the money injection process or additionally make it uneven, meaning benefiting some at the expense of others from the start, in order to generate additional transactions.

Even and Nontransparent Money Injection

Let us now assume that the same magical increase in everybody's money balances occurs, but that this time people don't know whether everybody else has also received an additional 10 percent of their previous cash holdings. Although objectively the situation is exactly the same as in the first scenario, the outcome will be different, as now there is room for error.

We can split the economic agents in our economy in two groups. The first group will interpret the situation correctly and therefore not change their consumption and production pattern but only adjust nominal prices. In their role as producers, these individuals will charge an extra 10 percent for goods and services produced; in their roles as consumers, they will accept to pay an extra 10 percent in goods and services consumed. The second group misinterprets the situation. Members of this group believe that only their own cash positions have changed and that their economic position has now been altered relative to that of other members of society. Even if they appreciate that a magical increase in their own cash balances has not made society overall richer in goods and services, they believe (erroneously) that their relative position is now better. More of the medium of exchange is now in their hands. They believe they have become relatively wealthier. In their role as consumers, members of this group will now increase their spending.

What will they increase their spending on? It is clear that they will not simply buy 10 percent more of whatever they used to consume before. According to what economists call the law of marginal utility, a person will spend extra money on those goods and services, that on the person's subjective value scale are just below all the goods and services that the person has already bought when on a smaller budget, but that are at the top of the scale of goods and services that the person does not yet own as the person previously lacked the necessary funds. Just as a person who has lost some of his money balances, perhaps as a result of theft, would not sell a fraction of every one of his assets to restore a certain desired money balance but would sell the least desired asset or cut back outlays on the least desired consumption or investment expenditure, a person that receives extra money will spend it on that most desired asset (or consumption or investment item) that was previously just outside the person's financial reach. Therefore, the new money will flow to producers that provide these new desired goods and services. Additional consumption demand has now materialized.

For these producers, the extra demand for their goods and services is difficult to interpret. Is it the result simply of more money going around, or is it the result of a genuine rise in consumer demand that reflects either changed consumer preferences or a better competitive position of these producers vis-à-vis other suppliers of similar goods and services? If producers think it is the latter, that is, a genuine rise in demand for their produce, they may reasonably expect this new demand to last and may make additional investments in their business. This will lead to an additional increase in economic activity. However, this is evidently the wrong interpretation of the situation. Neither have consumer preferences changed, nor have these producers beat their competitors.

As we have seen, the consumers who engage in additional spending have not changed their personal value scale but simply, and wrongly, believe they have additional spending power. As prices all around begin to rise, these consumers will soon have to increase their outlays on those goods and services that they always consumed and which rank higher on their value scale than the goods and services they intended to spend the new money on. We have to remember that they planned to spend in addition to what they had spent previously, rather than change their consumption pattern. As the prices for more and more goods tend to go up, they will soon realize that they are not richer and that they misjudged the situation. They will have to abandon their new spending plans. The extra consumption will thus ultimately evaporate. Consequently, the producers who wrongly expected this consumption to reflect lasting changes in consumption behavior will also have to abandon their investment projects.

Those individuals who make the original mistake of believing that only they have received extra money, are not just consumers, they are also, in a different capacity, producers. Thus, we have to assume that some producers believe that their customers' spending power has not changed and that these producers, out of fear of losing business to the competition, will not lift the prices of their goods and services initially.

Consequently, these producers are also likely to experience extra demand for their goods and services, simply because they will be selling at lower prices than their competitors who interpret the situation correctly. If they do not quickly realize their mistake, they may also think they are benefiting from changing consumer preferences or a better competitive position and may even invest in their business in order to expand it. But these producers are selling at prices that are below what they would be if the producers had all the relevant information. As prices all around tend to go up, they will soon have to pay higher prices when purchasing investment and consumption goods and they will realize that they are selling their products "below market." By misinterpreting the situation for longer than others, they based their economic calculations on incorrect inputs and ended up selling their goods and services at what must now appear to them to be "incorrect" prices. Those, however, who shifted their purchases temporarily to those producers who were adjusting too slowly to the new environment of rising prices, benefited at their expense. As a general rule, control over some economic resources will have shifted from those who interpreted the situation at first incorrectly to those who interpreted it correctly from the start.

It is obvious that in the stylized world of our highly theoretical models the scope for these mistakes is fairly limited. The quick and, indeed, instantaneous change in most prices that can be assumed in a model economy will communicate the facts quickly to everybody. The time and space for some consumers and some producers to err and to develop the patterns described above is very restricted in the context of pure models. However, the more we move away from the unrealistic model assumptions and consider a real-life economy, in which spending is not ongoing but discontinuous and intermittent, and price-discovery therefore periodic, these processes will be unavoidable. In any case, the imperfections of a real-life economy, when compared to the purity of the theoretical model, enhance the phenomena we just described; they do not cause them. What causes the processes described here is the lack of full transparency, which leads to potential misinterpretation. Some economic agents will confuse additional nominal spending with a rise in real demand that can only result from changes in consumer preferences or true entrepreneurial success. This confusion leads to additional economic activity. It is evident that in this scenario the economy undergoes a period of adjustment, in which additional economic transactions are being undertaken.

If the money producer again sets out to achieve the standard macroeconomic responses that are today associated with an expanding money supply, namely higher GDP growth and higher inflation, he will be happier than after the attempt in scenario one. By allocating money evenly but by simply decreasing transparency, the money producer has caused some economic agents to misinterpret the situation. Their errors generated additional activity and these additional transactions will have temporarily lifted GDP. As a result of these transactions, at the end of the process some will be richer (the ones that interpreted the situation correctly and bought from those who were adjusting slowly) and others will be poorer (those that increased the prices they demand for their goods and services too late). The allocation of resources and the distribution of incomes have now been permanently altered. It is therefore inevitable that the composition of goods and services in the economy has changed as well. Some people now have more economic means, others less. It follows that the structure of production will be changed as well and, because of this, it is inevitable that the increase in the price level is no longer proportional to the increase in money. An overall tendency toward higher prices has developed, although by how much prices rose on average is now unclear. Different prices will have responded differently.

The temporary rise in GDP leaves a somewhat bitter aftertaste, however, as it is clearly of a different quality than what we would normally expect from the occurrence of new voluntary transactions. In a free and uninhibited market, the voluntary exchange of goods and services by private property owners is, by definition, to the benefit of both parties or at least to what they perceive to be their benefit at the time; otherwise no voluntary exchange would occur. A rising GDP number for such a free and uninhibited market economy indicates that the number of transactions, of goods and services bought and sold, has increased and that more mutually beneficial exchanges among members of society have occurred. Consequently, more material needs have been fulfilled and more people have marginally improved their material well-being.

However, we can draw none of these conclusions in the case of the adjustment activity that was stimulated temporarily by the injection of money. The additional transactions that our money producer initiated crucially rely on error. If everybody had full knowledge of the even injection of new money, nobody would have seen any reason to change their behavior. As we already saw in Chapter 1, the quantity of monetary assets available to society is immaterial for the number of economic transactions that society can engage in. More money does not mean more economic activity; and more economic activity does not require more money. What has, in scenario two, generated additional economic activity is not more money per se, but the specific process of money injection. This process has disoriented some consumers and producers, and their errors have caused adjustment activity that has temporarily lifted the number of economic transactions that make up the GDP statistics. While the boost to growth is transitory, the changes to resource allocation and income distribution are permanent. The money injection has caused a growth blip. It also created winners and losers.

Uneven and Nontransparent Money Injection

Our money producer can obviously achieve similar results if he does not increase everybody's money holdings to the same extent and at the same time but if he only gives newly created money to a select few. This process has also the advantage that it doesn't require magic. The money producer can simply print the money and use it to transact with others in the economy. He simply spends it. The first recipients of the new money are those that the money creator buys from. Those will spend at least some of the money in turn on the purchase of goods and services from others, as it cannot be assumed that their demand for money has simultaneously risen by the exact amount they have received from the money creator. So the money is distributed to the next group of producers, and so forth. This process unfolds until the new money is completely dispersed throughout the economy. In contrast to the earlier, less realistic models, not everybody will get money instantly. That additional transactions occur—which will necessarily boost the

GDP statistics—is without question in this scenario. But other effects must result, too.

It is clear that this is how new money is in essence circulated in real life. Indeed, it is the only way in which new money can be brought into circulation in the real economy. Any injection of money will have to start at a particular point in the economy and the new money will get distributed in a process that takes time and involves numerous transactions. In real life, new money can never reach everybody, or even large sections of society, at the same time, but only through a step-by-step process, which will inevitably change the allocation of resources and the distribution of the ownership of economic means.

It is immediately clear that an instant and proportional adjustment of the overall price level is now completely out of the question. It is impossible. As the new money does not reach everybody instantly, it is impossible for everybody to simply move prices up. How prices will ultimately be affected will only be clear at the end of an extended and complicated process. Consequently, the redistribution effects will now be larger.

That this process creates winners and losers is without question. The biggest beneficiary of the process is certainly the money creator himself, as he brings the money into existence at almost zero cost and buys goods and services that others have produced. But even the recipients of the new money in the first couple of stages of the distribution chain derive substantial benefit from it. They enjoy the extra monetary income early in the process, before many other prices in the economy have responded to the inflow and gone up. The producers at the next stage of the money distribution process receive new money, naturally, from those who received it before them and who, because their money demand has not gone up at the same time, spend some of it on goods and services. When the new money reaches a group of producers, they will be able to sell their goods and services at slightly higher prices because of the additional demand for what they have to offer, and the higher nominal spending power of those who are one stage ahead of them in the money distribution chain, and who they sell to.

Thus, at each step, a marginal upward pressure on prices will be applied and over time, more and more prices will be lifted. It is evidently advantageous to be close to the money producer in this money distribution chain. The earlier one receives some of the new money, the higher its purchasing power still is. Many prices will at this point not have gone up yet. The winners in this process are thus those who get hold of the new money before the full effects on prices that will ultimately result from the money injection have materialized. Those who receive the new money early will benefit at the expense of those who receive the new money later. The redistribution of income and ownership of resources will be more pronounced than in our previous and less realistic example. It will also no longer be driven by individual error or misjudgment but be mainly the result of where one happens to be located in the money distribution chain. A redistribution of economic means is the logical consequence of any real life injection of new money into an economy.

From what we said earlier about money demand it also follows that, as more and more prices rise, the distribution process will slow down as a result of the public's growing demand for the monetary asset. This demand rises naturally in response to money's progressive loss of purchasing power. Thus, fewer and fewer people will pass the money on to the next stage. As we know, the additional money that was injected but not demanded can be placed with the public only via a drop in money's purchasing power. As more and more prices rise during the money distribution process, the demand for money goes up and the additional money will increasingly be held as part of voluntary cash holdings, rather than passed on.

At the earlier stages of this process, when the monetary unit still enjoys its full purchasing power, the opportunity cost of holding on to the extra money is very high. Most prices have not gone up yet, so the early recipients of the money have every incentive to spend it. But as the new money spreads throughout the economy and more prices rise, the desire to keep more of the medium of exchange as part of one's cash holdings will rise, too. This will, over time, slow down the money distribution process until it comes to a standstill. The multitude of transactions by which the new money makes its way through the economy and by which economic means get redistributed will have led to a temporary increase in GDP. Now that the money distribution process is concluded and the extra money is held voluntarily as part of individual cash holdings, it does no longer stimulate additional transactions. No further boost to economic activity emanates from it. The GDP statistics were lifted temporarily but this effect has now run its course. The reallocation of economic means is permanent, however.

Every injection of money must reallocate resources. These reallocation effects are not reflected and cannot be gauged from the changes in the standard macroeconomic aggregates, such as the price average (the price level) and the number and size of economic transactions (GDP). The former will rise, albeit not in proportion to the money injection, and the latter will rise as well, albeit only temporarily, as the distribution of the new money must induce a set of new transactions. Whether any of this is beneficial to society is debatable. The standard discussions about economic policy, along the lines of how much inflation should be tolerated for a certain boost to growth, give the impression that everybody shares in the benefits of growth and everybody suffers the disadvantage of higher prices, and that therefore a balance between these two effects can be established that is advantageous for society overall. This is decidedly not the case. Money injections always redistribute control over economic means. They must always create winners and losers. The losers do not benefit at all from this policy, regardless of how big a temporary GDP blip is being manufactured. The losers can rightfully claim that they are deprived of economic means for the sake of a boost to the GDP statistics that is short-lived and has no lasting benefit for society overall.

As we have already seen in the preceding scenario, the nature of the temporary boost to overall economic activity is very different from what we would normally expect when the talk is of generating higher GDP numbers. With better economic growth we associate that more economic needs have been met, that more people have bettered their economic position, even if only marginally. We expect that more mutually beneficial transactions have occurred. More growth means to us better supply with goods and services, more wealth and more economic opportunity. We expect that more people fulfill their economic potential in a growing economy. All of this is usually expected from rising GDP statistics. But there is no reason to think that this has occurred uniformly in the case of simple money injections.

The statistical measure GDP can measure only the number of economic transactions and the nominal amounts involved in them. In an

entirely free market it would indeed be reasonable to assume that all of
the above expectations as to what a higher GDP entails are essentially
met. In a free market in which no monopolist of coercion and compulsion exists, every transaction must be engaged in voluntarily by both
parties and must therefore be deemed beneficial to both sides. Thus, a
rise in the number of transactions means that mutually beneficial cooperation on markets has intensified and a better supply with goods and
services has been achieved. In a free market that is entirely constituted
by voluntary cooperation, consistently high GDP readings can rightly
be interpreted to indicate rising wealth, better fulfillment of individual
economic potential, more efficient resource use, innovation, and capital
accumulation.

But none of this has occurred as a result of money injection. Sure,
additional transactions have been initiated and the money producer can
rightfully claim to have boosted GDP, if only temporarily. But this
growth in GDP is of an entirely different nature. Just as throwing a
stone into a lake causes numerous ripples on the water's surface, so has
the arbitrary injection of new money—money that was not needed and
not demanded and that has no implication for the economy's ability to
produce goods and services in the long run—set off a number of transactions by which the economy adapted to this discretionary interference. This process will redistribute the ownership over economic
means. It will lift GDP statistics temporarily, never lastingly. It will not
lead to a better use of resources, to better human cooperation on
markets. It will not lead to innovation, creativity, or more entrepre-
neurship. It is a trick that the money producer plays on the economy
for short-term effect, and it cannot increase the efficiency and productivity of the economy.

Chapter 4

Money Injections via Credit Markets

In this chapter we will further enhance the realism of our model of money injections from Chapter 3. We will now introduce the market for credit. Most money creation today occurs via the fractional-reserve banking industry or the central bank. Banks operate in the loan market, and this is where money is being injected into the economy in the real world. A functioning loan market would obviously also exist in a world of inflexible commodity money and without fractional-reserve or central banks. The loan market is one of the institutions that help channel savings into investments, which is an essential part of any capitalistic economy. To imagine how this would work without banks, one only has to look at today's fund management industry, which also operates in the loan market (and the equity market) and which cannot print money.

In order to integrate bank credit into our model, we have to briefly clarify a few key concepts, such as investment, saving, capital goods, and interest. Even those readers who are knowledgeable about economics and familiar with these notions may benefit from the following explanation as it works out the features most relevant to our discussion and also refutes some common misconceptions about these concepts.

Consumption, Saving, and Investing

Everybody makes consumption and saving decisions. These are decisions about the use of economic resources, namely how much of what is at our disposal today should we use for meeting present-day consumption needs and thus consume, and how much should we set aside for meeting future consumption needs. It is clear, although it often gets overlooked in macroeconomic debates, that what we save does not drop out of the economy. We ultimately still want to use these resources for consumption but for as long as we do not want to consume them, others can use them for production purposes. By putting our savings in a bank or investing them via the bond or equity market, they become investments and help build a stock of capital goods.[1]

Everything in an economy is ultimately directed toward meeting the needs of people. As we have already seen, only goods and services can fulfill people's desires. Money as such cannot do it, and neither can most production goods, like machines, tools, and office buildings, but the latter can help produce and deliver the consumption goods and services that people ultimately want. Therefore, every economic activity is ultimately directed at producing consumption goods and services. By setting aside some resources for meeting future consumption needs, we invest them. They can become the capital goods that allow us to produce more and better consumption goods for the future and, in many cases, to produce consumption goods that would be inconceivable if the economy did not have a substantial capital stock. In everyday life we think of saving, and therefore of investing, purely in monetary terms, as money facilitates the exchange of goods and services and as any economic calculation requires money prices. It is evident, however, that ultimately it is goods and services that get exchanged and allocated.

A society can invest only those resources for investment purposes that are not needed by the consumers today in order to meet their present consumption needs.

It is the mark of poor societies that they need most or all of their available resources for present consumption, often literally for feeding, clothing, and sheltering the population. Richer societies have resources that are not needed for present consumption, that are saved, invested, and become capital goods. The purpose of capital goods is to produce consumption goods, but the capital goods now allow for production processes that have a higher physical productivity. Labor incomes in rich countries are higher than in poor countries because rich countries have a larger capital stock to work with. After many generations of saving, investing, and building a productive capital stock, the marginal productivity of labor is substantially higher than in poor countries.

Ultimately, the decisions on saving and investment are decisions about the use in society of real resources. Money facilitates the exchange of real goods and services, which is what any economy is ultimately about, and this includes transactions by which resources are allocated toward consumption purposes or saving/investment purposes. Just as an economy does not need more money in order to produce more goods and services, an economy does not need more money to have more investment and more savings or more capital. If that were the case, poor countries could become richer by simply printing more money.

Interest

The analysis of money injections via the loan market requires understanding of the concept of interest. Somewhat contrary to the views of the general public, interest is not a feature only of money lending. Indeed, interest is an integral part of human action. The underlying concept of interest would be detectable even in a human society that did not know money and did not have a market for loans. Because even in such a society every person would certainly value the same good or service differently depending on whether it were available today or only at a later point in time. This is called time preference and is an essential component of any act of valuation. "Present goods are valued higher than future goods of the same kind and quantity" (Mises).[2]

This statement is a priori. It must be true whenever all other factors affecting the valuation process are identical. If a person were indifferent to whether to enjoy the pleasure of consuming a certain good today or tomorrow, that person would tomorrow logically be indifferent to whether to consume it on that day or a day later. Consequently, that person would be indifferent to whether to consume the good at all. This means that the person does not value the good and that the good, therefore, does not even constitute a good to that person. "All other things being equal, to want something is to want it sooner rather than later" (George Reisman).[3] If things in some remote future were as valuable to me as anything today, I would never get up and try to obtain anything. Human action necessitates time preference.[4]

Interest is, first and foremost, simply the ratio of the value assigned to present goods over future goods. We can think of the interest rate as the discount rate at which the two values would be equal. Interest is therefore a ratio of prices, not a price in itself.[5] Interest always involves an act of valuation, which, by definition, is subjective and bound to change over time and from person to person. Therefore, interest reflects the current value assessment of economic agents, specifically, how they value goods and services of the same kind at specific points in time. Interest is then the direct expression of time preference. If time preference is high, meaning the value assigned to the satisfaction of present needs is high, interest will be high and future goods will be assigned a more heavily discounted value compared to present goods. If time preference is low, meaning the value assigned to the satisfaction of future needs is not much lower than the value assigned to the satisfaction of present needs, interest will be low and future goods will now be discounted less heavily.

This can be illustrated further by looking again at two societies, one rich and one poor. Members of a poor society are likely to have a high time preference. Given the limited means at people's disposal, many immediate consumption needs will still go unfulfilled and the value of future goods, which can only fulfill needs in the more remote future, will be assigned a much lower value than present goods. In a poor society interest rates will therefore tend to be high. By contrast, in a rich society many people will have the means to fulfill their most urgent present consumption needs and are now extending their economic planning into the more distant future. Arranging their resources to prepare for the education of their children, their own retirement, or even for future generations are now part of their considerations, and the value they assign to future goods is therefore relatively high. People in rich societies tend to have a low time preference, and interest rates tend to be low.

This is a conceptual analysis of interest. The interest rates that we observe in financial markets or in loan contracts naturally include additional elements, an entrepreneurial element and risk premiums for the risk of loan losses or for a loss in money's purchasing power. But it is clear that at the core of market rates is still the rate of interest that we describe here, which is the constituting element of market interest rates, and which Ludwig von Mises called "originary" interest in order to distinguish it from the interest rates observable on the loan market.[6]

This confirms a point established earlier in consideration of the principles of money production: The level of interest rates does not depend on the amount of money in the economy. An economy that has more money does not have lower interest rates. The level of interest depends on the time preference of the economic agents, their subjective valuation of present goods versus future goods. Equally, the level of interest does not depend on any attributes of the existing capital stock, such as its physical productivity, as was believed by classical economists. The idea that the productivity of the existing capital stock determines the level of real interest rates, that is, market rates adjusted for an inflation risk premium, is still widespread among financial market professionals today. This productivity approach to real interest rates is an entirely erroneous concept. It can be easily refuted.

The underlying assumption appears to be that in the process of bargaining between lenders and borrowers on capital markets over the temporary control of resources, the borrowers, who usually are entrepreneurs in need of resources to facilitate their investment projects, are willing and able to pay higher interest rates if the capital goods they acquire with the borrowed funds have a higher productivity. In that case, each of these capital goods of higher productivity helps produce, every year, more goods that the entrepreneurs can sell on the market, than the capital goods of lower productivity would. Consequently, it is assumed that rising productivity leads to higher market rates for the temporary control over resources, that is, to higher real interest rates on the loan market. The fatal flaw in this reasoning is that it ignores the present price of capital goods. Capital goods with a higher productivity must—all else being equal—also have a higher price.

We have already established that all economic activity is ultimately directed toward meeting consumption needs. Capital goods, such as tools and machinery, have value only to the extent that they help produce consumption goods, which in turn are demanded by consumers. Let us assume a machine is physically capable of producing, over its lifespan of 10 years, a total of 100,000 units of consumption good "p," and that the machine cannot be employed for any alternative purpose. If the demand for the good "p" were suddenly exhausted and no more units of "p" could be sold at any price, the machine would, of course, become instantly worthless. Conversely, if demand for consumption good "p" were to increase and its price to rise, then—all else being equal—the price of the machine would tend to rise, too. Although the exact price of the machine will, at any moment in time, be the result of many market factors, it is undeniable that its value to its owner and thus its price on the market must stand in a close relationship to the price of the good that it helps produce. If we now assume that the demand for "p" is still relatively strong and that more of "p" could be sold to the consumer at only marginally lower prices for "p," then we must assume that a new machine that is now capable of producing 150,000 units of "p" over a 10-year period would also demand a higher price. If the price of capital goods is derived from the price of the goods they help produce, then capital goods of higher productivity must have a higher price than capital goods of lower productivity, again assuming that all else is unchanged. It therefore follows that the internal rate of return on the investment in machinery will not necessarily be higher simply because the machinery has now a higher physical productivity. The new machine can produce more of good "p," but it will also require a bigger outlay for the entrepreneur to acquire this machine. The ability of any piece of the capital stock to help generate sellable consumption goods is fully encompassed in its present price.

We may further illustrate the inadequacy of the productivity approach to interest rates by envisioning an event that would dramatically change the population's time preference but not the productivity of the capital stock. If it became known that a giant asteroid were to hit the earth in three months and wipe out all life on the planet, it is clear that nobody would plan beyond three months and that the value of future goods and services would immediately drop to zero. This means that interest rates would suddenly not only be very high, but that they would have to be infinitely high. All available resources would instantly be redirected, to the extent possible, toward present consumption, and nobody would direct any resources to the satisfaction of consumer needs beyond three months. However, the physical productivity of the capital stock would obviously not have changed at all, but time preference and, therefore, interest rates would certainly have changed enormously.

An opposing, if somewhat less graphic example, would be the following: If the people living in some reasonably wealthy country, meaning a country where already many resources get allocated to meeting needs in the remote future, were to learn that their life expectancy had suddenly been drastically prolonged, it would be reasonable to assume that interest rates would tend to decline. The provision for the future would now become a relatively more important task, and the satisfaction of present consumption needs a relatively less important one. Time preference would have been lowered and the value assigned to future goods and services would have risen. Again, the physical productivity of the existing capital stock would not have changed at all, but time preference would have changed and that would have necessitated a change in the rate of interest. While in the scenario of the asteroid disaster, the tendency to consume rose sharply and the tendency to save practically vanished, in this example, the tendency to consume declined while the tendency to save increased. The physical productivity of the capital stock, however, was unchanged in both cases.

Although the originary rate of interest is not identical to the market rate of interest, it is apparent that the two are closely connected and that, if we rule out any disturbances on the loan market, a change in originary interest will cause the equivalent change in the market rate. To illustrate this let us again assume that time preference has declined, something that should be fairly normal in the development of a growing economy in which people get wealthier on trend. To say that time preference has dropped is identical to saying that the originary rate of interest has dropped or that future goods are now valued at a marginally smaller discount relative to present goods. People will direct some resources away from meeting present consumption needs and toward meeting future consumption needs. They consume less and save more. The additional savings are offered to entrepreneurs on the loan market where they will lower the market interest rate. At the lower interest rate, investment projects that have thus far not been viable due to the previously higher rate of interest now become marginally profitable. The lower interest rate thus encourages entrepreneurs to take temporary control of the additional resources saved by the consumers and to employ them in production processes. Via a drop in interest rates, the changed time preference leads to a reallocation of resources in the economy, away from consumption and toward investment.

To the extent that interest rates on the loans market correctly communicate changes in the originary rate of interest, they help shift the economy's resources into the forms of employment that are in accordance with the time preferences of the consumers. If their time preference is relatively low and the satisfaction of present-day consumption needs less of a priority, more resources get allocated to the production apparatus of the economy where these resources will not satisfy immediate consumption needs but where they help produce future goods and services. The extension of the production processes that the new capital allows enhances overall productivity. By employing more capital, the economy will not simply deliver the same goods and services in the future that it delivers today, but it also can now produce more or better goods with the same input, or the same goods with less input. This is one of only two possible ways of increasing society's material wealth, namely the increase of the per-capita use of capital, the other being the division of labor.

It also becomes evident why societies that have acquired a certain capital stock will exhibit a tendency to become ever wealthier. By employing more resources in production processes of higher productivity, more goods and services can be produced; this makes it even easier to fulfill present consumption needs and the wealthier population will now have—all else being equal—an even lower time preference, which leads to a larger share of the now enhanced supply of goods and services being directed toward production. This powerful tendency causes rich countries to get richer.

For any society that prefers more goods and services to fewer goods and services, a high savings rate and low interest rates are certainly desirable, as these two will help build and maintain the capital stock that allows for high-productivity production processes. Yet, it is also clear that any attempt to force interest rates lower through market intervention is dangerous and ultimately futile. Low interest rates are of no use but, indeed, harmful if they do not correspond with the population's time preference. If the government of a poor country managed to artificially lower the interest rates on the loan market with the aim of encouraging borrowing, investing, and the expansion of a wealth-enhancing capital stock, they would certainly not do their population any favors. The low rates would cause the reallocation of scarce resources away from where they help meet present consumption needs to where they will deliver future and better and cheaper goods. However, the time preference of the population is still high. Meeting the needs of the present is still a priority, and only higher interest rates will communicate these preferences correctly and ensure the appropriate use of resources. In an extreme scenario, we could imagine people having to go without food, clothes, or shelter while resources get shifted to building factories and office buildings.

As important and desirable as the latter are for an advanced economy, at this moment the population simply has other priorities. If market prices, including interest rates, do not reflect those priorities accurately, resources will be employed in ways that are of lesser importance to the population and will be wasted. From this, it follows that the path from being a poor country to being a wealthy one is likely to be slow and arduous. It will require, as its starting point, the voluntary lowering of time preference, most likely very marginally at first, that will allow at least some resources to get saved and shifted to production. These constitute the seeds of a nascent capital stock. If they are kept alive and nourished they should deliver at least a modest increase in income, which in turn should help lower time preference further. Thus, it can be hoped that the first rungs have been climbed on the ladder that leads to a lower time preference, higher savings rates, higher productivity, and, therefore, increasing wealth.

What is also clear from our analysis is that a one-off investment in productive capacity is not sufficient. A capital stock does not only need to come into existence, but it also needs to be maintained. The higher income that results from the higher productivity of using more capital should go some way toward making the maintenance of existing capital less of a burden. However, if time preference is not lastingly lowered, resources will ultimately have to be redirected again toward meeting imminent consumption needs. In this case, investment projects that were started by a temporary surge in savings will not be seen through to their completion or will not receive the steady reinvestment of resources that is required to keep them functional. The resulting disinvestment will reduce the capital stock again.

The level of interest rates in an economy is the result of an act of valuation on the part of the economic agents. In order for the investment in productive capital to increase, consumers must voluntarily free up these resources and allow their redirection toward capital formation. A change in consumer preferences is therefore the prime mover of an increase in investment. The relative valuation of present goods and services versus future goods and services has changed in such a way that the consumers are now willing to forgo the use of some of their resources for present consumption. This change in preferences is communicated to other economic agents in their role as entrepreneurs via lower interest rates. The lower interest rates will encourage the entrepreneurs to invest additional resources for the benefit of producing future goods and services. In short, increased investment is not the result of lower interest rates but of increased voluntary saving on the part of consumers. Lower interest rates indicate the increased propensity to save and assure that increased saving leads to increased investment. The driving force behind the increase in investment is a change in valuations by the consumer.

Money Injection via the Loan Market

As described in Chapter 2, in order to expand their loan business, fractional-reserve banks lower the interest rate on new loans and, as more loans are extended, bring new money into existence. Since the effect on the loan market is identical to an increase in voluntary savings, the entrepreneurs who take up the extra funds and invest them have no way of distinguishing one from the other. An increase in available credit as a result of additional true savings and an increase in available credit as a result of more paper money in response to the banks' lowering of their reserve ratios look identical to those who borrow from the loan market. In both cases, more funds become available and interest rates decline.

The new funds will not go to all businesses and industries alike but naturally will fund those projects that were marginally unprofitable at previous interest rates. As in the preceding scenario, the new money will not affect everybody at the same time and certainly not raise all prices instantly and to the same degree. The key beneficiaries of the new money are obviously the banks themselves and then the first recipients of the new money, meaning those bank clients to whom the new loans will be extended. They can use the new money to acquire goods and services before the price-raising capability of the new money has fully run its course. The new money allows its recipients to bid away resources from other economic agents. As in the case of a voluntary increase in savings, resources now get reallocated from consumption to investment. The capital stock gets extended.

The problem, however, is that no change has occurred in the time preference of consumers, in their propensity to save, and in the originary rate of interest. Nobody has, via an act of voluntary saving, freed up economic resources from their employment in satisfying imminent consumption needs, and made them available for production purposes that can only deliver consumption goods and services later. The urgency to consume now is still unchanged. The allocation of resources that is about to take shape as a result of the increased lending and the extension of the capital stock is not in accordance with consumer preferences.

It is evident that, just as in our earlier models, some prices will have to rise in response to the inflow of new money. It is also clear that without the support from changed consumer preferences the extended capital structure that is beginning to evolve as a result of the money injection cannot be maintained. The projects that were previously unprofitable are in fact still unprofitable. They would have a chance of being realized only if more resources were available for production, but that is not the case as consumers still demand these resources for consumption. The lowering of interest rates on the loan market has fooled entrepreneurs into thinking that consumers have decided to consume less and save more and that more resources are now available to be employed in additional production processes. The extension of the capital structure is based on the erroneous assumption that the public has lowered its time preference and is happy to see more resources employed in an extended production apparatus.[7]

As in our previous models, the injection of money has the character of a disturbance of the market process. This does not come as a surprise if money is correctly understood as a medium of exchange that facilitates transactions but does not bring new goods and services into existence. Money does not change the elementary valuations at the core of the market process, namely the wishes and preferences of the consumer, among them, importantly, time preference. More money is not needed for a growing economy, for an expanding productive sector, for saving and investment, and for the creation of wealth. But expanding the supply of money disturbs relative prices, first and foremost interest rates, and disorients market participants.

The Process in More Detail

Let us look at the process of money injection via the loan market in more detail. Assume that, at the starting point, the economy is in a state of equilibrium. This idea of equilibrium is a mental construct that we need because only an economy in equilibrium would not be subject to any inherent forces that change it. This notion thus allows us to isolate the effects of changes that we introduce for analytical purposes. No such state of equilibrium will ever be attained in reality, although economic processes certainly tend toward equilibrium. This is simply an analytical tool, albeit an indispensible one.

In this economy the size of the present productive structure reflects the prevailing time preference of the consumer. This means the extent to which available resources are allocated toward production rather than imminent consumption reflects prevailing time preference, and this is communicated to everybody in the economy via interest rates. Now an injection of new money from the banking industry via the loan market occurs. Inevitably, the new money at lower interest rates will encourage entrepreneurs to start new and more capital-intensive investment projects. Lower interest rates mean that the element of time becomes less of a constraining factor. Processes that require outlays today but only generate returns tomorrow, or deliver consumable goods tomorrow, are now more easily realizable. Tying up economic resources in longer-lasting production processes is the very essence of capital creation.

Let us assume that entrepreneurs start investing in plants and machinery that will ultimately allow the production of the very same consumer items that are in demand today but allow a more efficient production of them. We have already seen that this is likely to be the case as the use of more capital increases productivity. From a technological point of view this is a very sensible endeavor indeed, as a shift toward more capital-intensive production is essential for any society whose members want to get wealthier. The increased money leads to increased investment, which helps meet the same consumer needs more efficiently. This sounds rather good. What can go wrong?

The entrepreneurs will inevitably use the newly available funds to bid away resources from others in the economy. More specifically, the new money will allow the new entrepreneurs to pay other producers to produce the intermediate goods—such as machines and tools—that they need for their new investment projects. This means that some producers who previously employed scarce resources, including labor, in the production of consumer goods, albeit at relatively lower levels of productivity, will now shift these resources toward the production of producers' goods, that is, the tools and machinery that the new entrepreneurs need for their projects. Obviously, they will do this only if they are paid more than what they received in their previous line of business, and this is possible only because of the newly created money in the hands of the new entrepreneurs. What we see here again, in the context of a more complex and more realistic model this time, are the reallocation effects of money injections that we already encountered in the earlier and more primitive models. The new money has not filtered through to the consumer goods market yet. But, in this first stage, it allows its first recipients, the new entrepreneurs, to pay higher wages and higher factor prices for the labor and the intermediate goods they need for their investment projects. The prices of certain investment goods will now go up.

Initially, there are still enough already produced consumer goods available for consumption to proceed undisturbed. At this first stage, a rise in overall economic activity will undoubtedly be recorded as unchanged consumption that can for a while coincide with increased investment activity. The GDP statistics of our model economy will pick up at first.

After some time, however, the redirection of productive resources will be felt on the market for consumer goods. The stream of readily available consumption goods will lessen as productive capacity is being redeployed toward delivering the machines and tools that the entrepreneurs need for their new projects. Fewer readily available consumer goods arrive on the market. At this point, the fact that credit expansion was funded by money printing rather than by true saving comes into play and begins to develop forces that will work in the opposite direction of the ones at work so far. If the whole process had been kickstarted by an act of voluntary saving on the part of consumers, the marginal drop in supply of consumer goods would not be a problem. Increased saving would have meant a lessened demand for consumption goods but this was not the case in this scenario. A shrinking supply of consumer goods coupled with an unchanged urge to consume can mean only that an upward pressure on consumer goods prices will now develop. But how can consumers pay the higher prices? The newly printed money has not dispersed through the entire economy yet but is still circulating among various producers. The short answer is, they cannot, or at least not right away.

The producers of the new intermediate goods will, of course, receive higher money incomes. This means they will be the first to be able to pay higher prices for consumption goods. Naturally, this includes the workers who work for these producers. As they work in one of the sectors that benefit from the infusion of new money first, they stand a better chance than workers in other industries of demanding higher wages to compensate them for the rising prices of consumption goods. We see here another example of the redistributive power of money injections. But it is clear that not all consumers will be able to raise their money income in response to the price pressures in the consumption goods market. How they can respond to this, we will address shortly.

In any case, it is evident that prices for investment goods rise earlier and, until the later stages of this process, also more strongly than the prices for consumer goods. The investment goods market is the market on which the new money arrives first. It is the rise in the prices of capital goods that encourages some producers to redirect their efforts from producing consumption goods to producing capital goods (machinery, tools) for the new entrepreneurs, and this will later lead to the rise in prices for consumption goods. Inflation measures that focus on consumer prices are therefore likely to pick up the price effects of money injections via the loan market only at a late stage of the process.

Many popular presentations of the money injection process appear to imply that new money spreads quickly to every corner of the economy. These models tend to ignore the redistributive effects of money injections because they disregard the very process by which money gets dispersed throughout the economy. With the new money not spreading instantly and magically to everybody in the economy, it has the power to shift resources into different employment for some time. In our scenario, the new money reaches a specific group of producers first who can only realize their projects if they pay other producers who thereby become the second recipients of the money. As the money filters through the economy, resources will get reallocated. For a while the productive structure that is beginning to take shape makes it look indeed as though additional saving has occurred. In the absence of shifts in consumer preferences, however, the resulting structure is unsustainable.

For the outside observer and, equally, for all the actors in the economy, there is simply no way of telling whether what is occurring is in response to money printing or in response to voluntary saving. Of course, the by now familiar results of a near-term boost to GDP (spending) and a trend toward higher overall prices (inflation) will be evident. In a way, money injections via the loan market combine elements of our previous two models. There is an indisputable element of deception involved. Savings have not increased and preferences have not changed, but market signals have become distorted in a way that makes economic agents believe that these changes have indeed occurred. Equally, this process involves a decidedly uneven distribution of the new money. Both effects combine to disorient decision makers and to have them engage in processes that have no support from underlying consumer preferences. Money injections lead borrowers onto the thin ice of investment projects for which the fellow members of society are not willing to supply resources, at least not as readily and inexpensively as artificially lowered interest rates on the loan market suggest.

Surely, the economy exhibits all the symptoms of genuine vibrancy at first. There are new and better paying jobs in the expanding industries, and there is an increase in investment activity. Ultimately—but only at a later stage in this process—will the prices of consumer goods begin to rise. We now turn back to the question of how consumers cope with the diminishing supply of consumption goods and the rising price pressures. Besides rising wage income, which we discussed previously, the consumers have other means of raising the funds to pay higher prices. To the extent that they have been savers before, they now have an incentive to reduce active saving from ongoing income, and also to liquidate existing savings and spend the money on consumption. Some of their consumption needs went unfulfilled at old prices and can be met only at higher cost. Simultaneously, the interest they get for lending their existing savings on the loan market has dropped as a result of artificially lower interest rates. Consequently, the actions that consumers take in response to the changing price structure and reduced supply of consumer goods are directed toward driving both consumer prices and interest rates higher. Because the shift in resources was not in accordance with their preferences, it should not come as a surprise that the activities of consumers—their consumption decisions as well as their saving decisions—will tend to counteract the trends that have been initiated by the arbitrary injection of new money. Interest rates reflect the time preference of economic agents, and as the prevailing rate on the market for loans has been artificially lowered, the liquidation of savings is one mechanism by which the rate can be raised again to reflect the true underlying "originary" rate of interest.

The rise in interest rates is meaningful in another way. So far in the analysis, we have assumed that the originary rate is unchanged and that only the loan rate has been changed, that is, depressed by money production. However, we have to presume that in response to the effects of money injection described before, the originary rate of interest has in fact gone up, rather than stayed unchanged. Because of the money-induced changes in resource allocation, certain consumption needs remain unfulfilled, which means time preference is now higher than it was at the start of the money injection process. Consumers should assign an even lower value to future goods relative to present goods than before. Their time preference must have risen in response to the new undersupply of consumption goods. The desire to liquidate savings or refrain from saving is not only the result of the artificially depressed loan market rate, but it is also the natural expression of a higher time preference that is the direct result of the insufficient supply of consumer goods.

Rising consumer prices and rising interest rates are now beginning to derail the very process that the money injection had set in motion. For the producers who began to redirect their efforts away from delivering consumer goods and toward producing the intermediate goods (machinery and tools) for the new entrepreneurs, it is now less compelling to do so. Sticking to their previous business of producing consumer goods looks relatively more attractive again given the higher prices of consumer goods. To the extent that the new entrepreneurs need new loans or need to roll over existing loans at current interest rates, they are now facing higher funding costs.

The combination of higher consumer prices and higher interest rates sends an unmistakable signal to every producer in the economy: Time preference is high. Consumers need more consumption goods and they need them fast. Building a more elaborate production structure, whatever its technological benefits might be, is a luxury that society cannot or does not want to afford itself at this stage. It is therefore likely that the investment projects that were started are discontinued. At least some of the new entrepreneurs will fail as their projects were based on erroneous assumptions. The error was, however, not one of poor judgment on their part but was the unavoidable result of a distorted market signal. The lowering of the loan rate had fooled the entrepreneurs into believing that new resources had become available for extending the capital structure, when all that happened was that more money had been printed.

We have tried to analyze the process by which the investment boom is started and then aborted in some detail and what we see at its core is again the principle that any injection of new money temporarily increases the purchasing power of its recipients for as long as and to the degree that the price-raising capabilities of the new money have not run their course. Once that is the case, the preferences of the economic agents, which are the ultimate drivers of any voluntary activity and any sustainable resource allocation, come to the surface again and when that happens resources will again be reallocated. What matters to an economy is always the same: the available resources, both nature-given and previously produced (the capital stock), the technological know-how, and the preferences, attitudes, and wishes of the economic actors. None of this is changed by the trickery of money injection.

Obviously, the effects of money injection do not have to be as short-lived as in our scenario, which, for the sake of keeping the analysis simple, assumed a one-off act of discretionary money injection. If the banks are willing, they might extend their money-creation activities over a longer period and just as the first dose of money is beginning to lose its power to shift resources another injection of money might occur, further extending the process just described. If money creation is continuous, the build-up of the capital structure beyond what consumer preferences ultimately allow can be much more extensive. Indeed, this is what is likely to happen in reality. Fractional-reserve banks go through periods of more risk taking and less risk taking and, considering today's monetary infrastructure, they are unlikely to cancel one another out in the process.

If one or more banks decide to lower rates to expand their loan operations through a lower reserve ratio and increased money production, this is bound to generate two conflicting tendencies. On the one hand, it will exert pressure on competing banks to do likewise as they risk losing business by not matching the lower loan rates of their competitors. This factor is bound to make money creation more broad-based and lasting. On the other hand, lowering reserve ratios increases the risk of bank runs and to the extent that other banks do not join in, the ones that are more advanced in the money creation process risk increasing outflows of reserve money to their more conservative competitors, which increases their business risk substantially.

In an entirely free market, in which the monetary asset is a non-replicable commodity, and in which no central bank and state support infrastructure exists, the scope for money creation through fractional-reserve banking is strictly limited as just explained. Today's monetary arrangements, however, with their lender-of-last-resort central banks, elastic and unlimited reserve money, and state guarantees for depositors, have greatly diminished the risks that were usually inherent in joining other banks in a credit boom. Importantly, the various measures that were designed to make banking safer for the banks have invariably desensitized bank customers to the balance sheet risk of the individual bank. Consequently, little or nothing is to be gained for the management of any bank from running a higher reserve ratio and a more conservative balance sheet policy. There can be little doubt that, in aggregate, today's regulatory and financial support structure for banks has substantially increased the tendency of banks to expand balance sheets together. Under present arrangements, it is much more likely that banks mutually reinforce their tendencies to reduce reserves, lower rates, and create more money.

The very impression of economic vibrancy that is generated in the early phase of the process will also encourage more banks to join others in their creation of money and credit and turn it into an economy-wide trend. Overall business conditions appear good, which in turn makes the risk of lending seem small. If anything, in these conditions banks will tend to lower their reserve ratios further. Obviously, under contemporary arrangements, the central bank has to, at a minimum, tolerate the expansion of money and credit by the banks. But this appears highly probable given that most central banks today have a mandate to support economic growth and allow ongoing moderate inflation.

These are the basic elements of a credit cycle, in which a period of expanding money encourages additional investment but leads to an unsustainable structure of the production side of the economy and to a distorted structure of relative prices. These structures are distorted and unsustainable because they are at odds with the preferences of consumers. Only continuous injections of money by which the money producer tries to stay a step ahead of the attempts of the consumers to reestablish the prices and the productive structure that reflect their preferences keeps the boom going. Whenever the inflow of new money ceases, or only slows down meaningfully, a recession ensues; at least some of the new investment projects get dismantled and resources are again reallocated and prices readjusted. A recession has in fact become unavoidable once money creation has meaningfully affected prices and resource allocation. The recession is the necessary process of adjustment by which the economy is cleansed of the accumulated mispricings and misallocations of resources from the preceding, artificial boom. Naturally, the correction will be more severe the longer and the more extensive the preceding money-induced boom has been and the larger the dislocations in the economy have become.

The phenomena that characterize a period of recession are a decline in economic activity and a fall in certain prices. Activity declines because many of the investment projects that previously benefited from the money injections are discontinued. Additionally, those prices that were artificially boosted by money injections during the boom will tend to recede. Painful as they might be to some in the economy, these corrections are necessary to bring prices, resource allocation, and economic activity back in line with the preferences of all members of society. This process is therefore in the interest of everybody. It is indispensible for the continuing smooth operation of the extensive division of labor that the extended market economy makes possible. There is simply no alternative to going through a readjustment of prices and resource use once money injections have led economic structures astray. It is also evident that the recession will not go on forever, as is often feared. There is no reason to assume that the recessionary forces will somehow feed on themselves and lead to ever worsening conditions. The recession will end when structures are again more closely aligned with the preferences of consumers.

Policy Implications of the Austrian Theory

As mentioned previously, what we describe here is a business cycle theory, usually called the Austrian theory of the business cycle. I give

a stylized and compressed version of the theory, which should be sufficient for our purposes but necessarily neglects some of the finer points
of the theory. This theory is called the Austrian theory because it was
first formulated by Viennese economists working in the methodological
tradition of Carl Menger (1840–1921), who elaborated the principles
of what became the Austrian School of Economics in the latter part of
the nineteenth century.[8] Building on Menger's methodological foundation, Eugen von Boehm-Bawerk (1851–1914) made crucial advances
in the theory of capital and interest,[9] and Ludwig von Mises (1881–
1973), who became the leading intellectual light of the Austrian School
in the twentieth century, did seminal work in several areas, among them
notably the theory of money. It was in particular von Mises' 1912 book
on money and fiduciary media that laid the foundation for what became
the Austrian business cycle theory.[10]

In contrast to practically all other cycle theories, the Austrian theory
manages to explain the phenomena of boom and bust on the basis of
a discretionary disruption of the market's pricing process via the injection of money. It does not have to rely on arbitrary disturbances that
in other economic theories often appear to spring up randomly, such
as a lack of "animal spirits," a drop in aggregate demand, a sudden lack
of investment opportunities, or an excessive propensity to save or to
hoard money. Once the expansion of money and the artificial lowering
of interest rates have sufficiently dislocated the allocation of resources,
a recession has become inevitable because it is required to get resource
allocation back to sustainable structures. The conclusion for policy
makers is clear: Do not try to artificially lower interest rates and create
extra growth through cheap credit. After a short-term boom you will
face a recession. If you want to avoid a recession, you have to keep the
supply of money inelastic and allow voluntary saving to determine
interest and credit on an unhampered market. We have already shown
that this was decidedly not the course policy makers took throughout
the twentieth century.

Public debate and policy today are largely guided by macroeconomic theories that portray the recession as an almost isolated event
driven by uncontrollable exogenous forces. These theories fail to appreciate that the roots of the recession lie in the preceding false boom.
A lot of the blame for this has to go to the change in the focus of

economic enquiry, namely from a micro-perspective that starts every analysis with the individual actor, to the macro-perspective of statistical aggregates. The latter has come to dominate economics in the twentieth century. The macro variables that now rule economic debate, such as GDP or the consumer price level, are incapable of capturing the all-important effects of money injections on relative prices and resource allocation. The corresponding theories cannot account for new money's power to redirect activity and reallocate income and resources because they only deal with money's impact on the large wholes of national account statistics. Consequently, they fail to identify the most potent reasons for recessions, which are the dislocations that are unavoidable by-products of the money-induced boom. Guided by these theories, economic policy today is destined to fight the symptoms. Policy constantly tries to abort or delay the necessary adjustment process, and to maintain or even expand existing relative prices and resource allocations through market interventions such as further money injections (easy monetary policy) or state-enforced resource use (fiscal policy).

And in a world of limitless paper money and lender-of-last-resort central banks, this means that whenever the dislocations created by easy money and artificially low interest rates begin to derail the economy, a credit correction is avoided by a renewed administrative lowering of rates by the central bank and, if required, further additional injections of money. The idea behind this is obvious: The boom is good and should just be enjoyed; the correction is bad and must be avoided at all cost. And with money being now fully elastic, why ever suffer a credit contraction?

However, we know from the Austrian analysis that this cannot solve the underlying problems. Easy monetary policy in a recession simply obstructs or stops the adjustment process. The misallocations of capital from the previous boom do not get corrected and instead are carried forward into the next money-induced expansion in which additional misallocations are added to the existing ones. The next time a recession occurs—and it will, of course, only be a question of time—the need for a cleansing correction will be even more intense, and it will consequently require an even larger injection of money and even lower interest rates than previously to postpone the correction again and to manufacture another boom with the help of artificially low interest rates. There can be no doubt that this is a process that must make the economy progressively more unbalanced. Recessions will get more protracted, recoveries will be more difficult to engineer and will be shallower and more fragile. As the distortions that need liquidating get bigger, it will be politically ever more difficult to allow the correction to unfold. And as the policy establishment has long maintained that "under a paper money system, a determined government can always generate higher spending and hence positive inflation" (Bernanke),[11] the short-term fix of more money will be applied in ever larger doses. If this policy framework is not ultimately abandoned, it must finally undermine the confidence of the public in the state's paper money and lead to complete currency collapse.

We have to remember that the Austrian School developed its cycle theory in the context of a gold standard. Under a gold standard, the type of active monetary policy that short-circuits recessions and extends the cycle was not possible. Recessions were, by and large, allowed to properly cleanse the economy of misallocations and bring the economy back into some form of balance. It was therefore indeed appropriate to speak of a cycle. But this is no longer the case. A cycle implies that the system returns somehow to its previous position, or at least somewhere near its previous position. A business cycle describes fluctuations around a mean. This mean can be stable, or ascending or descending. But crucially, the cyclical factors are independent from the trend development of the mean. They do not describe any long-term trend at all but simply the ups and downs of fluctuations around the trend. In this sense, it is no longer appropriate to speak of a cycle. The introduction of a complete paper money system has transformed the factors that drove the business cycle into factors that drive ongoing decline of the overall system. Imbalances and dislocations get bigger, and in a desperate quest for short-term relief, policy makers are bound to accelerate this trend of monetary disintegration. In contrast to the cycle, this development has an endgame.

What the endgame for our present system may look like, we will investigate in one of the following chapters. Before we do this, we will first have a look at the mainstream's fixation with the "price index" and with the policy of price level stabilization, a fixation that in many ways distracts from the true innate problems of fully elastic money. We will then take a look at the sad history of state paper money systems, which shows that all previous attempts by governments to run uncon-strained paper money systems have failed—without exception. Then we will take a look at the broader intellectual superstructure of present arrangements to finally sketch the system's most probable path toward collapse.

Summary

Injections of money do not improve the productive capacity of an economy. This is not surprising, considering that we have already established that money is simply a medium of exchange and that it is in the nature of a medium of exchange that practically any supply of it is sufficient to deliver all the services a medium of exchange ever can deliver. More money is not needed for the economy to produce and trade more goods and services. Thus, the productivity of an economy cannot be permanently enhanced by the injection of addi-tional money. However, this does not mean that money injections have no effects.

Today's macroeconomic mainstream stresses two effects of money injections. Money injections elevate the price level, and they boost spending, that is, GDP. Our systematic analysis of money injections revealed that the former effect always occurs. Of course, this is under the important assumption, essential for formulating any economic theory, that all else is equal. If we remove that assumption and consider a situation in which the demand for money happens to increase simul-taneously, it is conceivable that the price-lifting effect of the money injection may be partially or fully compensated by the price-lowering effect of rising money demand. In such a situation, the statistical mea-sures of inflation may remain broadly unchanged. This is a scenario that we will consider in more detail in the next chapter. However, none of this detracts from the essential truth of the statement that an expanding supply of money, all else being equal, will lead to a drop in the pur-chasing power of the monetary unit.

Our analysis has revealed a couple of additional facts about the new money's effect on prices. In every even marginally realistic scenario of money injection, the effect on prices will neither be uniform nor proportional to the expansion of the money supply. This means that it is inconceivable that a 10 percent expansion of money will lead to all prices rising by 10 percent, or even a relatively broad average of prices rising by 10 percent. The reason for this is simply that money will always be injected at a specific point in the economy, and that it will then begin to disperse via a number of transactions. This is the "GDP-lifting" effect of money injections that we will discuss next. But because new money always changes relative prices and therefore resource allocation and wealth distribution, it is impossible for prices to change uniformly and in exact proportion to the size of the inflow. An expanding money supply will lead to a drop in money's purchasing power but some prices will respond more than others.

As to the GDP-boosting effect of money injections, it is indisputable that these are temporary effects only. It is impossible for money injections to lift the economy's growth potential to a higher plateau and to lastingly improve the economy's productivity. However, the mainstream is not wrong in maintaining that money injections lead to additional economic transactions and therefore to a temporary lift of GDP statistics. We have to remember, though, that all that the GDP statistics do is to record the number of economic transactions and the notional amounts involved. The type of additional activity that money injections initiate is rather different from what most people would normally associate with a rising GDP. The additional transactions are adjustment activity by which the economy adapts to the disturbance of a discretionary injection of money. The transactions result from the uneven distribution of the new money and from the desire of the early recipients of the money to take advantage of their privileged position by buying cheaply from those that still sell at lower prices. Additional transactions occur also because of errors that market participants make in response to some of the changes in relative prices that the new money creates early in the process.

Not only does the inflow of money not improve the market's core function, which is to bring together individuals for mutually beneficial economic exchange, but it also invariably disorients market participants and allows those in an advantageous position in the money-distribution chain to benefit at the expense of those in a less advantageous position.

Early recipients of the new money are always the winners, late recipients always the losers. We have to admit that as a consequence of all of this, the GDP statistics will record additional transactions for a while but it is clear that GDP loses its status as a measure of economic health under these circumstances. GDP has risen but lasting real wealth has not, and neither has the efficiency of resource use. And if money is injected via credit markets, which is the most common procedure of money creation today, the efficiency of resource use will even decline.

In this case, the new money must disturb the essential price relationship that is interest. Interest is the relationship of present prices to future prices, and is essential for the allocation of scarce resources between consumption and investment. An expansion of money lowers interest rates artificially and thereby encourages a level of investment activity that goes beyond what would be justified by voluntary saving. The resulting shifts in resource use and the extension of the capital stock are therefore unsustainable. The resulting boom is misguided and will end in a correction. Again, error is at work. The spurt of growth that is kick-started by the injection of money is based on an illusion. Economic actors are tricked into believing that a larger amount of resources has been freed up from their previous employment in close proximity to immediate consumption and has been made available for employment farther away from immediate consumption, thus allowing a more extended productive sector or the production of more longer-lasting consumption goods, like houses. Those who take up the new money loans offered at lower rates on the loan market, and use them to invest, do so under the false impression that what they do is in accordance with the wishes and preferences of the other members of society who appear to have signaled a lower time preference and therefore a willingness to support an extended capital structure. The additional growth occurs only because actors are misled into forms of economic activity that would deliver the hoped-for results only if consumer preferences had shifted. That, however, has not been the case. The rise in GDP is manufactured via a misallocation of resources. The boom must end in a bust.

There is no escape from the conclusion that a recession will not be avoided but, at best, be postponed by artificially lowering interest rates again and by injecting even more money when the initial boom peters out. The recession is the inevitable and necessary, if painful, process by which prices and productive structures get realigned with consumer preferences. The economy gets cleansed of the misallocations of resources and the misdirection of economic activity that were the necessary precondition of the false boom. If monetary policy tries to avoid or short-circuit the recession by injecting more money, as is now standard practice for all paper money central banks, it will only postpone the necessary adjustment. This will also make the ultimate recession even bigger, as the extra money injection will lead to the accumulation of additional dislocations.

Thus, one of the key arguments supporting the present arrangements—paper money, fractional-reserve, and central banking—namely, that they allow a swift and effective policy response to recessions, collapses entirely. A pro-growth monetary policy works everywhere and always via resource misallocation. It can therefore never be the solution to an economic crisis but only its origin. An expansionary monetary policy, even when applied after a crisis and during recession, and even at times of stable or falling price levels, misdirects resources away from the underlying preferences of society. Such a policy has to operate via distortions to generate a boost to growth. Misallocation of resources is the only way for new money to generate additional economic activity.

In part one of our investigation we established conclusively that a form of elastic money, which allows the constant expansion of the money supply, is not needed. Elastic money is superfluous. In part two we established that expanding money is always disruptive. If money injections are continued for an extended period, economic imbalances of substantial proportion must accumulate. The obvious question now is, what is the endgame? But before we turn to this question, we need to analyse the belief system that supports the present infrastructure. This will help us understand why the true source of growing economic instability is so regularly not correctly diagnosed, and why economic policy will most probably continue to destabilize the system further. We will also take a look at experiences with paper money systems. This will show that complete collapse has historically been the norm rather than the exception when it comes to the termination of paper money systems. First, however, we will take a look at the issue of price level stability and ask how good an indicator of monetary stability a stable price average is, and to what degree price level stability is achievable under paper and commodity money. This is an important part of our investigation, as the price level plays such a crucial role in today's debates on monetary matters.

Part Three

FALLACIES ABOUT THE PRICE LEVEL AND PRICE LEVEL STABILIZATION

Chapter 5

Common Misconceptions Regarding the Price Level

Toorday, in any discussion about monetary affairs in academia, in financial markets, and among policy makers, the price level is of inordinate importance. "Price level" here means any of the broad-based statistical averages of prices in the economy, such as the consumer price index or the producer price index, that are considered good representations of money's purchasing power.

The Price Level and Monetary Stability

It would not be an exaggeration to say that a reasonably stable price level has become the accepted definition of good money. Of course, this does not mean that complete price level stability is sought by policy makers or by the economists who advise them. The shift from inelastic commodity money to elastic paper money was consummated precisely in order to allow the constant expansion of the money supply, and, as we have seen and as is not contested by the mainstream, this will lead to an ongoing decline in money's purchasing power. Today's macro-economic consensus maintains that this is helpful for growth. In the preceding chapters we have seen that this is not the case. Be that as it may, a too-rapid decline in money's purchasing power is deemed undesirable and "good money" is thus defined as money the purchasing power of which diminishes constantly but at a moderate pace.

The fixation with the price level is understandable if we consider that an accelerating decay in money's purchasing power has the potential to cause complete loss of confidence in fiat money. Since immaterial money is based on nothing but confidence, a loss of confidence is, unquestionably, the biggest risk to the survival of any paper money system. As we will see in the next part of our investigation, every paper money system in history has, after some time, experienced rising inflation. In fact, no paper money system in history has survived. Either a voluntary return to commodity money was accomplished before a complete currency meltdown occurred, or the system collapsed in hyperinflation and economic and social chaos. We are frequently told that this time is different. Policy makers assure us that they have learned the lessons of history and will now pay close attention to the inflation rate. Thus, we may appreciate why the price level has achieved such extraordinary importance in policy debates today. This focus, however, has been the source of new and dangerous fallacies.

Although it is certainly true that elastic money with a rapidly diminishing purchasing power is "bad" money, it does not follow that money with only a moderate decline in purchasing power is necessarily "good" money. To put this differently, the distortions that expanding money must necessarily generate, and that we just analyzed, occur whenever the money supply is expanded, even if certain other developments should mitigate the impact of this monetary expansion on the price level, and if therefore the price level does not rise much or not rise at all. What could these compensating factors be? It is clear that if the demand for money rises at the same time as additional money is being injected into the economy, the price index may remain fairly stable.

From this, today's macroeconomic consensus concludes that the additional money is nondisruptive. The extra money just satisfies additional demand for money. As the price level remains relatively stable, no overissuance of money has occurred and, therefore, no economic imbalances have been generated. This is a dangerous misconception as we can clearly see from our analysis.

We have seen that injections of money lead to misallocations of capital, which, in turn, create first a boom and then a bust. These misallocations are the result of distorted relative prices, in particular artificially lowered interest rates, as a direct consequence of the money injection. They are distinctly not the result of a change in the price level. The statistical averages of prices may indeed remain fairly unchanged even after an injection of new money, but this does not mean that relative prices were not distorted by the money injection and that therefore capital misallocations have not occurred.

By definition, a price average cannot reflect changes in relative prices, but it is distortions in relative prices that lead money injections to cause capital misallocations. The price average may remain broadly unchanged in a scenario in which rising demand for money is depressing certain prices in the economy, while an injection of money is simultaneously lifting other prices. We have to remember that neither phenomenon affects all prices in the same way, affects them instantly, or affects them to the same extent. In such a scenario, the price index is unchanged but the effects on resource allocation are identical to what we saw in the models in the previous chapters. Because of compensating factors, money injections may not succeed in lifting the overall price level but they will still disrupt relative prices and lead to capital misallocations.

We see here a fundamental problem with macroeconomics. The assumption of those who consider the price average a good benchmark of monetary stability is that the rising demand for money on the one hand and the rising supply of money on the other hand would simply meet in the market and smoothly offset one another. But a look underneath the broad aggregates makes it clear that this is not only unlikely, but it is also practically impossible. The reason is that those who produce the extra money, that is, the banks and the central bank, do not deal with those whose demand for money has increased. Those who have a higher demand for money, as we have seen, become sellers of goods and services. In order to raise money holdings, either they will liquidate some of their possessions, that is, sell assets, or they will reduce ongoing outlays, which means they will cut back on spending on the acquisition of new consumption goods or new investment goods. By either selling assets or reducing consumption or saving, they will try to increase their holdings of money and thereby satisfy their increased demand for the medium of exchange.

In order to directly meet this demand for money via an increased supply of money—evidently a superfluous exercise as the extra demand would be met naturally and automatically by an adjustment to the purchasing power of the monetary asset—a process would have to exist by which the central bank or private banks would directly engage with these people, buy assets from them, and thus supply them with more money. No such process exists. As we have seen, the central bank and assorted private banks place the new money on the loan market. Borrowers on the loan market, however, have no demand for money but a strong demand for goods and services. That is why they borrow and incur the extra expense of interest. Once they got hold of the money through the loan, they immediately spend it. Only very few people who have genuine demand for money will borrow money at interest on the loan market in order to maintain a higher cash balance. While such behavior cannot be excluded entirely, it is evident that the usual procedure for anyone wanting to increase cash balances is still to sell assets or reduce money outlays. Those who will be encouraged by the lowering of interest rates on the loan market and the production of extra money by the banks to take out additional loans, and who are therefore the first recipients of the new money, constitute, most certainly, a different subset of the public than those who experience a rising demand for money. Thus, the increased demand for money cannot be satisfied directly by central bank and banking sector, in contrast to what the simple juxtaposition of aggregate money demand and aggregate money supply in macroeconomic models tends to suggest. The extra money may reach those who have extra demand for money in a roundabout way, but in the meantime the extra money will lead to all the dislocations that we analyzed previously.

If we assume that a central bank had, over a given period, allowed the money supply to expand but that the price index had, by the end of this period, not moved much, we may agree with the mainstream that the effect of the extra money on the price average had been compensated by the opposing effect of a rising demand for money. We may also agree that, if the central bank had not allowed an expansion of the money supply, the price level would most likely have declined. However, we cannot agree with the conclusion that the money injection had thus sustained a greater monetary and economic stability. The extra money that the banking sector produced was not handed directly to those with a higher demand for money, it was placed in the loan market where it propagated a drop in interest rates, thereby encouraged additional borrowing and additional investment, and initiated economic activity and resource use that would ultimately not be backed by the public's true propensity to save. All these disruptive effects still unfolded. None of them were rendered harmless just because, somewhere else in the economy, a rising demand for money suppressed certain prices, thereby allowing the price average to remain broadly unchanged. In fact, the destabilizing effects of money injections would have been avoided only if the central bank and assorted private banks had not artificially lowered rates and injected more money, and had instead allowed the increased demand for money to be satisfied naturally by a rise in money's purchasing power. From the point of view of overall economic stability, the drop in the price level in response to a rise in money demand, that is, a period of deflation, would certainly have been preferable to the maintenance of price level stability via additional money injection.

The notion that the price level is an accurate and reliable indicator of monetary stability and therefore economic stability is wrong and dangerous. Money injections must distort interest rates and other relative prices and lead to suboptimal resource use. This is what makes an elastic money supply so disruptive and what causes the boom–bust cycle. We explained these effects in detail in the preceding chapters. None of these disturbances is neutralized by the rise in money demand. All that the rise in money demand does is mitigate the effect of the money injection on the price average.

Bitter experience with paper money inflations has made the public more aware of the risk of loss of purchasing power. But today's obsession with statistical inflation measures, while understandable, brings new risks. First of all, there is the risk that these measures have been constructed inappropriately. In particular, they may be too narrow, and focusing on, for example, a limited set of consumer prices, which, as we have seen, respond usually fairly late in the money expansion process, may provide an incomplete image of money-induced price distortions. But even if they are reasonably broad and not too misleading, these price averages are still unable to capture the full effects of money expansion. In particular, a rising demand for money may contain the impact of the monetary expansion on such a price average but will not diminish the potential of the money injection to distort relative prices and to misallocate resources. A fairly stable price aggregate can instil an unjustified sense of security and stability in the public and make the public tolerant of ongoing money expansion, when in fact such money injections must be destabilizing for the economy and must set it up for an unpleasant correction.

A Historical Perspective on Price Level Stability

Inelastic commodity money has everywhere been replaced with fully elastic paper money under government control. The driving motivation for this has been, and still is, the desire to constantly expand money and thus allow credit expansion without saving. This has, as we have seen, deleterious consequences, many of which are today not fully understood or appreciated by the public. The one negative consequence that is appreciated, however, is the ongoing loss of money's purchasing power. Consequently, most central banks today have a mandate, whether implicit or explicit, to manage and control this ongoing decline. According to current consensus opinion, "good" paper money is paper money that loses its purchasing power at a moderate pace and in an orderly and predictable fashion, with the predictability of this process seen as particularly important. This has now led to the widespread view that such a form of money is even superior to commodity money. Because the purchasing power of the latter is, of course, not controlled or managed by any institution, and must necessarily adjust to any changes in money demand or to other market forces, occasionally even abruptly, it is commonly believed today that the exchange value of commodity money must be very unstable. This has led to the bizarre situation that what is essentially one of elastic paper money's key weaknesses, its declining exchange value, which makes some form of inflation-management by the central bank a requirement, has been transformed into one of paper money's alleged advantages. Well-managed paper money, so states today's macroeconomic consensus, is not only better than poorly managed paper money, but it is also even better than commodity money, which is not managed at all. Many mainstream economists today readily quote price level stability as a reason in favor of a paper money system under government control rather than against it.

This line of reasoning is remarkable considering that any destabilizing volatility in money's purchasing power, and certainly any ongoing decline in purchasing power, has never been a serious problem under a commodity money system. It is a fact of history that commodity money has never been abandoned and replaced with paper money for the purpose of providing society with a more stable medium of exchange. No historical example is known of the money users in society either coming together voluntarily to create, among themselves, a noncommodity form of money, or asking their government to create a non-commodity form of money because they thought that the existing commodity money was deemed too volatile to be of use for commerce. Paper money was introduced regularly by states in order to improve their own finances (most commonly for the purpose of waging war) and, to a lesser degree, to provide "elastic money" in aid of fractional-reserve banking. Undoubtedly, this often appealed to sections of the population but not because they were hoping for greater purchasing power stability but because they shared the erroneous belief that "easy" money meant more prosperity.

The suggestion that, under a paper money system, a medium of exchange of greater purchasing power stability could be delivered flies in the face of all historic experience. Throughout history and without exception, exactly the opposite has been the case. Whenever commodity money was replaced with state paper money, sooner or later, the monetary unit began to lose purchasing power. Indeed, volatility of the price level has only ever been discussed as an economic problem in paper money systems, or in watered-down commodity money systems with rapidly expanding fractional-reserve banking. While commodity money has a remarkable record of stability, state fiat monies have, without exception, led to rising inflation and frequently ended in total inflationary meltdown.

In his study *Monetary Regimes and Inflation,* Peter Bernholz looks at long-run statistics of the cost of living in Britain, Switzerland, France, and the United States.[1] No upward or downward trends are discernible at all from 1750 to 1914. Clear upward trends in the cost of living materialized after 1914, when some governments left the Classical Gold Standard to allow for inflationary war financing. These trends become more marked after 1933 and in particular after 1971, when the United States took the dollar off gold internationally and a complete paper money system was established globally.

There can be no doubt that the intellectual trends of the twentieth century were exceptionally adverse to the concept of commodity money and very favorable to state-controlled paper money. This was the century of big state ideologies, of socialism and communism, of fascism and Nazism, and, after the Second World War, of social democracy, that is, of "capitalism" under the control of a democratically legitimized state. The notion that the ambitions of state authority should be subjugated to the strict confines of a commodity money system, or that a society's monetary affairs should be outside political control, did not resonate much with the zeitgeist. It is no surprise that of the 30 superinflations that meet the modern statisticians definition of a hyper-inflation, that is, a monthly rise in consumer prices of more than 50 percent, 29 occurred in the twentieth century.[2] Of the pre–twentieth century paper money collapses, only the meltdown of the assignats, the paper money of revolutionary France, makes the cut.

The two oldest currencies in the world today, the pound and the dollar, ever experienced persistent inflation episodes only when they were taken off gold or silver, and when they temporarily existed as pure paper monies. None of these inflationary intervals was more damaging to their purchasing power than the one in the last century. In the first third of the twentieth century, consumer prices in the United States and in Britain increased by a factor of about 1.6 to 1.7.[3] By 1965 prices had risen almost fourfold in the United States and more than sixfold in the United Kingdom from their levels at the start of the century. But once the dollar's last link to gold was severed, inflation accelerated sharply to levels never seen before in the entire history of these currencies. By the beginning of the twenty-first century, prices had risen by a factor of roughly 20 in the United States and an astonishing 70 percent in the United Kingdom. By 2007, consumer prices were about 25 times higher in the United States and 88 times higher in the United Kingdom from their levels in 1900.[4] These inflations by far surpassed any of the inflations in these currencies during previous off-gold periods.

On any scale that encompasses these colossal post-1971 inflations, the milder swings in purchasing power before 1914 appear only as blips. Again, the bigger ones of these shifts were not deflations but inflations, and they occurred at times when the respective currency was taken temporarily off gold or off silver. In the case of the dollar, this was, most notably, the period after the War of 1812 and around the Civil War.[5] For sterling this was in particular the period during and after the Napoleonic Wars, when the British government under William Pitt used the Bank of England to fund the war with France. In 1797, the Bank was asked to suspend redemption in specie, and the pound was put on a de facto paper standard for 24 years. The country experienced an inflation that at the time was unprecedented.[6] Between 1792 and 1813 goods prices appear to have almost doubled,[7] which would mean a per annum inflation rate of slightly more than 3 percent, not a lot by the degraded standards of today's paper money systems but noteworthy at the time. It was so noteworthy, in fact, that, as we discussed in Chapter 2, this inflation initiated an important and lengthy debate about its causes among the economists of the time.

Outside of paper money episodes, inflations were recorded when metallic money was debased, that is, when the state reduced the metal content of the money without changing the nominal value. Before states established themselves as paper money producers with territorial money monopolies, this was a common stealth tactic to fund state spending, again most frequently the army and war. Additionally, inflations were recorded at times when new deposits of gold or silver were discovered and exploited, and the money supply was expanded more meaningfully. However, it is significant that all these inflations pale into insignificance if compared with the inflations of the later systems of fully elastic state paper money.[8]

There is simply no basis in the historical record for the popular fear that in a commodity money environment the price level would fluctuate widely with every little change in mining activity or any new discovery of gold or silver deposits. As we have already explained conceptually, the notion of a completely stable purchasing power of money is, of course, a fantasy. Complete price level stability is a mental construct in economic models. In a commodity money system, changes in money demand must affect the purchasing power of the monetary unit. We will see shortly that this must also be the case in a paper money system, even a theoretically well-managed one. Over the more than 2,000 years of the use of money, predominantly in commodity form, money's purchasing power has at times gone up and at times gone down. However, the historical record is very clear on one point: Major and economically disruptive changes in money's purchasing power have occurred only in the form of inflations, sometimes followed by corrective deflations, and these have always taken place during paper money episodes. Inflation and deflation as an economic problem were unknown to commodity money societies. In terms of price level stability, commodity money systems have been remarkably sound, while paper money systems have been unstable in the extreme.

A widespread concern about commodity money systems seems to be that they have a tendency toward ongoing deflation. Under a system of inflexible commodity money, a growing economy that constantly expands its production of goods and services should experience an on-trend decline in the price level. This is at least conceptually correct, although there is no reason to believe that this phenomenon constitutes a problem. Indeed, as we will see, this type of secular deflation has many advantages. Historically, it also has been of minor relevance.

After the United States joined Britain on what became the Classical Gold Standard in 1879, prices declined on trend for the next 19 years at an annual average rate of just over 1 percent.[9] This compares with a still positive inflation rate of 0.3 percent in Japan over the 20 years after that country's money-induced real-estate bubble burst in 1990.[10] Japan is today regularly cited by mainstream economists as an example of the evils of persistent deflation. Yet, the United States, during its two decades of gold-standard deflation, experienced solid growth and rises in income and wealth. In fact, even prior to joining the gold standard, the United States had gone through 12 years of almost no money supply growth and had experienced an almost halving of the price level from the elevated levels that prices had reached during the Civil War inflation. But still, U.S. economic performance was vibrant during this time, causing even such prominent advocates of state-paper money and central banking as Milton Friedman and Anna Schwarz to conclude that this constellation "casts serious doubts on the validity of the now widely held view that secular price deflation and rapid economic growth are incompatible."[11]

During the second half of the Classical Gold Standard, between 1897 and 1914, prices rose in the United States on average by about 2 percent,[12] which can be explained predominantly by the expansion of fiduciary media through fractional reserve banking (as described in Chapter 2). Fractional-reserve banking received increasingly political backing as part of a policy to economize on gold and, in particular with the founding of the Fed in 1913, to support money-induced credit creation. Thus, the foundation was being laid for substantial money-driven boom-bust cycles and, finally, the replacement of a gold standard with fully elastic state paper money.

We conclude that historically, the most stable form of money has been commodity money, while elastic paper money was an invariably unstable form of money. Whoever wants to provide society with a medium of exchange of reasonable purchasing power stability as a basis for balanced and continuous economic growth, and who has to base his decision on the historical record alone, will undoubtedly have to choose commodity money over paper money. However, our argument has to rest ultimately on a conceptual analysis, and not on an interpretation of past experience. Only a systematic, fundamental analysis can deliver conclusions that have to be accepted as universally valid. History can ever tell us only what happened and not what must happen. We will now conduct such a conceptual analysis and will start with a question: What factors could cause a system of entirely inflexible commodity money to exhibit purchasing power instability? On the basis of this analysis we can then test the popular claim of the advocates of state paper money that a well-managed and inflation-controlled form of fiat money can provide, at least in theory, superior price level stability to commodity money. It will be shown on conceptual grounds that this, too, is a fallacy.

Why Would Commodity Money Be Unstable?

It has been shown that commodity money has historically been reasonably stable in terms of its purchasing power. This is not surprising if we analyze it conceptually. We will do this by addressing the three potential reasons for concern about price level stability under a commodity money system. First, could commodity money be unstable because of influences on its exchange value that emanate from the monetary commodity's remaining use in industrial applications? Second, as the money supply does not expand with the growth of the economy, will there be constant deflation? What problems does this cause, if any? And third, how disruptive will changes in the demand for money be if they have to be fully absorbed by money's purchasing power?

First, we will look at a situation in which the monetary commodity is still being employed in other, nonmonetary applications in addition to its use as money. It cannot be denied that the remaining industrial use of the monetary commodity continues to exercise an influence on its price formation. For example, if the demand for the commodity in its nonmonetary uses rises, its price will, in principle, be bid up until some of the existing quantity of the commodity will get redirected from monetary to nonmonetary use. Naturally, the reverse will happen if the demand for the commodity in its nonmonetary function decreases. Extra supply of the commodity will then become available for monetary use and will have to be absorbed via a drop in the monetary unit's purchasing power. These processes introduce, potentially, an additional source of fluctuations in money's purchasing power independent from changes in the demand for money. However, excessive volatility appears unlikely, and the reason for this lies in the unique nature of money demand.

Demand for money is always demand for readily usable purchasing power. If demand for the money commodity in its industrial application goes up, the price of the money commodity goes up, and the purchasing power of every monetary unit increases. But if money demand has not changed simultaneously (and this is necessarily the "all else being equal" assumption we have to make), it must mean that money users must immediately feel the urge to reduce their holdings of the monetary asset. As the purchasing power of every unit of the monetary asset has increased, the money users can hold the same overall purchasing power with fewer units of the monetary asset. Putting this differently, the opportunity costs of holding a certain quantity of the monetary asset has increased, as every unit of it can be exchanged for more goods and services. Consequently, as the demand for the monetary asset in its nonmonetary uses goes up and begins to exert upward pressure on its price, demand for the commodity in its monetary use must go down. This will in turn put downward pressure on the exchange value of the monetary unit. The users of money will quickly make additional quantities of the money commodity available for other uses if its purchasing power begins to rise. Conversely, the users of money will quickly absorb additional quantities of the monetary commodity if its price begins to drop because those who use it in its industrial application have less demand for it and sell it. This extraordinarily high responsiveness to price changes is unique to the monetary commodity, which is ever demanded only for its exchange value and not for any use-value that comes with its physical properties. This will smooth out price volatility much more than is feasible for any other good that is subject to competing demands that all originate from its use-value.

We can illustrate this further by looking at a good that is demanded only for its use-value. Let us take steel. If the demand for steel goes up in one of the industries that use steel, and this puts upward pressure on the steel price, other industries will certainly have an incentive to replace steel with other materials. But usually, there are technical limits to such substitutions, and there is a high probability that other industries will have no choice but to pay the higher steel price. The ceteris paribus rule of economic analysis, the assumption that all else remains unchanged, requires that, in the case of all goods that only have use-value, if demand goes up in one application, demand in other applications remains unchanged. But in the case of the money commodity this is fundamentally different. There is always one user, the money user (and this is indeed everybody in the economy), whose demand for physical quantities of the commodity will immediately drop if anybody else starts bidding up the price of the money commodity. The demand for physical quantities of the money commodity in its monetary use must decline if the commodity's price rises in response to a higher demand for it in nonmonetary applications. The reverse happens if money's price declines. This is a unique feature of the monetary asset. Consequently, the price of the money commodity will not be as sensitive to a rise in physical demand in one specific (nonmonetary) application as is the case with all other goods that, by definition, have only use-value. Here we have the conceptual explanation for the remarkable purchasing power stability of commodity money that the historical record shows.

The second concern we have to address conceptually is the notion that money of essentially fixed supply means the economy is in a permanent state of deflation. As an expanding economy creates more goods and services to be exchanged for money, but with the supply of money essentially fixed, the purchasing power of every unit of money must constantly appreciate.

This notion is essentially correct, although it is worthwhile to consider all consequences associated with a rise in productivity in an economy with an unchanging money supply. Two opposing effects should be at work in such a scenario. The first effect is usually neglected in general discussions. It is analogous to what we discussed in the preceding paragraphs: As prices begin to decline and money's purchasing power rises, people will begin to sell some of the monetary asset because the opportunity costs of holding wealth in this form increase. As we have seen, money does not fulfill any needs directly, nor does it generate a return. With the rise in money's purchasing power, every unit of money now buys more goods and services that do fulfill needs directly or do generate returns. It is therefore reasonable to assume, at least initially, that people reduce their money holdings. The selling of the monetary asset will again put downward pressure on its purchasing power,[13] which will counteract some of the rise in purchasing power from higher productivity. It seems, however, unlikely that the two will offset each other completely. Why is that the case?

The answer is simply this: The demand for money should in this scenario not remain unchanged but in fact rise. If the economy produces a larger quantity of goods and services than before, and money users get, on average, wealthier, it is only logical to assume that the money users want to hold more purchasing power in readily spendable form. Indeed, it would be somewhat unrealistic to assume that, although more goods and services are now on offer, the individual money user would not have a higher demand for the flexibility to spontaneously engage in economic transactions. To the extent that this is the outcome, a monetary system with a money commodity of essentially fixed supply will experience secular deflation. A growing economy with an entirely inflexible money supply will exhibit a tendency for prices to decline on trend and for money's purchasing to steadily increase. But the key question now is why should this be a problem?

We have already seen that, historically, secular deflation was rather minor and that it certainly never appeared to present any serious economic difficulties. No correlation between deflation and economic recession or stagnation is evident under commodity money systems. We will now show that there are no reasons on conceptual grounds to consider deflation to be a problem either. There is nothing fundamentally disruptive or problematic about a gradual trend decline in the price level.

First, for the single purpose of rational economic calculation based on money prices, an ongoing moderate deflation is neither better nor worse than the ongoing moderate inflation that is widely advocated today under state-managed paper money. In particular, there is no reason to fear any disruption to production or efficient resource allocation. The on-trend decline in prices will simply come to be expected by economic agents and be part of their economic planning.

The widespread belief that deflation hurts borrowers on the loan market is unfounded. This view stems from the specific situation of an economic crisis, in which a sudden and unexpected drop in many prices can cause problems for those in debt, as it requires more real goods and real services to repay a nominal loan amount. Although this would then provide a windfall gain for the creditors. But what we discuss here is not a sudden, crisis-induced (or money-demand induced) deflation but trend or secular deflation as a feature of commodity money, which emanates from rising productivity and thus gradually rising money demand. And in this context, there is no reason to believe that, when agreeing to the terms of a loan, borrowers would disregard probable trend-deflation any less than lenders disregard probable trend-inflation in today's monetary system. Unexpected inflation is usually good for borrowers and bad for lenders and unexpected deflation usually bad for borrowers and good for lenders (as long as the borrowers can still pay), but any discernible, moderate, and stable trend in either direction will simply be anticipated and incorporated into the market rate of the loan agreement by both sides.

Second, if we move beyond the use of money prices in economic calculation, deflation has considerable advantages. In an environment of ongoing secular deflation money has an inherent return. In this scenario, cash holdings can function as a store of value and thus as an instrument of saving. Money balances will give their owners not only the highest flexibility to engage in transactions spontaneously but also a positive return, which stems from the on-trend increase in the purchasing power of the monetary unit. Of course, it is to be expected that most savings will still be channeled into financial or other assets that provide superior returns, but those members of the public who want to save but lack the expertise to invest in debt claims or equity claims will have a reasonable—if usually low yielding—alternative to such investment vehicles in the form of the monetary asset. By contrast, in today's environment, characterized by a constant decline in money's purchasing power, cash balances cannot fulfill this function and every member of society who wants to save has to engage in some form of speculation. We have previously seen that fractional-reserve banking attracts depositors with the prospect of combining, in the form of a bank deposit, the full flexibility of ownership of money with the positive return of ownership of a debt instrument. Banks make this promise by creating multiple claims on the same original quantity of money, which makes this procedure inherently risky and destabilizing for banks and the economy alike. In a commodity money system with ongoing secular deflation, cash holdings do in fact provide the flexibility of the most fungible good and a small return at the same time, and they do so without any of the risks and instabilities of fractional-reserve banking.

One of the popular yet entirely unjustified concerns about deflation is the idea that in an economy with declining prices, spending decisions would be deferred ever further into the future as a postponement of any purchase always means that more goods and services can be bought later. This is nonsense. This view completely neglects the essential concept of time preference. As we have seen, to want something means, all else being equal, to want it sooner rather than later. When making a spending decision, every decision maker in the economy simply contrasts his personal time preference with the benefit he would receive from the additional goods and services he could obtain if he deferred his purchase and waited for prices to decline. That is all.

This situation is not fundamentally different from an inflationary environment in which real interest rates, that is, inflation-adjusted interest rates, are positive. In such an inflationary economy, the consumer can obtain interest income for his savings in excess of inflation. In this situation, too, a postponement of an act of spending and the investment of the funds at positive real interest rates in the interim will give everybody the opportunity to buy more in the future. The disadvantage of not being able to consume today simply has to be compared with the advantage of being able to consume more tomorrow. As everybody can quickly confirm from own experience, none of this will stop present consumption and none of this is an obstacle to a growing and vibrant economy.

An additional illustration of time preference and of the misconception that deflation drains present demand is provided today by those sectors in which productivity gains are so rapid and competition so intense that nominal prices for these goods tend to decrease over time even in a generally inflationary environment. In recent years, this has been the case for many products in the area of consumer technology, such as personal computers, laptops, mobile phones, and other handheld devices. In general, these sectors have experienced strong growth on the back of solid customer demand, despite the fact that every buyer knows full well that by not buying any of these goods today he stands a good chance of buying the same, or even a more advanced product, for a lower price in the future. This is in fact a good example of personal time preference in action.

We conclude that today's widespread fear of deflation is unfounded. It appears that after almost a hundred years of global inflation, the possibility of an ongoing rise in the monetary unit's purchasing power has become a strange and discomforting concept to many people, making them susceptible to the scaremongering of parties who have a vested interest in ongoing money expansion and inflation. However, if one thinks about it dispassionately and rationally, a continuous decline in nominal prices seems to be a more natural condition for a growing economy in which people get, on trend, wealthier, than the artificial weakening of money's purchasing power through its constant overissuance by those who control the money supply.

For a society to become richer means that things become more affordable. Today, a worker in an industrialized economy has to work, on average, fewer hours to be able to afford a new refrigerator or TV set than a worker 20 or 50 years ago, and today he would also acquire a hugely advanced specimen of this product. In a commodity money system with secular deflation, these advances in the efficiency of society's resource use, the growth in its productive capacity, would be reflected in declining nominal prices. Instead, the discretionary and essentially arbitrary injections of substantial amounts of money, to the benefit of the money producers and unchecked by a limited demand for it from the public, constantly cause the medium of exchange to lose exchange value and cause prices to rise. Not only is this inflation in itself unnecessary and disruptive, but, as we have seen, the unavoidable distortions in relative prices that result from any money injection, and in particular from the vast ongoing money expansion common today, must also lead to economic dislocations and a progressively unbalanced economy. In any case, the stark contrast between what a rational assessment of deflation on the basis of economic theory and historical experience tells us, and how deflation is portrayed and in fact caricatured by central bankers and many mainstream economists makes one wonder if this portrayal is the consequence of intellectual error alone.

Third, there is another and more sophisticated argument about potential instabilities created by commodity money, and that is that the unavoidable, if historically minor, volatility in its purchasing power as a result of any changes in money demand could, in itself, be a source of economic instability. Defenders of paper money will request that this issue is duly taken into account when contrasting the two systems. In the absence of a flexible money supply, sudden changes in money demand will have to be fully absorbed by changes in money's purchasing power. One could argue that this, too, has the potential to disrupt the otherwise smooth operation of the economy. Indeed, as we have seen, this phenomenon will also affect the prices of different goods differently. People will not sell or buy equal parts of everything when money demand rises. Relative prices must change. Additionally, people will be affected differently depending on how much cash they hold at the time the change in purchasing power occurs. A change in the demand for money will change overall prices but also relative prices and therefore the relative position of economic actors and the allocation of resources in the economy. All of this is true but it must lead to a different question: Is any of this avoidable in a system of elastic paper money? If consequences of changes in money demand exist that can justifiably be labeled disruptive, the point is then whether such disruptive effects could be avoided in a system of elastic paper money. This will be the focus of our investigation in a later chapter. However, a couple of general observations can already be made here.

First, changes in purchasing power that emanate from changes in money demand can be in either direction. Money demand may increase at certain times and at other times decline. We may characterize these occasional swings as disturbances but they cannot have the lasting, systematic effect on resource allocation and, in particular, the size and structure of the productive side of the economy that must result from a constantly expanding supply of paper money. A one-off change in money demand has similar effects as a one-off injection of money. But even an ongoing gradual rise in money demand cannot have the same disturbing effect. It will cause a tendency for prices to decline, but it does not systematically change relative prices in one specific direction. There is no reason to assume that a rising demand for money will constantly distort the price relationship between present goods and future goods of the same type, that is, distort interest rates. This is the key difference to the present paper money system, which has an inherent tendency to artificially lower interest rates. Constant money injection continuously interferes with market interest rates and therefore leads to disruptions of the saving-investment equation. The point is not that commodity money is perfect by the unrealistic expectation of some economic model of perfect efficiency. The point is that paper money is always disadvantageous relative to inelastic commodity money. In fact, its drawbacks are so colossal that a paper money system cannot be made to be stable and to last.

The danger is that the present obsession with price-level-stability and the misguided notion that a stable price-level is, in itself, a sign of economic stability, leads to the belief that "good" paper money could be "neutral" money, that is, money that does not at all interfere with the real economy. This would indeed be a grave error. Money is never neutral, has never been neutral, and can never be made to be neutral. From the moment that human society made the transition from direct trade (barter) to indirect trade via media of exchange, a new element entered economic relationships. Money allowed great advances in human cooperation on markets, but money has its own dynamics and inevitably also constitutes a source of occasional disturbance and of economic volatility. There is simply no point in arguing that a monetary system would be conceivable in which money was simply a veil that would float over the "real" processes of the economy and that had no impact on the use of real resources. We therefore readily admit that no system of commodity money can guarantee complete stability of prices and an unvarying purchasing power of the monetary unit. But such a system would be fundamentally incompatible with a market economy anyway. In a market economy, any notion of complete stability or predictability is unrealistic. Nobody can argue that commodity money will satisfy the lofty demands of some theoretical notion of perfect monetary stability, but its historical record is not only remarkably good, but it also is vastly superior to that of paper money. Our conceptual analysis has shown why this is the case. All that is now left to do is to show that even on purely theoretical and conceptual grounds, paper money under control of a central bank can never deliver superior purchasing power stability compared with inflexible commodity money.

■ ■ ■

For the following analysis we will disregard the disastrous history of paper money and the vested interests of the paper money producers and the early beneficiaries of money injections. We will, for arguments' sake, assume that achieving the highest possible price level stability is a reasonable objective for a monetary constitution, in theory at least. We will further assume that an independent central bank could be put in charge of the money franchise and would focus exclusively on offsetting any volatility in money's purchasing power stemming from changes in money demand and thus endeavor to deliver a better stability than inflexible and unmanaged commodity money. It will be shown that even under such idealized conditions, the goal of superior stability of the price level is unattainable.

Chapter 6

The Policy
of
Stabilization

To begin the discussion in this chapter, we need to define the objective of a policy of price level stabilization. The advocates of price level stabilization and of central bank–controlled moderate inflation can have no objection to any moderate, trending, and therefore largely predictable changes in purchasing power, such as the secular deflation of commodity money. Their very own model entails just such on-trend purchasing power changes. What their system must achieve is to smooth out the potentially abrupt changes in purchasing power that may stem from sudden changes in money demand.

Problems with Price Index Stabilization

The first point to note is that once we made the transition from inflexible commodity money to practically unlimited, elastic fiat money the predictability of the price level has decreased, rather than increased. The notion that the price level could now be forced to be stable or predictable rests entirely on political will and state intervention. If left to their own devices, the fractional-reserve banks, which are the dominant money producers in a paper money system, have no incentive to produce exactly the amount of money that keeps the price level stable or on some predetermined path. In fact, they could not guarantee such an outcome even if they wanted to. Their interest must be to use the privilege of money production to their benefit (i.e., that of their shareholders) by lowering the interest rate on the loan market enough to encourage more borrowing, which they can fund out of new money production. They have to balance the benefit of the extra income against the risk of having to pay out some of their deposits in form of bank reserves that they cannot produce themselves. It is evident that in this arrangement the notion of the price level does not even enter, and cannot enter, the deliberations of the fractional-reserve banks. It is rational for these banks to expand their operations as much as appears reasonable based on their limited reserves at present and the probability of receiving additional reserves from the central bank in the future. It therefore follows that any tendency of this system to deliver a stable or otherwise predictable price level must rest entirely on a political decision, which is by definition an arbitrary decision and can be changed at any time. And whether this objective will be realized will depend on the ability of the political institution, the central bank, to use its monopoly powers over the private banks in such a way as to steer the production of fiat money to attain the desired price level stability.

Commodity money may not be perfect, but the reasonable stability it provides rests on its inherent qualities and the laws of economics. Previously we were able to explain the historic record of reasonable price level stability conceptually. It is in the nature of commodity money. Elastic state fiat money, by contrast, offers no inherent stability at all. Any stability, let alone one that is superior to that of commodity money, rests entirely on political will and its execution via the central bank. That this is a rather optimistic or even naïve starting point for the design of a monetary system does not require further elaboration. Nevertheless, in the following examples we will assume that those in control of the money franchise will indeed try their utmost to deliver a monetary unit of superior purchasing power stability.

The advocates of price level stabilization argue thus: As relative prices are all-important in directing resource-use toward meeting the most urgent needs of the consumer, it is essential for economic agents to always be able to distinguish changes in prices that result from the sphere of goods and services from changes in prices that result from a change in money demand or money supply. In a commodity money system, in which the supply of the monetary asset is essentially fixed, how can economic agents isolate price changes that result from changing consumer preferences or a changing supply of certain goods and services, from changes in prices that simply result from changes in the demand for money? As this is not possible in an economy with inelastic money, economic agents must frequently err in their economic calculations. They are bound to misinterpret price changes because they cannot distinguish between price changes that result from "real" factors (changes in tastes, technology, or scarcity) from those that result from changes in the demand for the inelastic medium of exchange. If all price changes that result only from the money side of the economy could be eliminated, then all remaining price changes could firmly be attributed to the goods side of the economy, that is, to real factors. Economic planning and economic calculation could thus be made more reliable and the allocation of scarce resources be made more efficient. Therefore, a monetary unit of stable or at least predictably changing purchasing power would provide a unit for economic calculation superior to commodity money that remains necessarily subject to shifts in purchasing power due to changes in money demand. If the supply of money is fixed, its purchasing power must be allowed to fluctuate. But if the money supply is essentially elastic, its purchasing power can, at least in principle, be held steady. In order to achieve this, the money supply must, of course, be manipulated by a central authority, for certainly no automatism exists by which a stable purchasing power would be achieved otherwise.

The first problem for such a program is the measurement of money's purchasing power. This is a fundamental problem for any policy of purchasing power management. We have spoken about money's purchasing power and the price level as theoretical concepts to explain a very complex reality. The way in which we used these terms for theoretical discussion has been in the somewhat stylized form that all economists resort to when analyzing and illustrating economic phenomena: It is the ceteris paribus approach, the assumption that, as we look at a specific phenomenon, such as a change in the purchasing power of money or a change in money demand, we assume that all else remains unchanged. Only under this rather unrealistic condition can we mentally isolate the money-induced price changes from the goods-induced price changes.[1] This approach is not only common in scientific inquiry, but it is indeed indispensible. However, in the real world it is impossible to isolate money-induced price changes from goods-induced price changes. "All else being equal" never works in the real world. But this is the indispensible precondition for a successful price level stabilization policy.

To illustrate this point, let us look again at a model society with a monetary asset (m) and a range of goods and services (p, q, r, s, t, u, v). In the first period the voluntary interaction of the members of this society has resulted in the following exchange relationships:

$$3p = 2q = 4r = 1s = 0.5t = 2.2u = 2v = 2m.$$

In a dynamic economy, such exchange relationships cannot be expected to remain unchanged. Let us assume that after a while the following new exchange relationships have materialized:

$$4p = 1.5q = 4.3r = 0.8s = 0.7t = 2u = 2.5v = 2.5m.$$

It is immediately apparent that it is impossible for any observer of this economy, and indeed for anybody operating in this economy, to isolate a change in money demand from any of the other factors that has contributed to changes in exchange relationships. Certain goods have become cheaper versus some goods and more expensive versus other goods. The same is true for the monetary asset, which is just one good among many. As different goods are of different importance to different people, for some people the purchasing power of their money holdings will have risen, and for others it might have declined or stayed roughly unchanged.

The idea that there is such a thing as one specific and identifiable purchasing power of money, one universally applicable price level, is a fantasy. Every exchange relationship between the monetary asset and any good or service that money is being exchanged for is as good a representative of money's purchasing power as any other. In a dynamic economy, money's purchasing power may frequently rise versus one good, stay unchanged versus another, and drop versus yet another. This must be the case because the exchange relationships between the various goods that money is exchanged for cannot be expected to remain unchanged. When analyzing monetary phenomena, the economist makes the ceteris paribus assumption. He pretends that the exchange relationships between all other goods and services are fixed, and only the relationship between the monetary asset and these goods and services changes. This is an indispensible mental tool for scientific analysis. But when the economist or economic statistician calculates a price index in the real world, he implicitly pretends that the ceteris paribus assumption also holds in reality. This is baseless and indefensible, and it puts the whole project of price level stabilization on shaky conceptual ground from the start.

Once we drop the all-else-being-equal assumption and move to the real world, it is clear that money-induced price changes cannot be distinguished from goods-induced price changes. Only in extreme scenarios, like a major inflation, when the change in purchasing power of the monetary asset is very rapid and occurs over an extended period in the same direction, and in a magnitude that overwhelms any other relative price changes, can the two at least partially be distinguished. But the goal of price level stabilization is not to avoid major inflations or deflations. Commodity money can do an entirely adequate job at this. The alleged advantage of well-managed state paper money is precisely that it should provide an even greater stability in terms of its purchasing power.

Of course, it is mathematically possible to calculate some average of the exchange relationships between the monetary asset and the various goods and services in our model economy. The question is how sensible the result of such an exercise can be. Despite the widespread use and the general acceptance of price indices today, all of them stand, conceptually, on thin ice. In fact, they may distort and obscure more than they reveal.

Additionally, various alternative procedures for the calculation of such an average exist and they will necessarily lead to different results. Should an arithmetic mean or a geometric mean be used? Are all the prices of equal importance for calculating money's purchasing power? It is clear that each result will be different and that reasonable people may disagree over which standard is more appropriate. Rather than embodying the definitive measure of money's real purchasing power, which is a theoretical concept and not a definitive real-world entity, the chosen price level standard will have to be a compromise, reflecting considerations of practicality and convenience and politics. Different groups in society have different interests concerning how price level stability should be defined. That these index numbers represent a definite economic entity is a dangerous misconception.

Let us now assume that a statistical method has been agreed upon to calculate a price level for measuring money's purchasing power. Even in our model economy of only seven goods and services plus the monetary asset, it will now be extremely difficult for the money producer to inject precisely enough money to keep the agreed-upon statistical average stable or, as is more common today, to keep it advancing at a steady pace of, say, 2 percent per annum. In a modern economy with millions of goods and services and ongoing changes in preferences and in economic conditions, initiated by innovation and entrepreneurial activity, the task is even more difficult.

Defenders of paper money and price stabilization will argue that the money producer can still identify certain trends in such variables as economic growth and wealth and, therefore, in money demand. If only the money producer forecasts these trends correctly, he stands a good chance of achieving stability over the medium to long term. Most inflation-targeting central banks today allow for a certain amount of near-term volatility around their aimed-at inflation rate, anyway. But again, for as long as money demand develops in a stable and somewhat predictable fashion, it does not pose a particular challenge for a commodity currency of fixed supply either. If we assume that an economy experiences a steady rise in the demand for money of about, for example, 2 percent per annum, in a commodity money system with an essentially fixed money supply everybody could simply adjust monetary calculations for the tendency of an ongoing deflation of 2 percent per year. In terms of calculation-efficiency, a steady and reliable tendency of all prices to fall by 2 percent is no better or worse than a reliable tendency of prices to rise by 2 percent every year, courtesy of the money producer. It follows that a money producer whose money creation only accommodates long-term trends in money demand (to the extent that it is realistic to assume that these long run trends do indeed exist and can be correctly identified) does not provide a form of money that is superior in reliability for monetary calculation to inelastic commodity money. The Achilles heel of the latter, in theory, is precisely that exogenous and sudden changes in money demand will have to be fully absorbed by changes in money prices for goods and services, and that this will affect different prices differently and affect economic agents differently.

However, this particular problem is fundamentally insolvable for the fiat money producer. If a sudden change in money demand occurs, money users will immediately respond to it. They can and will adjust their money holdings very flexibly through minor changes in their buying and selling of goods and services. This will instantly affect prices in a paper money economy, too, and, once the purchasing power of the monetary unit has responded, no additional changes are required. The change in prices constitutes the full and efficient satisfaction of the new money demand. For the fiat money producer to avoid this effect, he would have to anticipate sudden (nonlinear) changes in money demand before they impact money's purchasing power. He would have to know of a coming change in the demand for money before even the individual economic agents know of it. This is theoretically and practically an impossibility. If, for example, a sudden rise in money demand occurs, it will immediately cause a drop in the price average. As a result, the money producer will undershoot his inflation target for a period, but there is no reason for him to compensate this effect with increased money production in the next period. First, the change in money demand may have reasonably been a one-off event, rather than a trend change. Second, the shock of a move in the price level has now occurred and additional money creation will not undo it. And third, the overall demand for and supply of money are again in equilibrium. At the higher purchasing power of the monetary unit, no demand for money goes unfulfilled. No additional action from the money producer is needed.

And finally, even if we assume that all of this were possible, and that the goal of a medium of exchange of steadily declining, but in its decline perfectly predictable, purchasing power had been realized, we would still have to conclude that superior monetary stability had not been achieved. The ongoing money injections necessary to manufacture steady inflation will necessarily dislocate the loan market, artificially lower rates, and thus help build an investment structure that is not aligned with ongoing voluntary savings. As we have shown conclusively, money injections cause economic dislocations that manifest themselves in a credit-driven business cycle even if the purchasing power of the monetary unit is stable or falling gradually in a predictable manner. The two are entirely different phenomena. Price level stability is not synonymous with monetary stability. In creating a monetary unit that is stable or in any case predictably changing in terms of its purchasing power, the money producer still creates economic instability through the constant injection of new money.

Money injections via the loan market must channel the new money first to those who do not have a high demand for cash balances but a high demand for goods and services. Only in a roundabout way will the new money finally reach those with a heightened demand for cash. In his attempt to give the economy a monetary asset of stable purchasing power, the fiat money producer inevitably obstructs one of the market economy's most important mechanisms, that of coordinating the future-oriented activities in the economy with the time-preferences of the members of society.

The agenda of the advocates of price level stabilization is therefore illogical. It is absurd to suggest that resource allocation efficiency can be enhanced via money injection when money injection itself disturbs efficient resource allocation. The idea of giving all economic agents a stable price level so that they can better identify relative price changes is superficially appealing but collapses entirely as a realistic policy agenda once it becomes apparent that price level stabilization can be achieved only by ongoing money production and ongoing money production will itself always be a source of resource misallocation.

Summary

It is claimed by today's macroeconomic mainstream and widely accepted by the public that the purchasing power of money can be accurately measured and then managed by the central bank, so that a monetary unit of superior stability can be delivered. It is therefore readily believed that paper money should be a better, because more predictable, medium of exchange than commodity money, the supply of which is not managed by any institution. Additionally, as the supply of commodity money is fairly static and as there is no reason to expect that the supply will keep up with advances in productivity, an economy that uses commodity money is likely to experience ongoing secular deflation.

As we have seen, no procedure exists by which money's purchasing power can be accurately and definitively measured. The concept of a measurable relationship between money and a broad aggregate of goods and services implies stability of exchange relationships between the individual goods and services, which is a fiction. Price indices are no better than guesses and should be treated with the utmost skepticism. Furthermore, even a paper money producer with the best of intentions can ever only hope to identify long-term trends in money demand, to the extent that these exist and are reasonably stable, and try to manage his supply accordingly. In a paper money system, too, any sudden changes in the demand for money will directly affect money's purchasing power, just as they would in a commodity money system. The paper money central bank has no means by which to anticipate these before they have an impact on the purchasing power of money. Demand for money is not demand for loans, and the paper money infrastructure with its central bank and fractional-reserve banks has no mechanism for satisfying this demand before it has satisfied itself naturally by the selling and buying of money and the automatic adjustment of money's purchasing power.

In terms of the predictability of price trends, the moderate inflation officially targeted in paper money systems today has no advantages over the moderate secular deflation in a commodity money system. But in all other respects, and in sharp contrast to generally held beliefs today, secular deflation has many advantages. In a commodity money system, the monetary asset is likely to provide a small steady return through the on-trend decline in prices, which allows those without investment expertise (or the means to purchase investment advice) to save through cash holdings. On the other hand, the constant injection of new money in a paper money system has to lead to the distortions of interest rates and to the misallocations of capital that we analyzed earlier and that will progressively unbalance the overall economy. This has to be the case even if the goal of a steadily and moderately declining purchasing power is realized. The paper money producers have no means by which to satisfy the demand for money directly but always have to give new money first to borrowers on the loan market, thus initiating the distortions in capital allocation explained earlier. A reasonably stable or predictably rising price level is no guarantee of underlying monetary and economic stability. A growing demand for money may offset the price-raising effects of money injections on the chosen price statistics but will not render the disruptive potential of money injections harmless.

There is no reason on the basis of fundamental economic analysis to assume that paper money could ever provide a more stable or otherwise advantageous medium of exchange to inflexible commodity money. The historical record in fact provides an even more devastating verdict on paper money. Commodity money has, through the ages, consistently provided a medium of exchange of reasonable stability. Large swings in purchasing power were largely unknown to commodity money societies and occurred only under paper money systems, when they invariably took the form of inflations, sometimes followed by corrective deflations. All paper money systems have resulted in high and accelerating inflation and ended in a return to commodity money or total currency collapse.

To suggest that our present paper money system is a superior guarantor of monetary and therefore economic stability is nonsense. Not only is there no evidence to support such an allegation, but also everything points toward the opposite being the case. Elastic paper money is today the biggest threat to a smoothly functioning economy and rising prosperity. It must lead to growing instabilities and ultimately to economic collapse. Before we chart the likely path of the present system toward its inevitable endgame, we will first have a look at the history of paper money systems to show how they came about and how they finally collapsed. Following this, we will look at the present system more closely, in particular by revealing its main beneficiaries and the intellectual support structure that keeps it in place. Then we will be ready to look at the approaching monetary breakdown of our present paper money system.

Part Four

HISTORY OF
PAPER MONEY
A Legacy of Failure

Chapter 7

A Brief History of State Paper Money

O nce a commodity of essentially fixed supply becomes generally accepted as a medium of exchange, society can reap all
the benefits from the use of money and all the advantages
from indirect exchange by using this type of money. Nothing can be
gained from ongoing money production, whether private or public,
from competing currency providers, from the customization of money
or from an active market in alternative monies. Obviously, competition
and innovation still matter for all sorts of financial services related to
money. Here the same rules apply that apply to all goods and services
that have use-value. But no economy needs an expanding supply of the
medium of exchange. People buy and sell the monetary asset according
to their individual demand for money, and this will lead to changes in
the purchasing power of the monetary asset, which are necessarily

sufficient to align demand for money with the fixed supply of money.

On the other hand, we have seen that replacing inelastic commodity money with elastic paper money must lead to economic dislocations, to the obstruction of the pricing process, to ongoing decline in money's purchasing power, and increasingly to economic disintegration.

So how can we explain that practically all economies are operating under paper money standards today? If money users derive no advantage from the abandonment of commodity money and the switch to paper money, how could the paper standard completely replace commodity money? It has been shown that a type of paper money was issued in the form of fiduciary media by fractional-reserve banks a long time ago. It has also been shown that this issuance was not in response to any additional demand for money but simply a by-product of contentious banking techniques, and that this form of money never replaced commodity money. So how was commodity money replaced with paper money?

The answer is clear and unambiguous on the grounds of both theory and history: Paper money systems are creations of the state. History does not provide a single example of privately issued paper money replacing commodity money simply as the result of the spontaneous and voluntary interaction of private citizens.[1] Fiat money is, has always been, and always will be state money. It therefore deserves special scrutiny. Unlike other elementary social institutions, like private property, market exchange, and commodity money, paper money cannot claim to be the result of voluntary interaction. It was not adopted because its benefits were obvious to the mass of money users who then voluntarily chose to use it. Since it has been introduced by political means and for political purposes, the specific doctrines that support it require close attention. Various reasons are cited today for the alleged advantages of fiat money, but, as we have seen, none of them stands up to critical inspection. Historically, the reason for why paper money was introduced has—consistently, very straightforwardly, and often by official admission—been this one: to fund state expenditure, predominantly to finance war.

Paper Money Experiments

All states enjoy the privilege of funding themselves via taxation, meaning the expropriation of resources from private wealth owners and market-income earners. All other persons and entities in society have to obtain the goods and services of others by contributing to the production of goods and services themselves and then engaging in voluntary exchange. The state can take by force or by the threat of force. Openly taxing wealth and income of the private sector, however, is rarely popular and thus comes with natural limitations. Printing money opened up an additional avenue for funding the state. Without exception this was the reason for all experiments with paper money in the history of mankind. In every case, the supply of paper money was constantly expanded and the purchasing power of the monetary unit eroded. The system always led to high inflation, ending either in the total collapse of the financial system with catastrophic effects for economy and society, or in the timely abandonment of paper money and the return to commodity money.

We have already come across many paper money experiments in history in the course of our investigation. It should still be instructive to line them up again in chronological order to make their common features stand out more clearly and to show that the coming breakdown of our present paper money system, as dramatic and inconceivable as it may appear to today's mainstream, will constitute nothing unusual or unique. Based on any cool-headed analysis of history and theory, it is simply what the rational observer has to expect.

As we have mentioned, China was first to experiment with full-fledged paper money systems. Between the early twelfth and the late fifteenth centuries, state-issued paper money was used in the Southern Song Dynasty (1127–1279), the Jin Dynasty (1115–1234), the Yuan Dynasty (1271–1368), and during the early reign of the Ming Dynasty (1368–1644).[2] Naturally, the Chinese dynasties issued paper money to generate income for government expenditure. Although payment in kind was still widespread at the time, the governments encouraged the use of paper money among the public by demanding that taxes be paid with this money. The Chinese governments also used their paper money to pay their own employees, mainly the standing armies. Initially, issuance was fairly moderate in each case, but over time ever more paper money was circulated and the purchasing power of money inevitably began to decline. Sooner or later, all Chinese dynasties experienced inflation and indeed progressively rising inflation. Various policy measures were taken to fight the symptoms and to keep the currency in circulation. The Yuan Dynasty first restricted and then banned private trading in gold and silver. It also undertook various currency reforms by which new paper money with new denominations was circulated. The Jin Dynasty attempted price controls. The paper monies of the Jin and Yuan Dynasties ended up being worthless by 1223 and 1356, respectively, preceding the downfall of the dynasties themselves by only a few years (1234 and 1368). The Southern Song Dynasty was spared the fate of complete currency collapse only by its occupation and then dissolution at the hands of the Mongols. The Ming Dynasty is the exception. After introducing paper money and experiencing the regular pattern of growing issuance and rising inflation, the Ming rulers abandoned the paper money experiment altogether and returned to commodity money. Remarkably, after 1500 China did not return to paper money but remained on commodity money until paper money was reintroduced as part of westernization in the nineteenth and twentieth centuries.[3]

In 1690 Massachusetts, at the time a British colony, started issuing paper money to pay its soldiers for military expeditions against French Quebec.[4] The trend caught on in other North American colonies until all of them issued paper money. The result was in all cases a steep decline of the purchasing power of the monetary unit. The British parliament put an end to this experiment with paper money in 1764.[5]

The Bank of England, often called the mother of all central banks, was established in 1694 for the specific purpose of lending to the state. A multitude of legal privileges was bestowed on the Bank, which gave it an exalted status from the start. Anticipating the policy of all modern central banks, the Bank of England issued bank notes against liabilities of the Crown, which means it monetized government debt.[6] During the first hundred years of its existence, the Bank was permitted on several occasions to default on its promise to repay notes in physical gold and still continue as a going concern.[7]

France issued paper money under the famous scheme of the Scottish gambler and monetary theorist John Law between 1716 and 1720 in order to shore up public finances. "Saddled with enormous public debt as a result of the wars of Louis XIV, the government was on the brink of its third bankruptcy in less than a century" (Ferguson).[8] The issuance of paper money led to a speculative stock market boom (the Mississippi Bubble). The inevitable crash and the decline in the value of bank notes brought turmoil to the French economy but failed to ease France's fiscal predicament.[9]

In 1775 the North American colonies resumed the issuance of paper money in the form of continentals, named after the Continental Congress, this time to fund the Revolutionary War. Six years later, continentals were practically worthless.[10]

France's next paper currency was the assignats, issued during the revolution to fund another bankrupt government. They lasted from 1790 to 1803 and ended in complete worthlessness.[11] The paper money collapse of the assignats is the first recorded inflation that made the modern statistical definition of hyperinflation, that is, a rise in prices of more than 50 percent in a single month.[12] In 1803 Napoleon introduced the franc.

The period from 1793 to 1821 saw international conflict on an unprecedented scale, involving much of Europe and, at times, America in what are called the Napoleonic Wars. In Britain, the government of William Pitt increasingly used the Bank of England to fund the war with France. Excessive credit creation lead to the outflow of gold and in 1797 the Bank was asked to suspend redemption in specie. Britain remained off gold for 24 years and experienced unprecedented price inflation.[13] In 1821, Britain returned to the gold standard.

To fund the War of 1812 between the United States of America and the British Empire, the U.S. government issued substantial amounts of Treasury notes, borrowed heavily from the growing banking sector, and in 1814 allowed the banks to suspend specie payment. Resumption of specie payment took place in 1817, but it was again suspended in 1819.[14] The next major experiment with paper money was initiated by the Civil War. The United States was again taken off gold in December 1861, when specie payment was suspended. This was followed, over the next three years, by substantial issuance of new paper money, new

"United States notes" that were soon known as "greenbacks." As should be expected, greenbacks quickly began to lose purchasing power and declined sharply versus gold. Greenbacks were declared legal tender, and in 1863 and 1864 various measures were taken to disrupt the gold market. The goal of these policies was to suppress the price of gold and to discourage the use of gold as a basis for contractual exchange.[15] The Resumption Act was passed in January 1875, but the full resumption of specie payment did not occur until 1879.[16] In that year, the United States joined the Classical Gold Standard, a global monetary arrangement that, while not perfect, saw an unprecedented and as of today unrepeated period of fast global growth, free trade, and harmonious monetary relations that was ended by the First World War. Germany, Holland, and the Scandinavian countries had joined Britain on the gold standard already in the 1870s. Switzerland, Belgium, and France all followed in 1878. After the United States joined in 1879, Austria followed in 1892, Japan in 1897, Russia in 1899, and Italy in 1900.[17]

Quite naturally, the Classical Gold Standard coincided with the era of Classical Liberalism, of cultural and political attitudes that were conducive to free trade and limited state involvement in economic affairs, of laissez-faire. This era was brought to an end by the onset of World War I. Already in the second half of the gold standard era a distinct trend toward higher inflation had emerged, albeit still subdued by the standards of complete paper systems. This mild inflation was the result of official policy increasingly encouraging the issuance of fiduciary media by the banks, a trend that culminated in America establishing its first full-fledged lender-of-last-resort central bank in 1913, in the form of the Federal Reserve System. The promise by the state to backstop the banks in their creation of deposit money naturally provided a strong incentive for banks to create more money. This money creation resulted in the imbalances that made the Great Depression inevitable.

In the first half of the twentieth century, inflationism and expanding state power became global themes. A dislike of gold and a desire for state-controlled paper money were universal. Germany went off gold in 1914 to fund the war effort. After the war, Germany increasingly used the printing press to fund reparation payments and other government expenditure, which led by 1923 to one of the most spectacular hyperinflations in history. This currency catastrophe tore German society apart and impoverished the middle class.[18] The highest inflation per month recorded in Germany in 1923 was close to 30,000 percent.[19]

The revolutionary government in Russia confiscated gold in all forms in 1917.[20] In 1924 Keynes famously announced that the gold standard had already become a "barbaric relic." By executive order 6102 (April 5, 1933), President Roosevelt confiscated all gold held by U.S. citizens within the borders of the United States, sealed all private safe deposits, and outlawed the private ownership of gold.[21] Although the executive order expired, restrictions on gold ownership remained in place until 1974. At no time in history was the hostility toward commodity money so deep rooted and so lasting as in the twentieth century.

In Germany the Nazi economist Werner Daitz declared that "in future, gold will play no role as a basis for the European currencies, because a currency does not depend on what it is covered by, but rather it is dependent on the value which is given it by the state, or in this case by the economic order which is controlled by the state."[22]

After the Second World War, and in particular after the disintegration of the Communist Soviet Bloc after 1989, the dominant global model of society became parliamentary social democracy, which combines capitalist elements, in particular private ownership of the means of production, with a democratically legitimized, interventionist state. Democratic states have all experienced on-trend growing state expenditure, rising levels of taxation and rising public debt. Against this backdrop it should come as no surprise that the attempt to limit the power of the state by subjugating it to the strictures of an immovable and inflexible system of commodity money turned out to be short-lived. Since 1971 the world has been on a global state fiat money standard. Nixon's decision to default on the promise to foreign central banks to exchange dollars for gold was again in no small part due to war-related government spending, in this case for the Vietnam War. The global paper money system has since led to accelerated declines in money's purchasing power, a much larger financial and state sector, and substantial rises in overall indebtedness, not least that of the state. Since 1971 there has also been a marked increase in the number and magnitude of financial crises around the world.[23]

Summary

No matter how many disasters have been created and how much misery has been spread through false booms, severe recessions, and high inflation, often culminating in total currency collapse and societal breakdown, the representatives of the state and their advisors simply do not want to give up their privilege of creating money at will and of exercising inordinate control over society's economic resources and the direction of the economy. The problem with the numerous preceding currency disasters must have always been, according to the view of officialdom, with the execution of monetary policy in the specific case. If certain things had only been done differently, elastic money could have been made to contribute greatly to the community's welfare. We have shown conclusively that this is a myth.

Like all previous paper money systems, our present system is unsustainable. It will lead to ever-higher indebtedness, in particular that of the state, and increasingly economic instability. In fact, our present system has already progressed a long way on the road to inevitable demise. Before we predict its endgame, we will next take a look at the beneficiaries of this system and the belief system that props up public support for it, against the overwhelming evidence of history and theory.

Part Five

BEYOND THE CYCLE
Paper Money Collapse

Part Five

Chapter 8

The Beneficiaries of the Paper Money System

By now we have fully exposed the disadvantages and dangers of elastic money. We have demonstrated the inherent instability of a pure paper money system. In order to chart the further disintegration of our present system, it is useful to know and to understand the interested parties that benefit from this system and that support it. This should allow us to better predict how those in charge of the paper money franchise are likely to respond to the system's increasing instability and incoherence.

Paper Money and the Banks

It is not difficult to see how the banks and the wider financial industry benefit from the present paper money infrastructure. The fractional-reserve banks enjoy the privilege of creating money at no cost to themselves and lending it to nonbanks at interest. This is naturally very lucrative. The wider financial industry also reaps substantial benefits since it is usually the first recipient of new money. As we have seen, the early recipients of new money enjoy an as-yet fairly undiminished purchasing power while those who receive money later, when many prices are elevated, do not benefit at all. It is no surprise that since the introduction of fully flexible fiat money in 1971, the financial industry has greatly expanded. Since the late 1980s in particular, the expansion of money mainly has been channeled into the markets for financial assets and real estate, thereby benefiting the holders of such assets and those operating in the markets for these assets at the expense of other sections of society.

By replacing inflexible and apolitical commodity money with its own unlimited state fiat money, and by making its central bank a lender of last resort, the state has, to a large degree, socialized the risks of individual banks and allowed for the massive expansion of fractional-reserve banking, albeit now under the state's tutelage and control.

It would be wrong to assume that central banks and state fiat monies exist merely as a response to fractional-reserve banking. Throughout history, states have imposed their own paper monies on their populations and have run privileged state banks, clearly with the intent to fund state spending. But the present arrangement, which, as we have seen, really came to fruition in the course of the twentieth century, constitutes the ingenious pooling of the interests of the state and the fractional-reserve banking industry. Only with the full backing of the state can the banks conduct fractional-reserve banking on the considerable scale it is practiced today. Unlimited state paper money, legal tender laws, lender-of-last-resort central banks, state-backed deposit-insurance and, ironically, even government regulation, are indispensible for an extensive large-scale fractional-reserve banking industry. The state, in return, obtains full control over the monetary sphere of society and the privilege of running larger deficits than would otherwise be feasible, with the added bonus that the state's extraordinary powers in this area appear to large sections of the public as a necessary arrangement in the interest of the public. Somebody has to control the bankers and reign in their money printing!

The state-bank alliance necessarily involves the cartelization of the banks around the dominant central bank. Banks become to a large degree extensions of the state and instruments of economic policy. However, as has been shown, this system does not do away with cycles; it merely extends and magnifies them. In this system banks are bigger but not safer. In the inevitable downturn, the banking sector receives further state protection as bank failures are now even more painful in a massively inflated banking industry than they were before. Additionally, the banking sector plays an essential role in the government's anticrisis scheme. Any monetary stimulus has to go through the banking sector to reach the broader economy and hence constitutes a powerful subsidy to the banks. Neither state nor banks will initially have to suffer the full consequences of the boom and bust cycle that is the unavoidable outcome of their money-printing privilege. Bank bailouts, including bank nationalizations, and an expanding state are innate elements of a system of state paper money.

As the financial sector gets bigger its instability becomes ever more threatening to the overall economy, prompting ever more extensive, yet ultimately futile, involvement of the state. The endgame will be full nationalization of money and credit and ever more aggressive money creation to prevent the liquidation of the accumulated dislocations.

Paper Money and the State

As the territorial monopolist of coercion and compulsion and the ultimate decision maker in case of conflict, the state does not have to rely on voluntary exchange of goods and services to obtain resources but enjoys the privilege of legally expropriating the private property owners and market-income earners in its jurisdiction.[1] This is called taxation and is a unique feature of state power. In the course of the twentieth century all states, and certainly all democracies, managed a ceaseless expansion of state activity, so that today the share of government spending in overall economic activity is everywhere higher than it was 50 years ago and substantially higher than 100 years ago. This growth of the state has not been funded by taxation alone, albeit as a general rule, the number of taxes and the rates of taxation have risen dramatically. Governments have also relied heavily on borrowing on financial markets and, as a result, the amount of outstanding public debt has also risen on trend in all major democratic states.[2]

Ownership of the paper money monopoly has allowed the modern state to consistently incur outlays in excess of the revenues the state obtains through taxation. The privilege of printing money has given the state an additional advantage over private borrowers and allows it to crowd them out more easily. The ability of the state to meet obligations by simply printing more money means that any shortfall of revenue will not mean default, an event that would be to the complete detriment of the state's creditors. Instead, by issuing more money and in the process impairing the purchasing power of the monetary unit, the creditors can be repaid (at least at only a small real loss to them resulting from inflation) and the burden of meeting these obligations can be socialized and spread across the entire community of money users. Society overall is made to pay not only via the direct cost of a diminished purchasing power of its monetary assets but also indirectly via the numerous destabilizing second-round effects of monetary expansion that we just analyzed. But to the creditor it is evidently preferable to be repaid in money of a somewhat diminished exchange value than suffer the risk of default. There can be no doubt that fully elastic paper money under a territorial state monopoly greatly enhances the ability of the state to run deficits and borrow in financial markets. The explosion in public debt that occurred since the introduction of paper money systems is evident. That this is, in itself, a destabilizing effect of paper money systems is often not fully appreciated. If elastic money had no other consequence than allowing bigger government deficits and the accumulation of more government debt, it would be sufficient to reject it for this reason alone.

It is sometimes assumed that issuing government bonds is equivalent to borrowing from future generations. This is a fallacy. The present generation can obviously not transport resources through time and thus obtain, that is, borrow or steal, the resources of future generations. The present generation has only the presently available resources at its disposal. The only question is how to allocate these resources to the various alternative uses. By issuing government bonds, the state simply claims a larger control over the currently available amount of resources than it already obtains through taxation. If the government bonds were not issued, more resources would simply get allocated to different uses according to the wishes of private property owners. In particular, government bonds compete with privately issued debt-claims (corporate bonds) and privately issued equity-claims for the existing pool of savings. However, this competition does not occur on a level playing field, as we have just seen. The government can crowd out any private competition for savings. Unlike the private issuers of bonds and equities, who have to convince their investors that the projects they are funding stand a good chance of generating an attractive market income by producing something that the buying public will voluntarily purchase, the government is under no such scrutiny. The government simply invites its investors, not to share in entrepreneurial risk and opportunity, but to participate in the lucrative government privilege of taxation and the printing of money. As long as the government finds enough private property owners and market income-earners to expropriate in the future, and takers for its state paper money, it can repay its bonds, regardless of what it did in the meantime with the funds that were raised through the issuance of the bonds.

A large part of state expenditure today is used for funding redistributive programs. To the extent that this is how the funds raised via the issuance of government bonds are spent, government borrowing channels savings back into consumption, rather than into investment. A society with a large amount of outstanding equity claims and corporate debt claims can reasonably be expected (if we exclude for a moment the possibility of this being the result of extensive previous money creation) to have a large stock of voluntary savings that has been channelled via the financial system into a substantial stock of productive capital. By contrast, a society with a large amount of outstanding government debt can reasonably be assumed to have enjoyed a period of substantial consumption, which was to a large degree government-funded, so that a considerable portion of its accumulated savings are backed by mere promises of the state to let the bondholder partake in the state's privilege of future expropriation. It is therefore clear that high levels of government spending, which have to coincide with high levels of taxation and/or high levels of government borrowing, will undermine the wealth-generating capabilities of the economy.[3] As we have seen, the ability to print money allows the state to borrow more heavily and thus increase government spending beyond the levels supported by taxation. The results are further distortions in resource allocation, in particular the diversion of scarce resources from building a productive capital stock to government-directed present consumption.

Here is another aspect to the interest of the state and the banks in a system of continuous inflation: As has been shown, in a commodity money system with no or limited fractional-reserve banking and thus a fairly static supply of money, the monetary asset will provide its holders with a moderate return in the form of its gradually appreciating purchasing power. This allows those who have a low tolerance for risk or limited expertise in investing to obtain at least a marginal return for their savings if they save by accumulating money. In a paper money system with ongoing inflation, this option does not exist, and the closest alternative available to those who have a low tolerance for risk or limited knowledge of investing are bank deposits and government bonds. The members of the public who would, in a commodity money system with secular deflation, save through holding cash are turned, in a paper money system, into the natural holders of save deposits and government bonds and the reliable source of funds for the banks' fractional-reserve banking activities and the state's spending. Herein lies another reason for why the representatives of banks and states uniformly favor inflationary paper money and are always very keen to portray deflation as a great social evil. Money that has an essentially stable or on trend appreciating purchasing power would be powerful competition to fractional-reserve deposits and government debt.

Other components of the paper money infrastructure further enhance the state's control over economic resources. There is the state-owned central bank. Central banking is usually profitable. The central bank creates money at almost zero cost and lends it to the banking sector at interest or it buys interest-bearing securities with the newly created money. This gain usually goes to the state. Obviously, to the extent that the central bank buys government bonds, the government pays interest to the central bank first and then collects the central bank's profits later.

Furthermore, the direct monetization of government debt has been a constituting feature of central banks from the beginning. We have seen that it was one of the key objectives behind the founding of the Bank of England. From the start, the Bank of England was allowed to issue notes against obligations of the Crown. Central banks create money by buying things and paying for them by crediting the account of the seller with newly created money, thus monetizing whatever the central bank buys. Although this could, in theory, be practically anything, the state usually encourages the central bank to buy state debt. The official reason is that the central bank should not risk incurring losses by buying risky assets, and that it should thus mainly monetize safe government bonds. As we have seen, government bonds are indeed safer because of the state's monopoly of taxation. They do not have to be repaid through the uncertain process of meeting the changing demands of the buying public but can be met by taxing those who have, in the preceding period, taken market risk and have succeeded in an entrepreneurial endeavor. This, by itself and under the condition that all else is equal, makes government bonds safer than comparable corporate loans, at least for as long as government debt is not excessive. There is certainly a limit to how much any government can realistically expropriate from the productive part of society. Consequently, there are limits to the supposed safety of government bonds. There is undoubtedly a point at which the additional negative effects on the economy of higher taxes would be so overwhelming that the government may contemplate not meeting its obligations to bondholders rather than taxing the productive part of society further. The ability to also print money and to have the central bank monetize government debt thus provides an important second layer of safety to the bond investor. It is therefore not without irony that central banks are allowed to monetize government debt for the reason that government debt is supposed to be safe, when it is precisely the monetization of this debt by the central bank that, to a considerable degree, adds to government bonds' perceived safety. Furthermore, according to the government-imposed rules and regulations, the fractional-reserve banks in its jurisdiction are usually allowed to hold more government bonds and other public-sector securities on their balance sheets for each unit of capital than riskier loans to private-sector entities.

We see here the extensive interdependence between the state and the financial sector of a monetary system based on state paper money. Government bonds are declared safe and can thus provide the basis of money creation by the central bank, but it is precisely this monetization that substantially reduces risk of outright default. Fractional-reserve banks can extend credit on the basis of money creation, a process that, to the extent it is practiced today, requires substantial state backing. At the same time, the entity to which fractional-reserve banks can provide that credit most easily is the state itself.

The paper money infrastructure allows the state to grow in any economic climate. During good times the state collects more tax revenue, and during recessions its central bank lowers interest rates and injects reserve money into the banking system by buying government securities. Low rates and higher reserves encourage the banks to expand their balance sheets, but as loans to private entities are always risky, and particularly risky during recessions, and as the cost of capital is lower for holding government securities, it is likely that a lot of the new and artificially stimulated lending will again benefit the public sector.

One of the important and often underestimated benefits of the money-printing privilege for the state is the ability to create short-term booms in economic activity. As we have seen, growing government expenditure, which has almost become part of life in modern mass democracies, involves rising taxation and government borrowing, which in turn weaken the productive capacity of the economy. It has therefore been vital for governments to combine growing expenditure, taxation, and borrowing with ongoing inflationism, with the suppression of interest rates through money injections, thus creating the illusion of higher levels of voluntary savings and allowing for artificial investment booms.

Paper Money and the Professional Economist

To put professional economists next to the state and banks as beneficiaries of the present monetary system may appear strange at first. The latter two are powerful sectors of modern society with substantial control over economic resources. Professional economists are simply not in that category. But a system that is built on privilege and state protection requires an intellectual support structure, a widely shared belief system that secures public acceptance. We will analyze this intellectual foundation of the present system in the next chapter. It should already be clear, however, that the intellectual guardians of the contemporary monetary architecture are the professional economists. As will be explained shortly, it is not the entire body of economic theory but rather a specific subsector of it that provides, in its popularized form, large sections of the population, of the state bureaucracy, the political class, and the media with a framework for interpreting and debating economic phenomena today.

It would be naïve to simply assume that the exalted position of these theories in present debate is the result of their superiority in the realm of pure science. This is not meant as a conspiracy theory in the sense that professional economists are being hired specifically to develop useful theories for the privileged money producers in order to portray their money printing as universally beneficial. But it would be equally wrong to assume that the battle for ideas is fought only by dispassionate and objective truth-seekers in ivory towers and that only the best theories are handed down to the decision makers in the real world, and that therefore whatever forms the basis of current mainstream discussion must be the best and most accurate theory available. No science operates in a vacuum. The social sciences in particular are often influenced in terms of their focus and method of inquiry by larger cultural and intellectual trends in society. This is probably more readily accepted in the other major social science, history. What questions research asks of the historical record, what areas of inquiry are deemed most pressing and how historians go about historical analysis is often shaped by factors that lie outside the field of science proper and that reflect broader social and political forces.

Moreover, ever since mankind began writing its histories they have served political ends. History frequently provides a narrative for the polity that gives it a sense of identity or purpose, whether this is justified or not, and the dominant interpretations of history can be powerful influences on present politics. Similarly, certain economic theories have become to dominate debate on economic issues because they fit the zeitgeist and specific political ideologies. This is not to say that economics cannot be a pure, objective science. It certainly can and should be. Whether theories are correct or not must be decided by scientific inquiry and debate, and not in the arena of politics and public opinion. But it is certainly true that many economists do depend for their livelihoods on politics and public opinion, and that they cannot operate independently of them.

We will shed light on today's dominant economic doctrines, at least in their popularized forms, in the next chapter. Here we look at the benefits that the present monetary infrastructure has to offer to the economics profession. There can be little doubt that many economists truly believe that this is the best possible system, but it is also clear that it is in their own interest to do so. The alternative to the present financial infrastructure would be a system of denationalized inelastic commodity money. This would be a system without monetary policy and therefore without the need to constantly analyze, discuss, predict, and advise policy, which is how most economists earn a living today.

Many economists work in sectors that owe their size and importance if not their very existence to the fiat money system and its extensive bureaucracies, like the numerous central banks, the International Monetary Fund (IMF), the Bank for International Settlement (BIS), the World Bank, and the wider financial industry. Here, the economists either are policy makers themselves, advise policy makers, or provide research for policy makers. In the private sector, professional economists help investors, traders, and bankers anticipate what the policy makers are likely to do next. The highest paid jobs for economists are frequently offered on Wall Street or in the City of London and are thus provided by companies that directly or indirectly benefit from the paper money system, either by being paper money producers themselves or by being consistently early recipients of newly created money. Furthermore, these jobs often go to professionals who earned their stripes in government central banks or in institutions like the IMF, and whose special knowledge of the extended financial bureaucracy is precisely what makes them interesting for their private-sector employers. But even purely academic economists will find that their work achieves broader recognition if it can claim direct relevance to the present institutional arrangements.

This development is fairly recent but representative of what happened to the economics profession at large, as it has, in the course of the twentieth century, adapted to the needs of the large and ever-growing interventionist state. While the economist once strived to discover the laws that guide the cooperation of otherwise unconnected individuals on markets and that allow everyone to benefit from the extended division of labor—an endeavor that put him often in conflict with political powers and earned economics the epitaph "the dismal science"—the modern economist is now frequently a government advisor and an accomplice in ongoing market intervention. Economists themselves rarely work in the free market. In 2008 in the United States, the federal, state, and local governments accounted for more than 50 percent of total employment of economists. Additionally, with 300 economists, the Federal Reserve System alone accounted for more than 2 percent of them.[4]

This is not to say that economists are simply mouthpieces of the policy establishment. Many of them can be critical of policy makers, and many of them want to contribute to a better understanding of the system or genuinely strive toward its improvement. Yet, they work within self-imposed limits. Mainstream economists have little incentive to question the system itself, and they will rarely think outside of it.

Of course, none of these observations can tell us anything about the validity of the theories that these economists advocate. As made clear here, whether a theory is correct and valid or flawed and erroneous can be decided only by thorough theoretical investigation. A theory is not wrong because it serves those who propose it and is not correct because it is being advanced by disinterested truth-seekers. Only careful examination can reveal the merit of any theory, and this is what we aimed for in our systematic analysis above. However, it is a simple fact that a return to a system of inflexible commodity money, such as a proper gold standard, would deprive not only the state and banking industry of a source of power and profit but also the economics profession of positions of influence and income.

Chapter 9

The Intellectual Superstructure of the Present System

W hen crises occur they lead to debate, and debates always take place within an established framework, within a set of widely accepted theories and beliefs that are themselves no longer the subject of inquiry but are treated as established truths and are therefore being used as intellectual tools. In respect to economic crises, this framework is not, as many might believe, the science of economics as such but rather a specific subset of economic doctrines, a body of theories that have become dominant and that in their popularized form today provide the basis for most economic discussions.

The dominant trends in economic thinking in the twentieth century were the rise of macroeconomics and the related spread of mathematical and statistical techniques in economic analysis (econometrics). These trends brought not only new theories but also new ways of looking at economic phenomena, of framing economic problems and conducting economic analysis. Whether they constitute an improvement over earlier modes of economic thinking is a valid question that has to be answered in the realm of pure science. There can, however, be little doubt that in many ways a narrowing of perspective relative to older modes of economic thinking has occurred, mainly as the result of the strong emphasis of the "new" economics on large aggregates, in particular those that can be followed conveniently by national account statistics. Theories that center on the large entities of GDP, the price index, the unemployment rate, and so forth are fundamentally unable to capture the crucial processes of resource allocation and of the alignment of economic activity with consumer preferences. These processes, by definition, operate beneath such aggregates. The statistical aggregates can, if anything, give only a faint and often misleading image of them.

Nevertheless, these theories provide the theoretical paradigm that is now shared by the majority of those who participate in discussions on economic matters. Today almost everybody who participates in economic debate, whether he is a politician, central banker, or journalist, is, first and foremost, a macroeconomist and thus tacitly adopts a series of usually uncontested notions of the macro paradigm. While the wide acceptance of the mainstream doctrines provides everybody with a ready language to discuss economic problems in, it certainly poses an obstacle to the recognition of rival and less well-known theories that use a different paradigm.

Two representatives of the modern macro paradigm are central to a discussion of the fiat money system because they continue to have the biggest influence on the policy establishment, the media, and the financial industry whenever the topic is crisis and recession: Keynesianism and Monetarism. More than any individual aspect of these theories, it is the overall worldview behind them, the specific set of notions about what a market economy is and how it works, and about the origin of crises, which shapes today's debates on economic problems.

There is an alternative economic paradigm which does not hold similar sway over public economic debate. This alternative system is older. It has provided the basis for the analysis in this book and it will be presented first, before we take a look at the paradigm that the mainstream uses and that dominates discussion today.

The Alternative View: Individualism
and Laissez-Faire

The analysis of money injections presented in earlier chapters started from the key function of money as a medium of exchange and developed all its conclusions via logical deduction from this starting point. This approach has been called methodological individualism,[1] as its basis is the individual economic actor and what he is trying to achieve by his actions. In this case, an analysis of money started with individual money users, why they use money, and the effects that the use of money must have. The analysis did not rely on an interpretation of historical data (statistics) but was nevertheless empirical in that its starting point was the empirical fact that we use money to facilitate transactions. All further insights followed from there.

This methodological individualism, the focus on the individual decision maker as driver of economic processes, is consistent with a view of the market economy as a form of voluntary human cooperation, in which people participate to improve their supply with goods and services. The development of a complex market economy can be understood entirely from the self-interested actions of rational individuals. The foundation of the market economy is the realization on the part of its participants that division of labor enhances productivity, which benefits everybody, and that the wider this division of labor is, the better. If people had been content to live in self-sufficient isolation and enjoy only the fruits of their own labor and those of their immediate family or clan, the economic cooperation that is the market economy would not have come into existence. In order to extend the division of labor, new modes of human cooperation had to be developed. The narrow and hierarchically structured family or clan, in which uniform goals existed and work was coordinated by command, was supplemented with and partially replaced by the extended and contractually organized market economy, in which people cooperate via the exchange of goods and services, and in which activity is directed by market prices and the calculation of profit and loss. The precondition for trade was the recognition of private property, of an individual's personal sphere of exclusive control over resources. Once these essential building blocks were in place, other institutions and practices followed logically, each of them justified in its existence by recognizably benefiting those who used it: indirect exchange through money, saving, and investing, capital formation, capital markets, and so forth. The market economy exists and is maintained by its members because they see the benefits of participating in it.

The use of a medium of exchange, the introduction of indirect exchange through money, constituted a fundamental change in human cooperation. Individual human action can operate on ordinal systems. In order to act, I need to know only that I like "A" more than "B." Likewise for a simple exchange economy. When, in a barter economy, one farmer trades with another farmer one cow for two sheep, all they need to know is that one prefers owning two sheep to owning the extra cow, while the other prefers the cow to the two sheep. (It may be added here that, contrary to a widespread view, the two farmers do not agree that one cow is *worth* two sheep. Indeed, the trade takes place only because the two farmers value the one cow and the two sheep differently. That is why both of them gain from the transaction.) But, once goods are traded for money, money prices can be generated to reflect the valuations of many individuals, and economic activity can suddenly make use of cardinal numbers and of calculation. Costs and revenues can be computed and profit and loss calculated.[2] Private property and market prices are the precondition for rational economic activity, "rational" meaning the employment of scarce resources according to the valuations of the many individual members of society.

If the market economy is, rightly understood, a tool that can be used for the purpose of those who participate in it, it is clear that it fulfills its purpose as long as it provides a functioning framework for voluntary cooperation in pursuit of individual plans and ambitions. This is its only purpose. The market economy is not a superior organism that has its own goals. There is no overriding or unifying purpose. It is not the purpose of the market economy to generate positive GDP growth. It is just a tool, a framework, albeit the most important framework mankind has ever discovered, that allows everyone to better realize their own plans, and it is their own plans that matter.

It is true that most people prefer more goods and services to fewer goods and services, and this is precisely the reason they use the tool "market economy" to cooperate with others. And because of this, the growth in the statistical aggregate of GDP (national income) is, as long as the market is entirely uninhibited, a decent indicator that the economy is operating smoothly. But it is just that, an indicator. A higher GDP as such is not the goal of any of the individuals participating in the economy. Nobody will be made happy just because this statistical aggregate is higher in this period than in the previous period. People have specific goals and plans, and getting closer to realizing these plans is what cooperation on markets is all about. Government intervention can, for a short time but only for a short time, lift the GDP statistics. We have shown that this is possible through the discretionary injection of new money. However, in the process government intervention must obstruct the coordinating function of the market economy and thus frustrate many of the plans of those who participate in the economy. A smoothly functioning market economy should lead to a rise in GDP, but a state-manufactured rise in GDP does not lead to a smoothly functioning market economy.

What constitutes a crisis? According to this understanding of the market economy, the crisis is an unusually high rate of plan failure. It has been accurately called a "cluster of errors."[3] Errors are obviously a part of life. Even during so-called good times, many entrepreneurs will fail. They may misjudge consumer tastes or technological change; they may invest too little or too much, or for other reasons get replaced by more efficient competitors. Failure and bankruptcy are part and parcel of even the smoothly functioning market. What constitutes a crisis is the exceptional accumulation of errors, and this is what any good cycle theory needs to explain. It is clear that the type of collective misjudgment that results in a crisis can occur only if the market's essential pricing process has been corrupted. An elastic monetary system inevitably produces such large-scale disturbances.

Once an economy has developed an unsustainable structure of production and prices and has entered a recession, only one solution is logically possible for returning the economy back to stability, and that is to allow the complete and uninhibited liquidation of any unsustainable investment projects and the full correction of prices distorted by the previous money injection. If the root cause of the economic crisis is a distorted allocation of resources as a result of misleading price signals, only a reallocation of resources can logically constitute a solution.

The advisability of strict laissez-faire, even and in particular during recessions, does therefore not follow from any personal value judgment but is the logical consequence of the understanding of the market economy as a tool for large-scale human cooperation in a contractual society. By contrast, a policy of interventionism is not rational because it cannot improve upon the coordinating power of voluntary interaction on markets. Its goal of boosting the GDP statistics does not constitute a solution to the underlying problem because the underlying problem is not an insufficient number of transactions (a subpar GDP), but the accumulation of capital misallocations, which only a free market can lay bare and correct.

There exists a common misconception. It is sometimes presumed that those who advocate a policy of strict laissez-faire in a recession assign positive effects to deflation, or that they advocate deflationary policies. This is not necessarily the case. Once money injections have distorted prices and resource allocation, the damage is done. What is needed is not a new deflationary policy but simply a stop to the previous policy of injecting money and artificially lowering interest rates. Of course, the correction of inflated prices must be allowed to proceed, wherever and to whatever extent needed. A temporary drop in the statistical average of all prices cannot be excluded. Additionally, rising uncertainty in the crisis may lift the demand for cash holdings, which, in the absence of further money injections, will lead to a rise in the purchasing power of money. These deflationary processes must be allowed to proceed. They are part of a necessary readjustment of prices away from money-induced distortions and back toward market-clearing levels. However, no specific policies are necessary, such as shrinking the money supply or lowering prices to return to a specific price average or a previous gold price. All that is needed is simply a complete stop to money injections followed by the abstention from any interference with the market process.

Another misconception is that opposition to interventionist policies after a crisis must be based on considerations of moral hazard. According to this idea, interventions are bad because they allow those who made errors during the boom to escape the full consequences of their mistakes. State intervention always socializes the cost of business failure and thus encourages more reckless risk taking in the future, which will lead to more crises. The incentives for prudent risk taking are lowered if profits remain private but losses are socialized.

It cannot be denied that this is a problem. Yet, it is not the key argument for the noninterventionist position. The crisis occurs because resources have been misallocated and prices have been distorted. The market must be allowed to correct these dislocations. This is the only solution to the underlying economic problem. Providing short-term relief through interventionist policies must mean distorting prices again by keeping interest rates artificially low or by maintaining an inappropriate capital allocation by bailing-out failed companies. These policies cannot logically constitute a solution but must obstruct a return to more sustainable economic structures. Allowing the economy to cleanse itself of the misallocations of resources from the previous boom and to reorient itself according to consumer preferences is the only rational position, the only position that cannot simply be rejected on logical grounds.

The Mainstream View: Collectivism and Interventionism

Present-day discussions on economics and economic policy are based largely on a very different intellectual paradigm with different ideas about the market economy, the correct approach to economics and the role of policy. The methodological foundation of today's consensus is macroeconomics:

> The macroeconomic approach looks upon an arbitrarily selected segment of the market economy (as a rule: one nation) as if it were an integral unit. All that happens in this segment is actions of individuals and groups of individuals acting in concert. But macroeconomics proceeds as if all these individual actions were in fact the outcome of the mutual operation of one macroeconomic magnitude upon another such magnitude. (Mises)[4]

Macroeconomics is part of the broader intellectual trend of methodological collectivism, which treats "wholes like society or the economy, capitalism (as a given historical 'phase') or a particular industry or class or country as definitely given objects about which we can discover laws by observing their behavior as wholes" (Hayek).[5] Naturally, the macroeconomic approach lends itself to statistical and mathematical techniques but, more importantly, it appeals to those in politics.

On the foundation of methodological collectivism, the view of the economy has largely changed from that of a decentralized framework for voluntary, contractual human cooperation to one of an organism that has its own life and purpose. This organism has a quantifiable performance potential and in any given period it can be determined whether it achieves this potential or not. Thus, crises are no longer clusters of errors or high degrees of plan failure, which result from previous disruptions to resource allocation, but a suboptimal path of measured GDP. It only takes a small step from the idea that a set of statistical aggregates can tell us whether the economic organism is working at its full potential or not, to the notion that anything that brings those aggregates back to where the economist thinks they should be is already a solution to the underlying problem. A sudden drop in economic activity as measured by GDP is, to the individualist micro-economist, a symptom of the problem of distorted resource allocation that has now been exposed resulting in drastic adjustment of individual plans, but, to the mainstream macroeconomist, it is what constitutes the economic problem itself and what thus requires solution through intervention.

Once the economic problem has been redefined like this, the natural next step is to conceive of means to "stimulate the economy," a phrase that has become a standard, uncritically used term in economic policy debates but that is meaningless within the framework of an individualist concept of the economy. The term has its origin in physiology and psychology, where it relates to external influences on the operation of body and mind. First, it conveys the false impression that the recession is simply a form of fatigue of the economic organism that can be overcome if the organism is restimulated to a higher degree of activity. Second, it obfuscates the true effects of government intervention. In the case of a stimulus in biology, for example, the nerve cells that are subject to stimulation have only one clearly defined purpose and all that the stimulus does is to initiate the execution of the cells' unchanging faculties. Whatever is subject to external stimulus in biology will perform only the tasks that it is genetically designed to perform. This is not, and cannot, be the case with government intervention in the economy. "Stimulating" an economy, for example, by injecting new money into it, will change the economy. The same things will not be produced as before, only in larger quantity. New money will alter the economic process and lead to a different allocation of resources and a different income distribution. The same is necessarily true of fiscal policy, which always involves the redirection of resource employment from private use to public use. Nothing new is being added to the economy. Fiscal policy merely rearranges the already available resources away from how private property owners would have used them and toward how state officials and their economic advisors want them to be used.

The extent to which the public has accepted the notion of the policy stimulus is most certainly the result of its false portrayal as a process in which the government somehow brings something to the economy that was not there before, and the purpose of which is to stimulate the underlying economic procedures, that is, bolster what may unfold anyway, albeit less vigorously, without the intervention. But unlike the stimulus in physiology, the economic stimulus is an intervention that changes procedures rather than simply setting them in motion or amplifying them.

The goal of the policy stimulus is evidently to increase overall economic activity, to generate a positive growth in GDP statistics. The traditional Keynesian approach is to "stimulate aggregate demand" mainly through government spending programs. The typical Monetarist crisis measure is aimed at avoiding a drop in the money supply or at actively increasing the money supply and thereby avoiding deflation. How can the success or failure of these programs be measured? Obviously, these programs achieved their declared aims if, after their implementation, the money supply is expanding, the price level is rising, and GDP statistics show higher growth than in the previous period or even positive growth. As the obvious crisis symptoms have eased or disappeared, the depression is over.

However, a certain change in GDP statistics cannot say anything about efficient allocation of resources and the degree of individual plan fulfillment. We have seen this very clearly in our models of money injections, in which frequently new transactions were initiated by money injections with these transactions simply shifting control over resources but failing to add to overall wealth and failing to improve the use of available resources. Indeed, a temporarily higher GDP as a result of intervention, including money injections, will have been bought with further resource misallocations and the distortions of market signals, meaning ultimately with further frustrations for those who use the market as a tool to meet their goals.

The Political Appeal of Mainstream Macroeconomics

This view of the economy and of the origin of crises is attractive to those in politics. First, there is intellectual appeal. Although in reality economic interaction does not stop at political borders, the macroeconomist views the economy through the prism of national account statistics. Those perfectly correspond to areas of political control. Second, the political mind in general tends to struggle with the concept of the decentralized market order in which common goals are absent and in which a multitude of individual plans and aspirations are being coordinated spontaneously through market prices. The problem for the politician is that this system does not need politics. The market economy is indeed the very antithesis of politics, which depends on the existence of common goals, common values, and a common strategy. The politician must establish an agenda that unites people behind specific overarching purposes that all can share and identify with. Sociologically, it is tribal and closer to earlier and more primitive forms of human cooperation, like the hierarchically structured family or clan, rather than the decentralized contractual society based on market exchange.

But the macroeconomic concept of large units, of collectives that can be juxtaposed against one another, is much more appealing to political thinking, in particular if one can use this concept to formulate collective goals, like the need for a larger national product (GDP), increased levels of consumption or investment, a reduction in unemployment or a "socially beneficial" inflation rate. The decentralized complexity and spontaneous order of the market, with its multitude of individual plans, suddenly disappears and is replaced with a few statistical aggregates that can be monitored, to which targets can be assigned, and that can then be manipulated for the greater public good.

Third, there is the undeniable appeal to those in politics of the idea that anything is good that has the potential to instantly boost GDP. Keynesianism has introduced and popularized the notion of "aggregate demand" and the idea that what is at the heart of an economic recession is a lack of such aggregate demand. Obviously, the number and size of economic transactions that occur in aggregate over any specific period is of no benefit and, indeed, of no consequence whatsoever to the individual economic actor. Everybody uses the market economy for his or her own specific advantage, to realize or advance personal goals, or the goals and objectives of a group of people that one belongs to. If, for whatever reason, certain economic transactions that boosted GDP in the previous period are discontinued in the present period by those who previously voluntarily engaged in them, the specific benefit that those actors used to derive from these activities cannot be generated by some other activity conducted or initiated by the state bureaucracy with the aim to keep the statistical average of economic activity up. The peculiar notion that GDP is, in and of itself, the benchmark for economic health is used to justify practically any activity of the state bureaucracy.

As the state has greatly expanded the range of its responsibilities over the past 100 years, a considerable number of "public services" today constantly vie for more resources, spoiling the state for choice in its effort to stimulate aggregate demand by increased spending. A constantly expanding state apparatus is the inevitable consequence of this intellectual approach to economy and crisis.

The concept of aggregate demand is closely linked, albeit not identical to, another feature of the Keynesian framework that appeals to the state bureaucracy, and that is the antipathy toward saving. The peculiar idea that recessions are caused by too much saving and lack of consumption is hardly an invention of Keynes or his followers. It has, indeed, a very long tradition in economic folklore. Not surprisingly, it appeals to politicians who see it as a suitable excuse to run budget deficits and thus extend their control over economic resources beyond their take from taxation. We will revisit this notion when we discuss the theory of the "saving glut" later in this chapter.

Every market intervention must inevitably conflict with the framework that allows the coordination of private plan fulfillment. Every intervention replaces to a certain degree the spontaneous and multilayered interaction of all members of society on free markets with the targeted direction of resources by the state, which will inevitably benefit some at the expense of others. The state is by definition the monopolist of coercion and compulsion in society. Whenever the economist calls upon the state to use its powers to influence resource use and prices to bring about the desired constellation of macro variables, he acknowledges that the voluntary interaction of private property owners would bring about a different constellation and one that, in the view of the economist, is inferior. By definition, any intervention in the market must direct resources away from how private property owners would have employed them and toward how state officials and their economic advisors would like to see them employed. This is logically necessary because if the resource allocation and prices resulting from intervention reflected private preferences, no intervention would be required in the first place. The rationale for any intervention is that if private property owners were left alone to decide how to employ their resources, a suboptimal outcome would ensue. But how can one define what is a suboptimal and what is an optimal outcome? Obviously, this is impossible if we understand the market economy as a tool for economic cooperation. Then, no single goal exists and the voluntary cooperation of private property owners is always preferable to any state directive. But, in abandoning this view of the market economy and in defining a set of statistical aggregates as not only indicators but also as politically desirable outcomes, the modern macroeconomist has laid the intellectual groundwork for the state-directed economy. As Keynes himself declared in his preface to the German edition of *The General Theory of Employment, Interest, and Money*, published in late 1936:

> *The theory of aggregate production that is the goal of the following book can be much more easily applied to the conditions of a totalitarian state than the theory of the production and distribution of a given output*

turned out under the conditions of free competition and of a considerable degree of laissez faire.[6]

The Myth That Everybody Benefits from "Stimulus"

The idea of common economic goals is of course an illusion. Let us take the policy actions in response to the crisis that commenced in late 2007 in the United States as an example. It is only rational to assume that not everybody in U.S. society wants house prices to stay at elevated levels or, indeed, to rise. Marginal buyers of new homes would certainly prefer them to be lower. Not everybody wants interest rates to be low. Savers benefit from higher rates. Not everybody wants a very large part of society's resources allocated to the construction and maintenance of private homes. Many entrepreneurs have different ideas about the potential use of society's scarce resources, and many consumers may benefit from their ideas and support them. If it were in everybody's interest to have high house prices, low interest rates, and an ever-expanding housing stock, there would be no market pressure in the direction toward lower house prices and higher rates. There would simply be no crisis.

The process of liquidation of the excesses from the preceding credit and property boom is undoubtedly very painful for those who see their previous expectations disappointed and their plans fail. In this crisis, these are mainly the owners of property, in particular those who bought houses during the boom not as long-lasting consumption goods for their own use but for the purpose of selling them later at higher prices, and those who gave them loans. But it is an undeniable fact that the voluntary cooperation of all members of society does no longer support the previous expansion. It is lamentable that the injections of substantial amounts of money in the past had, for an extended time, distorted interest rates and thus made it appear as if the personal plans and the voluntary decisions of the rest of society did indeed warrant further real estate investment, even at rising prices. Those who suffer in the correction can, with some justification, claim to be victims of misleading signals. Low interest rates indicated an enormous future-orientedness of consumers, which meant that more resources could be committed to the provision of long lasting consumer goods. Given this evidently low time preference, it seemed reasonable to shift resources accordingly into areas such as housing, which deliver their full use-value only over a long period. Once the money expansion began to slow (partially triggered by the central bank itself tightening monetary conditions, although a slowing of the money flow would in any case have been unavoidable at some stage), it became apparent that true preferences were different from what low rates had signaled. In terms of its size, structure, and prices, the housing market turned out to be out of synch with the real preferences of the public. There was simply no alternative to a meaningful correction.

Coming to the aid of those whose expectations have been disappointed necessarily means maintaining a resource allocation and a price structure that was built on distorted signals and erroneous assumptions, and that is not supported by the wishes of the rest of society. Yet, in recent years, the U.S. state has taken it upon itself to keep interest rates again artificially low and, via political means, keep resources committed to the housing and mortgage market by, among other measures, the de facto nationalization of mortgage finance (through the conservatorship of the Federal National Mortgage Association (FNMA) and the Federal Home Loan Mortgage Corporation (FHLMC)) in 2008 and the buying of mortgage-backed securities by the state central bank.

The measures are sold to the public as being in everybody's interest because they are aimed at avoiding a near-term correction of GDP. But the idea that all of us share one single goal—a higher GDP—is false. There are always a multitude of competing potential uses for society's strictly limited means, and only the market can coordinate among them. Consequently, these measures will never solve the underlying problems. By obstructing the market from liquidating these misallocations of capital and correcting the mispricing of assets, these policies create an illusion of normality. They simply postpone the painful and inevitable liquidation into the future but, in the meantime, make the problem worse by continuing to distort market signals and to further encourage the accumulation of imbalances.

As a rule, the biggest beneficiaries of government intervention are usually the very same sectors that benefited disproportionately from the false boom, as these are now the sectors where the correction is most severely felt. Due to the ruling macroeconomic theories, policy is always concentrated on revitalising the very same drivers that were behind the preceding expansion, or at a minimum, to shield them from adverse market pressures. There is an inevitable element of conservatism in market intervention in that it always opposes the redirection of activity and the reallocation of resources to alternative employment. In the process, the interventionists must suppress the legitimate views and preferences of large sections of society. Those consumers, savers, and producers whose preferences favor alternative uses of resources, and who could voice their personal choices only through buying or selling in a free market where they would, on the margin at least, contribute to lower house prices, take a back seat to the existing owners of property and the existing lenders in the real estate market. Only the state as monopolist of legalized force can sideline these uncooperative economic actors and ensure that resources continue to be allocated to where they created the preceding boom. And to the extent that this state intervention comes in the form of money printing and low interest rates, which it always does, many of these sidelined constituencies are likely to end up the future victims of false market signals themselves. Entrepreneurs will again be disoriented by low interest rates and scale their investment projects to unrealistic assumptions about the availability of voluntary savings. Many of their projects will inevitably end in disappointment, too. The effect of every intervention is necessarily that old dislocations persist and new ones are generated.

Monetarism as Monetary Interventionism

In academia and in the world of think tanks, Keynesianism and Monetarism are regularly presented as archenemies but, in respect to the topics discussed here, the differences are at most marginal. Monetarists claim to be advocates of the free market and are generally critical of the heavy fiscal interventionism and deficit spending of the Keynesians. However, they combine their defense of the market order in most areas with the promotion of a state-run monetary system, which includes state paper money issued by the central bank and constant, albeit controlled, inflationism to aid growth.[7] Not surprisingly, most government advisors and financial market economists today are as happy at times of stress to advocate Keynesian deficit spending as they are to advocate Monetarist easy monetary policy. Consequently, in recent crises, most governments have fully embraced both sets of recipes. The media and the public have learnt to accept both policy prescriptions as the inseparable twins of modern anticrisis management. Deficit spending and money injections are simply what one does in recessions.

Intellectually, the two schools are very similar too. Both are part of the twentieth century's trend toward methodological collectivism and macroeconomics just described. Milton Friedman himself clearly perceived their common methodological foundation when he said that "in one sense, we are all Keynesians now; in another, no one is a Keynesian any longer. . . . We all use the Keynesian language and apparatus; none of us any longer accepts the initial Keynesian conclusions."[8] Furthermore, he declared: "I believe that Keynes' theory is the right kind of theory in its simplicity, its concentration on a few magnitudes, its potential fruitfulness. I have been led to reject it not on these grounds, but because I believe that it has been contradicted by experience."[9]

Somewhat ironically, Friedman's Monetarism became, in the eye of the public, the main representative and even the benchmark of free market ideology in the last third of the twentieth century, although it had completely abandoned the traditional libertarian position on money. Defense of freedom and personal liberty had for centuries been synonymous with the defense of commodity money. If political power should be restrained, politics had to be kept out of money and banking, and bankers had to be tied to hard money. This was possible only if money were a depoliticized and denationalized inflexible commodity, outside the influence of politicians.[10]

For the sake of completeness it should be mentioned that Friedman rejected fractional-reserve banking and proposed the introduction of 100 percent reserve requirements.[11] However, Friedman saw the problem with fractional-reserve banking less on the side of the bankers, who through a dubious conflation of deposits and loans circulated uncovered claims to boost the return on their loan portfolios, but more on the side of bank customers, who were likely to switch their holdings of money from bank deposits to physical currency at any moment and thus introduce instability into banking procedures. Be that as it may, the goal of his proposal for 100 percent reserve banking was not to provide the economy with hard and inflexible, let alone denationalized, money but to increase the level of control the central bank has over total money supply. Friedman's proposals are therefore different in spirit and objective to those of the Austrians but very close to those of another eminent American economist and monetary theorist, Irving Fisher, who also recommended 100 percent reserve requirements.[12] Fisher published his proposals at the height of the Great Depression, evidently motivated by the specter of collapsing banks and a shrinking money supply during a crisis. Like Friedman, Fisher advocated state-controlled paper money and its controlled expansion under a policy of moderate price level stabilization.

Friedman's influence on today's monetary policy establishment can hardly be overstated. His theories, again in a somewhat popularized form, shape public debate on monetary matters to a large degree today. They have a particularly strong hold on central bankers. With their concern about overall inflation and their proposal for measured growth in the money supply, these theories appear to address the main dangers of the elastic money system while simultaneously legitimizing elastic money as such. The most widely accepted tenets of modern central banking can be characterized as essentially Monetarist: the notion that a stable or moderately rising inflation rate indicates monetary stability; that this can be achieved by controlled and moderate expansion of the money supply; and the idea that at times of crisis, when inflation risks are low, the central bank should ease monetary policy aggressively in order to avoid a contraction of the overall money stock and deflation. The latter was the result mainly of Friedman's interpretation of historic events around the stock market crash of 1929 and the Great Depression of the 1930s, events to which the U.S. Federal Reserve should have responded, according to Friedman, with a more aggressively expansionary policy.[13] The lesson from history is that at times of panic and sharp asset price falls, the central bank needs to inject substantial amounts of reserve money to stop the contraction of the supply of deposit money and a rise in the purchasing power of the monetary unit. This is, in central bank and financial market circles, a largely uncontested notion today.[14] To the extent that these policy prescriptions are debated at all today, the discussion focuses mainly on the technical aspects of their implementation rather than on the underlying concepts. At what point should a central bank interfere and how aggressive can and should it be? For how long should the stimulus be implemented and at what point should the central bank tighten again? Elastic money itself, however, is seen, if handled correctly, as an important tool for stimulating the economy, for avoiding or shortening recessions and as a means to achieve higher economic stability.

However, as we have shown, money injections always affect relative prices, they must disorient the economic agents by sending wrong signals, in particular with respect to the true extent of available savings, and they will consequently encourage a price formation, a resource allocation, and a direction of economic activity that are not in synch with the true underlying preferences of society. Money injections always lead to economic dislocation. The ongoing moderate inflationism that Monetarism prescribes is far from benign. By sanctioning the ongoing injection of new money into the economy, a Monetarist policy will lead to the accumulation of dislocations that make a crisis at a later stage unavoidable. A stable or only marginally rising price index will convey a false picture of stability while the actual shifts in prices and resource allocation that the money injections create go undetected.

The Pattern of Economic Deterioration

The following pattern is almost certain to develop under such a policy and, indeed, has developed in all countries where the moderate inflationism that today's policy consensus advocates has been practiced. As long as the official inflation measure stays within the politically accepted band, the central bank supports ongoing money production by the fractional-reserve banks. Inevitably, dislocations accumulate in the form of capital misallocations although, on the surface and through the prism of national account statistics, the economy's performance appears solid. Sooner or later, the inflationist policy will affect the official inflation measure, causing the central bank to tighten. Although the tightening is moderate, the accumulated misallocations from the preceding monetary expansion cause the economy to respond very sensitively to higher rates and a slowing of the flow of new money. The economy enters a recession. Today, large parts of the public and practically the entire policy establishment subscribe to the alleged trade-off between inflation and growth and thus to the view that a recession is to be tolerated only when it is needed to correct unusually high inflation. Accordingly, it is now deemed unnecessary to suffer a recession, as inflation has only been elevated marginally. The central bank is criticized for its overly restrictive policy and has to revert course, not least because the official inflation measure appears to be declining again in response to the economic downturn. The central bank moves from moderately tight policy back to easy policy. The dissolution of capital misallocations that started in the recession is arrested and a new expansion is generated through further and now even larger money injections (mainly by the fractional-reserve banks, which benefit from the easy monetary policy of the central bank).

As the recession was not allowed to play out completely, some or most of the dislocations from the first expansion have not been unwound and are now carried forward into the next expansion, during which, of course, new dislocations are being accumulated. None of this is perceived by the macroeconomic consensus as the focus is on GDP and the official inflation measure, both of which might have dipped briefly but will soon resume their rise. Of course, at some stage, inflation readings will again cause uneasiness among the central bankers and lead to a moderate tightening of policy. The aforementioned pattern will be repeated, albeit with some minor changes. Now the economy responds even more sensitively to higher rates and a slowdown in the money flow. The misallocations of resources are now larger and the dependence on low rates and ongoing money injections is even more pronounced. Asset prices have been elevated and those sectors that benefit most from low rates play a larger role in the overall economy. Although the macro variables up to this point portrayed solid growth, the economy will quickly show signs of recession again. The central bank will have to abandon tight policy and adopt anew an outright expansionary stance. Compared to the last cycle, it will now take an even easier monetary policy to arrest the liquidation of the now larger misallocations and to generate another money-induced boom. As this pattern is repeated, dislocations will necessarily accumulate, making the economy on trend ever more vulnerable to higher rates and making an ever more aggressive policy intervention necessary to keep the money supply on an expansionary course.

The results of this policy are obvious: a lasting and persistent shift of resources to forms of employment that reflect a low time preference although the true preferences of the population are different. Resources are being allocated to the provision of future consumption goods, either by the accumulation of productive capital or the provision of long-lasting consumption goods (housing). The size and structure of this part of the economy are out of synch with voluntary savings but are being supported by an ever-expanding supply of money, which depresses interest rates and allows growth in investment and simultaneously sustained high levels of present-day consumption.

This inflationism, while it lasts, disproportionally benefits the holders of financial assets and property. Financial assets represent claims on future money balances and future consumption goods, and the persistent downward manipulation of interest rates will provide a continuous boost to their prices. This in turn affects income distribution, the direction of economic activity and the overall structure of the economy. A policy of ongoing inflationism leads to a disproportionate growth of the financial industry and bloated and ultimately poorly capitalized fractional-reserve banks. The level of indebtedness in the economy increases. At a later stage of the inflationary process it will be the debt of the state that grows most. One reason is that the expenditures of the modern welfare state are largely nondiscretionary, and that they not only cannot easily be cut in a recession, but even tend to rise, while tax receipts inevitably shrink. Another reason is that, given today's mainstream consensus elaborated here, the efforts to stimulate the economy usually include forms of Keynesian deficit spending, and as ever more policy intervention is required to avoid the necessary correction, the state's debt load will expand, made possible by the again and again revitalized credit expansion.

The boost to growth from more monetary easing and more deficit spending—naturally always transitory and the source of further misallocations of resources—will be ever more faint and short-lived. Instead of igniting a new false boom, a progressively larger share of the policy stimulus will simply evaporate in the service of maintaining the accumulated misallocations, of avoiding a correction of artificially raised asset prices and of bloated balance sheets. As the manufactured recoveries get weaker, fiscal deficits get larger as a result of the combination of ongoing welfare state outlays and futile Keynesian stimulus spending.

These developments were clearly observable in all developed economies over the past decades. In the late 1990s, it took the U.S. Federal Reserve only a few reductions in official interest rates in quick succession (after the collapse of the hedge fund LTCM in 1998) and a generous infusion of reserve money around the turn of the century to extend the credit cycle and ensure ongoing money creation by the fractional-reserve banks. After the collapse of the NASDAQ stock market boom and the 2001 recession, the Fed had to leave official rates at 1 percent for almost three years to generate the kind of statistical recovery that made the central bank feel comfortable with finally moving rates higher again. A few years earlier, an identical policy by the Bank of Japan had caused surprise and apprehension among international financial experts. Official rates of 1 percent had been considered an unusually accommodative policy by any standard. It was generally perceived that such a policy came with the risk of rising inflation and currency decline. Undoubtedly, it indicated substantial economic stress. International investors sold Japanese government bonds in fear of the inflationary consequences.

In the case of the United States, there can be little doubt that this accommodative policy stance, while only slowly generating the desired bounce in GDP, was instrumental in accelerating the rise of residential house prices and the expansion of the mortgage market.[15] Higher headline growth had to be bought with yet more leverage and capital misallocations. Naturally, the dependence of the price structure and of large parts of the economy on a steady flow of money at low interest rates had become so considerable that the next attempt to return to and sustain "normal" rates and a slower pace of money growth initiated another downturn and now even kicked off a severe financial crisis. This was the so-called subprime crisis that commenced in the summer of 2007.

Not surprisingly, the U.S. Federal Reserve did go again one step further, now adopting practically zero policy rates and conducting aggressive debt monetization, labeled "quantitative easing," a policy in which it was followed by the Bank of England. But again, Japan had preceded everybody by a few years, having conducted zero-rate policies and quantitative easing from 2001 to 2006. When Japan had done so, the policy had again been unprecedented and appeared extreme to financial market commentators. The policy establishment began to follow Japanese developments with increasing trepidation, frustration, and even anger. After all, the Japanese used the twentieth century's newfound policy equipment of money printing and deficit spending, the all-purpose policy tools that allegedly promised an end to any recession. Why were the results not better? Were the Japanese authorities too cautious in their application of this anticrisis policy?

At time of the writing, the United States has joined Japan in the next phase of the process: persistent fiscal deterioration. Not only did the U.S. government run record budget deficits in 2009 and 2010, but official budget projections, although based on a return to solid economic growth, also point toward substantial deficits in the future. It would therefore be wrong to assume that, unintentionally, a new equilibrium has been reached and that current policies can simply be maintained and current structures simply be frozen in a state of suspended collapse. The system is subject to an underlying dynamic that allows only a few conceivable endgames, which we will investigate in the final chapter of this book.

The persistent inflationism of our contemporary monetary system must lead to the accumulation of more and more dislocations over time. Only an end to money injections and an uninhibited market can reveal to what extent the level of asset prices has been artificially lifted, to what extent the structure of production and the size of the debt load and of the financial industry have been distorted. Those who argue for an end to the manipulation of the economy through easy money, rising indebtedness, and a larger state will find it ever more difficult to make themselves heard in the debate. Liquidation will appear a more and more frightening prospect, and the pain involved will be considered intolerable and unacceptable. It is overlooked that there is ultimately no alternative to liquidation of these misallocations and that the extent of the required correction is entirely a function of the size of the accumulated dislocations through money injections and other interventions. Restoring the economy to health would necessarily involve a stop to any inflationary policies and a position of strict laissez-faire toward the market-driven reallocation of resources and readjustment of prices, even if this meant tolerating a near-term contraction in overall economic activity and an overall drop in prices (deflation). However, this is precisely what the governments and central banks try to avoid with all means at their disposal. To the extent that their policy can claim success, it is only in postponing the necessary adjustment into the future and in making the dislocations larger in the interim. The hope is always that the next dose of extra money will ignite a self-sustaining recovery in which all the sins of the past will be miraculously forgiven and all previous dislocations painlessly corrected. This study has shown that this is an entirely irrational and futile hope.

There appears to be a necessary and obvious endgame to this process. The ultimate barrier to the ongoing profitable exploitation of the fractional-reserve privilege is the banks' limited capital base. There is, therefore, a point at which the "private" banks will find it difficult to continue their balance sheet expansion, regardless of how strong the incentives are from low refinancing rates and from an overly generous provision of reserves from the central bank. At that point the central bank will have to fund most of the money expansion directly, and this is when it truly becomes the lender of last resort and the money producer of last resort. Of course, the nationalization of the fractional-reserve banks and their provision with fresh bank capital via the expropriation of the taxpayer is an alternative by which the state can alleviate some of the strain on its central bank.

On the side of the borrowers, there is also a limit to ever-growing indebtedness as private firms and individuals will increasingly be reluctant to accumulate more debt despite enhanced incentives from policy to do so. Then the state will assume the role of borrower of last resort. Inflation is inevitable once growing state-expenditure is being funded directly by the printing press, but accelerating inflation might be ignited earlier simply by the public's loss of confidence in the state's paper money. Once the public realizes that an ever-increasing supply of paper money is the last arrow in the interventionists' quiver, they will attempt to reduce money holdings quickly and aggressively, thereby speeding up the decline in money's purchasing power.

There is only one way to avoid the full collapse of the paper money system: a timely return to a hard, inflexible form of commodity money. Given the current strong belief in the power of economic management by the state and the widespread scepticism toward the market and free-market money (i.e., gold), it appears extremely unlikely that such a course will be taken. The policy establishment, financial market participants, the media, and large sections of the public subscribe to the view that our economy can be made more stable with an elastic money system; that no matter what the extent of the misallocations of resources or the level of indebtedness, the economy can always be revived via more money production and state spending. A different endgame does therefore appear more probable, and we will elaborate on it in the final chapter of our investigation.

Before we do this, we will detour and take a brief look at an alternative explanation the mainstream has developed for how the present predicament and the large and palpable dislocations came about. According to a popular view, phenomena such as low interest rates, excessive borrowing, and substantial rises in the prices of certain asset classes are not the result of monetary expansion but, ultimately, of excess savings. It seems worthwhile to briefly analyze this alternative narrative for two reasons: First, it will be shown that the extent of savings can never provide a satisfactory explanation for why an economic crisis occurs. Second, an analysis of the "savings glut theory" provides a good illustration of international aspects of the current monetary infrastructure. In particular, it can show how domestic inflationism can be substantially extended via a de facto international coordination of monetary policy.

The Savings Glut Theory and the Myth of Underconsumption

The notion that recessions occur because people save too much and consume too little has a very long history. It has intuitive appeal to the broader public, who perceive the recession in the form of a drop in the quantity of goods and services sold and the accumulation of excess inventories. They therefore believe that these symptoms of the crisis are also the root causes of the crisis. If everybody simply went back to previous levels of spending, would the economy not be in better shape? Many economists over the past 250 years have proposed various "underconsumption" theories to explain business cycles, among them Robert Malthus, James Mill, Thorstein Veblen, Waddill Catchings, and William Trufant Foster.[16] Marxism has at its core its own underconsumption theory. Karl Marx's projection of the inevitable death of capitalism was based on his conclusion that an impoverished class of workers would be unable to purchase the growing output of the efficient capitalist economy.

Despite their intuitive appeal to the public and their appeal to politicians as excuses for running budget deficits, these theories did not stand up to scientific scrutiny. By 1928 Ludwig von Mises could confidently state that the only business cycle theory constituting the basis for serious discussion and research at the time was the monetary theory of the cycle. Recessions were the consequence of capital misallocations that resulted from money-induced disturbances. The origins of recessions were thus to be found in the previous expansion and the sphere of money. Such a crisis theory was first developed by the British Currency School in the nineteenth century but had found a full and satisfactory elaboration only through the Austrian School in the early twentieth century, not least by Mises himself.[17] But underconsumption theories were not dead. They once again rose to prominence in the form of Keynesianism in the 1930s, which has constituted the most influential underconsumption theory to this day.

All underconsumption theories suffer from an irrational fear of savings and a lack of appreciation of the pricing mechanism. Saving, consumption and investing are interconnected and coordinated via market prices, including interest rates. Saving is the basis for prosperity. No society has ever risen, nor could any society conceivably ever rise, out of poverty and into prosperity via consumption. It is saving and production that generate wealth. By shifting resources from meeting present consumption needs and by allocating them to productive uses to meet future consumption needs, that is, by saving and investing, society generates the capital stock that raises the productivity of labor and allows a larger supply of goods and services, and also different and better goods and services. What is being saved doesn't drop out of the economy. Of course, it exercises "effective demand." To save is to spend; it is simply spending on different things. He who saves does not never want to consume. He wants to consume later. And those who take his savings in the meantime and use it to build productive capital sell their produce practically to the same saver at the point when he finally wants to consume. Saving means postponing consumption, not nonconsumption. To explain the origin of a recession it is not sufficient to point to the level of savings, which by itself can never constitute a problem. One needs to explain why the pricing mechanism that coordinates the various activities in the economy fails, and for this, money is the prime candidate.

The so-called savings glut theory became popular before the recent financial crisis, not least because it was embraced by Ben Bernanke in a speech in 2005 before he became chairman of the Federal Reserve.[18] In this speech, Bernanke did not deal with the financial crisis, which at that time had not commenced, but with a set of perceived or real imbalances, which were widely debated at the time, in particular the large and widening U.S. current account deficit. A current account deficit is generally the result of the value of imports of goods and services into the domestic economy exceeding the value of exports of goods and services to foreign countries. This is called a trade deficit. As the domestic population consumes goods and services from foreign countries in excess of what it returns to those foreign countries in goods and services, it needs to "pay" the foreigners the difference in the form of claims against domestic assets or future production, that is, with IOUs. The country thus imports extra goods and services by exporting capital. The extra present consumption in the domestic economy has its pendant in extra present savings abroad. There, people consume less in the present period than they produce in the present period. They save by accumulating IOUs.

Bernanke's version of the savings glut theory stated that the primary mover of the U.S. current account deficit might not be, as was generally accepted, domestic consumption in the United States but high levels of saving abroad. The origin of the current account deficit might therefore not lie in excessively accommodative financial

conditions in the United States, which encourage the consumer to
borrow heavily and devour more and more goods from foreign countries for which he pays with the debt claims that the foreigners accept
as payment; rather, its origin might lie in those foreign countries that
save more than they invest locally and that push their "excess savings"
into the United States. The foreigners want to hold more dollar IOUs,
and they pay for them with the goods that they sell to the American
consumer.

In part, Bernanke's version of the theory is beyond reproach. It
deals with accounting identities, as one country's current account deficit
is another country's surplus. Naturally, we are at liberty to explain
changes in these balances from either side of the accounts. This point
is of no relevance to the topic discussed in this study. What is relevant
to our purposes, however, is that the savings glut theory later, after the
financial crisis had started, provided many commentators with a narrative of how the imbalances could have developed that played a role in
destabilizing the economy and making a recession inevitable, such as
persistent overly generous lending conditions in the United States, a
low savings rate, and the concurrence of high levels of consumption
with high levels of investment (mainly in residential real estate).
According to this interpretation of the savings glut theory, these phenomena could have resulted from excess savings abroad rather than from
domestic monetary arrangements and domestic monetary policy in the
United States. The theory has featured prominently in the discussion
about the recent crisis for this reason.[19] However, as a crisis theory it
is not of much use. The reason is simply that, to the extent that these
phenomena were indeed the result of true saving, they cannot explain
the crisis.

In contrast to older and more standard underconsumption theories,
this excess savings theory does not identify the problem as one of savings
being too high and, consequently, consumption too low relative to the
present production of consumption goods. The problem seems to be
that savings are too high relative to present investment activity in the
countries where people save. The surplus savings thus washes up on
U.S. shores, where it causes imbalances in the domestic economy. As
in previous excess savings theories, it is difficult to see a problem in this
for as long as the pricing mechanism works. The amount of saving and

the amount of investment are not two uncorrelated magnitudes that we must hope will somehow match. An uninhibited market and non-distorted interest rates coordinate the two. True savings mean that real resources have been freed up from meeting present consumption needs and have become available for investment purposes. Lower interest rates that result from true savings do not send wrong signals but they correctly communicate that more real resources are available for investing. At lower rates more investment projects appear profitable and will be initiated. Saving and investing are about the intertemporal use of society's resources, and as long as interest rates communicate the propensity to save correctly, investment activity will be aligned with voluntary saving.

Indeed, this must precisely be the point where a cycle theory has to locate the origin of disruptions, and this is exactly what the monetary theory of the business cycle does. What causes the crisis is not that there are somehow too many savings or too few savings, which obviously constitute the simple aggregation of many individual decisions, but that the pricing mechanism that coordinates saving with investment is disrupted. As we have shown in detail, a monetary system that constantly injects money via the loan market will systematically distort interest rates in a specific direction. This must lead to economic dislocations and ultimately to recessions. A rising propensity to save is by itself insufficient to cause economic disruptions, but money injections must always lead to economic dislocations.

The international aspect of the savings glut theory is equally insufficient to help explain a crisis. In an open economy it simply doesn't matter whether the savings are raised locally or abroad. To take the obvious example, if the Chinese lowered their present consumption demand and thus freed up resources for investment and then decided that there were not enough promising investment opportunities in China, and that it was preferable to entrust these resources for some time to the Americans, this would result in capital flowing to the United States (or the control over physical resources shifting to U.S. persons and corporations), it would lower interest rates in the United States and thus lower the return threshold for potential investment projects there. But none of this would constitute a disruption of the economy. Low rates would correctly reflect the availability of true savings, of additional resources not being needed for consumption in the near future and thus being available for investment. Whether these resources are freed up and redirected by domestic consumer-savers or by foreign consumer-savers is immaterial, as long as prices and interest rates reflect individual preferences correctly.

As an aside, we may add that this process is hindered by the existence of territorial paper currencies. If both the United States and China were on a gold standard and used the same form of money, this shift of resources would occur fairly easily and without friction. The international segregation of capital and goods markets by local fiat money monopolies, which are used by the local central banks to manipulate their domestic economies according to domestic political objectives, is an obstacle to international human cooperation, as just explained. However, any disturbances that originate from this aspect cannot be attributed to an excessive propensity to save, of course.

If Bernanke's core assumption was correct, namely that various phenomena in the U.S. economy at the time—low interest rates, generous funding conditions, ample availability of credit—were the result of substantial foreign savings, then these phenomena would not have constituted dislocations and not initiated a crisis. (We may recall that Bernanke did not propagate the savings glut theory to explain a crisis, which at that point had not started yet.) But if one wanted to use these phenomena as the basis for a crisis theory, then attributing them only to a high propensity to save in foreign countries would not be sufficient to explain how they could have disrupted the economy. One would have to elaborate on how the coordinating faculties of market prices and, in particular, interest rates had been corrupted to a degree that allowed investment and saving to be temporarily out of synch. At this point one would have again arrived at a monetary cycle theory. If the savings glut theory describes the result of voluntary savings then it cannot explain the crisis. If one wants to build a crisis theory on what the savings glut theory describes, one would have no choice but to use the monetary crisis theory again, rendering the savings glut theory superfluous in the first place.

Inflationism and International Policy Coordination

Indeed, international capital flows and the phenomena described by Bernanke's version of the savings glut theory can be integrated with the monetary crisis theory quite straightforwardly. To do this, we may take a step back and envision a time line on which we trace how the institutional arrangements of our contemporary monetary architecture came about and how each step appears to be deliberately designed to make money more elastic and to extend the life span of the credit boom a bit more.

The starting point is an economy with inflexible commodity money. The most likely trend in prices is moderate secular deflation, while any sudden changes in money demand will have to be absorbed by a change in the monetary unit's purchasing power. This money is not neutral. Changes in its supply and in demand for it will affect the relative position of the economic agents and affect relative prices. Money can never be only a veil that passively lies over the "real" economy and does not interfere with underlying economic processes. However, a systematic distortion in the economy's workings cannot originate from this form of money.

The next step of the development introduces just such distortions: banks begin to issue uncovered money substitutes, or fiduciary media. Fractional-reserve banking begins. As the banks issue the fiduciary media through their lending business, the coordination between saving and investment is systematically disrupted. A period of overinvestment (boom) is followed by a period of contraction and bank runs (bust). Credit-induced business cycles have arrived. However, while hardly pleasant, these cycles are constrained by the competition of independent banks, the absence of a lender-of-last-resort central bank and the inflexibility of the gold supply, which functions as reserve money (and indeed as money proper).

The next step introduces the state, which uses its unique privileges to support fractional-reserve banking and exploit it to its own advantage. A state-backed central bank is being created that cartelizes the private banks, that coordinates their money creation, and that issues its own central bank money, which the state declares eligible as reserve money for the private banks. The inflationary process of money creation—or at least the creation of fiduciary media, as money proper is still gold—can now be extended. The competition between domestic banks is substantially reduced, and the central bank provides at least a limited backstop to the fractional-reserve banks' money printing. A more extended money expansion and credit-induced boom will now occur, but as we have seen, a larger bust is necessarily the consequence. Once the accumulated misallocations of capital catch up with the speed of money creation, a recession becomes inevitable. Sooner or later, the state will thus be confronted with the overwhelming temptation to abandon the gold anchor altogether. This is likely to receive the full backing of the fractional-reserve banks as it allows a further extension of the credit boom.

One of the key constraining factors for money- and credit-expansion, for as long as money is still essentially a commodity, such as gold, is the potential outflow of that commodity. The money-induced economic boom will increase the demand for goods and services, and in an open economy this means also the demand for foreign goods and services. But the domestically created fiduciary media will not be accepted in foreign countries. Foreign suppliers of goods will have to be paid in gold. Increasing gold outflows will soon restrain the domestic banks' ability to create fiduciary media.

An additional factor leading to gold outflows is that under domestic legal arrangements the monetary units created by the fractional-reserve banks out of nothing continue to carry the same purchasing power as the gold money to which they represent claims and which remains strictly limited in its supply. The issuance of fiduciary media thus lowers the purchasing power of all forms of money, including gold money. Thus, Gresham's law kicks in and bad money drives out good money.[20] It makes sense for the domestic population to use the expanding supply of paper money for local trans-actions, naturally at rising prices, and sell the gold abroad, where its purchasing power remains higher because undiluted by the printing of paper claims to it. In any case, the outflow of gold makes the reserve position of the domestic banks increasingly precarious and will likely put the brakes on the credit expansion process. This is another factor that limits the extent of fractional-reserve banking in a commodity money system.

This restriction is overcome with the final step when redemption in specie is abandoned, both domestically and internationally. As we have pointed out, this final step toward a complete paper money system was taken in 1971, when the United States took the dollar off gold internationally. Now seemingly nothing stands in the way of ever-larger money creation. Yet, in analogy to what has been said about gold outflows, we may now add an international dimension to our analysis. The domestic credit boom can obviously no longer lead to outflows of gold and certainly not of paper money, which is not legal tender in other jurisdictions. If domestic residents want to buy foreign goods, they have to exchange their domestic money for foreign money on the foreign exchange market. This is obviously a suboptimal arrangement that introduces partial barter into the global economy and deprives international trade of the key advantages of money-based exchange (see Chapter 1). However, domestic inflationism, all else being equal, should lead to a decline of the currency's exchange value on the foreign exchange market and a drop in its international purchasing power. While this, in itself, will not have to cause domestic monetary authorities to tighten policy, it will certainly be another factor that makes the inflationary consequences of the present policy visible to the public. It is clear that the hard-to-conceal decline of a currency's foreign exchange value can be a further and important early warning signal, in particular for an open economy. Not unlike the competition between otherwise unconnected and independent fractional-reserve banks, which at the earlier stage of monetary history, before the introduction of central banks, constrained the banking sector's ability to create money, can the independence of a number of territorial money monopolists potentially provide an at least tentative check on overly aggressive domestic money creation. No country that wants to benefit from the international division of labor can entirely ignore the purchasing power of its monetary unit on international markets. To a degree at least, domestic inflationism can be exposed if other countries conduct a less inflationary policy.

Obviously, this restriction can be overcome if the monetary authorities in various countries coordinate their inflationary policies and agree, whether implicitly or explicitly, to expand the fiat money supply together in a joined effort. This is precisely what has occurred between the world's dominant paper money producer, the United States, and a number of Asian monetary authorities, most prominently those in China. This is not to say that an explicit agreement between the two sides exists, only that both sides have been able to create more of their domestic currencies for longer because they have conducted similar policies. It is this de facto coordinated inflationism that has led many observers to misinterpret the resulting phenomena as attributable to mythical excess savings.

Quite plainly, by pegging its currency to the U.S. dollar, Chinese authorities have committed themselves to matching United States inflationism for the sake of obtaining a larger share of U.S. consumer spending. Mirroring U.S. inflationary monetary policy is a development strategy for China. The growing supply of dollar-denominated IOUs that is the necessary result of ongoing U.S. money production has been absorbed, not by voluntary acts of saving on the part of independent foreign individuals, but by political authorities that have accumulated them as monetary reserves, and, via a de facto currency peg, monetized them by printing matching amounts of their own paper money. Thus, a drop in international purchasing power of the initially inflating currency has been arrested. Monetary expansion in the United States could proceed further without a loss of purchasing power for the dollar on international markets. At the same time, China used its own monetary expansion to build a larger productive sector that sells into Western markets, particularly into the United States.

Governments in both countries have interfered in their economies and guided the credit boom into specific sectors for political reasons. In the United States, this has been the residential housing market. The methods to achieve this include the long-standing preferential tax treatment of residential real estate and the ongoing and large-scale subsidization of mortgage lending via the government sponsored and now government-owned agencies, the Federal National Mortgage Association and the Federal Home Loan Mortgage Corporation. Also, there is regulatory enforcement of lower lending standards in the mortgage market for social engineering purposes, such as through the Community Reinvestment Act or the Home Mortgage Disclosure Act. In China, the matching credit boom has been directed toward an aggressive expansion of industrial capacity, which has guaranteed the American consumer undiminished purchasing power for his inflating dollars, at least in terms of Chinese produce. It is this internationally coordinated paper money production that explains all the phenomena that the savings glut theorists concern themselves with: the large United States current account deficit and the corresponding Asian surpluses; the con-currence of low savings and high levels of consumption with extensive investment in real estate in the United States, coupled with relatively low levels of official consumer goods inflation; and simultaneously, on the part of China, the extraordinary accumulation of foreign currency reserves and of Treasury securities holdings, and the explosion in domestic credit and in domestic investment activity. Whether this process was the outcome of the deliberate design of U.S. policy makers is immaterial. It may simply be that the dollar's status as a global reserve currency and the importance of the U.S. goods market for the export sectors of other countries lead to policies that furthered a de facto glob-ally coordinated money and credit boom.

Summary

In the context of the stylized history of state-sponsored fractional-reserve banking just described, the pinnacle of paper money production has now been reached. All inhibiting factors that have the power to short-circuit the artificial money–induced boom have now been removed: true interbank competition with real risk of bankruptcy, commodity money of strictly limited supply and outside the control of the state, and feedback from tight money regimes abroad. What has become possible over the past 30 years is the global credit megacycle; the result of a global paper money system, in which fractional-reserve banking is encouraged and fully supported by state-run central banks the world over, none of which is restrained by a commodity anchor, and all of which encourage one another to pursue coordinated global inflation.

The more the artificial credit boom can be extended, the more severe are the accumulated dislocations in the form of mispriced assets, misdirected economic activity, and excessive debt, and the larger will be the necessary and inevitable correction that must await the world at the end of this artificial global expansion fueled by paper money and cheap credit. No meaningful credit correction has occurred in the major economies (not even in Japan) since the early 1980s. Over the past 30 years, the credit megacycle has repeatedly been reactivated by central bank and government interventions, most importantly the frequent lowering of interest rates and the injection of reserve money. That this cycle has been extended for as long as it has is no reason for complacency. To the contrary, we must be concerned that an inevitable point of no return must be reached or, more likely, has already been reached, at which neither a further extension of the cycle nor an orderly and painless unwinding of the accumulated dislocations is a reasonable option. As we have outlined, efforts to keep money and credit growth going have already shown rapidly diminishing returns for the past decade, despite the increasing aggressiveness of the applied policy measures. The accumulation of imbalances is now palpable. It is therefore highly probable that the crisis that started in 2007 is a watershed for the present system, and that rather than think about the phenomena discussed in these pages purely in terms of recurring money-induced cycles, we must rather contemplate the endgame, the inevitable collapse of this system. This is a topic that we will turn to in the next, and final, chapter.

Chapter 10

Beyond the Cycle

Paper Money's Endgame

There is no means of avoiding the final collapse of a boom brought about by credit expansion. The alternative is only whether the crisis should come sooner as the result of a voluntary abandonment of further credit expansion, or later as a final and total catastrophe of the currency system involved.
—Ludwig von Mises[1]

When the latest financial crisis commenced in 2007 and comparisons with the Great Depression of the 1930s began to appear, one could frequently hear comments to the effect that such an outcome was unlikely. The reason given was that modern-day governments would simply not allow a repeat of these catastrophic events. The state, this was the confident prediction, had learned from past mistakes. It would now use active fiscal policy to avoid a collapse of aggregate demand. But most importantly, and this was a view that was shared across the political spectrum, the monetary policy apparatus had been greatly enhanced. Central banks were no longer tied down by inflexible commodity money. The "golden shackles" had come off and through the printing of new money—in potentially unlimited quantities—bank runs, asset price collapses, and a return of deflation could be prevented. Active monetary policy would provide a powerful counterbalance to the recessionary forces unleashed by the crisis, and would soon initiate a recovery.

The preceding chapters show that this assessment is untenable. The view of the elastic money system as a superior tool of government anticrisis policy is mistaken. To the contrary, the absence of hard money, of commodity money of essentially fixed supply, has inevitably led to the substantial dislocations and imbalances that have produced this crisis with inescapable necessity. Elastic money is the reason this crisis occurred, and it is the reason that previous major crises occurred. Once a recession becomes unavoidable, neither more money printing nor Keynesian deficit spending constitutes a solution.

It is true that, over the 30 years preceding the recent crisis, periodic minor recessions in the United States and Europe had been "managed" according to the modern blueprint of the interventionists, mainly by the timely lowering of interest rates and by new money injections from the central banks, and that this had indeed prevented more severe recessions in these economies. Recessions are corrections of previous misallocations of capital. It is because the cleansing of these misallocations, at least in their entirety, had always been stopped through extra money injections that recessions had appeared either relatively short or relatively shallow, often both. However, in the thus manufactured recoveries, new misallocations had necessarily been created and added to the old and unresolved dislocations of the previous cycles. These misallocations restricted the economy's potential for lasting self-sustained growth and made the economy increasingly sensitive to any slowing in the flow of new money. Ultimately, a big and unmanageable crisis had to occur as the inevitable end point of this process.

In this final chapter we will try to take a look into the future to assess the potential next developments of the present paper money system and its most likely endgame. The following is not just idle speculation. Past developments have created an irrevocable reality, a set of conditions that establishes very tight boundaries to the range of possible future scenarios. Political ideology and the accepted economic paradigm of today's mainstream also make certain developments considerably more likely than others.

The Size of the Dislocations

The extent of the correction the economy would face presently if there were no state intervention is difficult to ascertain but must roughly be proportional to the dislocations that have accrued. In comparison with the Great Depression of the 1930s, these misallocations are likely to be considerably larger today as the monetary infrastructure of the past 40 years has been much more conducive to ongoing money production than it was 80 or 100 years ago. Back then, the preconditions for the Great Depression were created by the extraordinary growth in fractional-reserve banking during the late nineteenth century and early twentieth century, in particular after it received full state backing in 1913 in form of a lender-of-last-resort central bank, the Federal Reserve. This laid the groundwork for the money-induced boom of the 1920s. The monetary architecture has since been developed further into an uninhibited paper money system. The last meaningful correction in the United States in which high real interest rates were allowed to cleanse the system of the dislocations of preceding money expansions occurred as far back as 1980. Misallocations of capital are most probably much larger today than they were at the end of the 1920s.

Statistical aggregates have been shown to provide incomplete and flawed images of the state of an economy. How big the dislocations in resource allocation and in resource pricing are today, can only be revealed conclusively by an end to money production and by price discovery on an uninhibited market. Nevertheless, statistics may give us an indication: Industrial production in the United States is about 12 times larger today than it was at the beginning of the Great Depression.[2] However, the amount of currency in circulation (notes and coins) is more than 200 times larger today (end of 2010).[3] The stock of money in the statistical definition of M1 is about 65 times larger and in the M2 definition about 150 times larger.[4] By the end of 2010, the Federal Reserve was on its second round of quantitative easing, which meant that the monetary base and bank reserves were more than 330 times larger than in October 1929.[5] Total net debt as a percent of GDP—which stood at about 150 percent when Nixon took the dollar off gold—reached a record high of 370 percent in the third quarter of 2009. At the time of the 1929 stock market crash, this ratio stood at less than 200 percent and was thus half of what it is today.[6]

It is part of the inherent logic of the present system that policy makers must do everything to avoid a rise in interest rates, as such a rise would reveal the true availability of savings, which naturally is much more limited than what artificially lowered interest rates have consistently projected. Higher interest rates would cause the current extended credit structure to contract rapidly and would cut off certain sectors of the economy from the steady flow of new money.

A rise in market interest rates is being prevented by a two-pronged strategy: On the part of the central bank there are the reduction in official rates, aggressive money injections, and purchases of assets that are at risk of steep price declines. On the part of other organs of the state, there are generous state guarantees for or nationalizations of companies, in particular financial companies, and injections of funds taken from the taxpayer or borrowed from savers and channeled to selected sectors. All of this is aimed at the compression of market risk premiums. The state underwrites private balance sheets and private debt in order to mask the scarcity of private capital and to keep prices of debt claims elevated and thereby their yields low.

These policy measures have succeeded in arresting, for the time being, the liquidation of excessive debt and of the accumulated misallocations of capital. We have to agree with the advocates of these polices that without them many prices (in particular asset prices) would be lower and much of the developed world would have already experienced overall deflation and a sharper drop in GDP. However, in that case, the world would at least be closer to the solution of the crisis, as the market would have been allowed to liquidate resource misallocations and adjust prices to reflect the true voluntary demand for assets, and the true availability of private savings. The antideflation policy that has been adopted is largely a policy of price fixing, a policy of preventing the market from exposing capital misallocations and then liquidating them. The root causes of the crisis remain in place and the underlying problems unaddressed.

For example, mortgage-backed securities worth billions have still not been placed at market-clearing levels with private investors but are being artificially supported either directly by the Federal Reserve or indirectly by the banking sector that has been encouraged with vast amounts of free money from the Fed to hold onto these securities. Without a free market and uninhibited price formation, there is simply no way of telling what the true demand for these securities is and which of them are supported by private capital and true savings. Two of the United States' largest financial institutions, the Federal National Mortgage Association (Fannie Mae) and the Federal Home Loan Mortgage Corporation (Freddie Mac), have been put under government conservatorship, which means that they have practically been nationalized, and that the vast majority of mortgage loans in the United States are now backed by the state. In other countries, too, financial institutions have been nationalized, have received funds taken from the taxpayer, and are being kept alive or kept from shrinking with substantial doses of new reserve money from their central banks. These policies are mere attempts at hiding the problems and creating illusions of stability.

The expectation seems to be that over time these problems will somehow solve themselves automatically, maybe due to the economy's ability to heal itself. But this remains an illusion for as long as policy actively sabotages the operation of the market. The economy cannot realistically be expected to rectify itself if the market is not allowed to liquidate capital misallocations and correct distorted prices. The state has erected a protective fence around the most dislocated sectors of the economy, trying to keep market forces outside. As long as this lasts, no true recovery is possible. Present policies cannot create a new reality in which the need for these adjustments magically disappears.

Those who believe that the crisis has been allowed to unfold and is soon behind us, and that therefore Mises' warning about ultimate currency collapse, expressed in the quote at the beginning of this chapter, does not apply to the present situation, make a fundamental error. Current policies have postponed the crisis and the necessary process of liquidation of misallocations of capital. They have not, and logically cannot, make them go away.

The Nationalization of Money and Credit

It cannot be ruled out, of course, that aggressive interventionist policy may, for a while at least, arrest the liquidation of misallocations and even create money-induced bubbles somewhere else in the economy. In this case, a bounce in the GDP statistics could indeed be manufactured once more, although for how long is difficult to assess. It would probably cause the interventionists to claim victory over depression and deflation and announce the success of their policies. This would be a misconception. New misallocations of capital and distortions of asset prices would have simply been piled upon the existing misallocations and price distortions, and, just as we have experienced numerous times before, a short-lived period of statistical recovery would be followed by yet another and even more severe downturn. In any case, this scenario cannot be considered the endgame of the process described here, as it cannot bring about the final dissolution of imbalances.

Moreover, this outcome is exceedingly unlikely. First, where should new bubbles occur? The assets that can most easily function as collateral for money-induced additional lending have already experienced substantial inflation: debt claims, equity claims, and real estate. The public will not as readily as before subscribe to the idea that further advances in the prices of these assets are the result of sound economic fundamentals rather than new money injections. Second, the extension of balance sheets in the private sector, in particular the financial sector, which is the corollary of the money-induced boom, has reached levels that make further leveraging difficult. To avoid credit contraction and deleveraging in the financial system, the interventionists already had to resort to increased lending directly from the central bank and increased borrowing by the public sector. It appears almost certain that this will not only have to continue but also that it will have to intensify if a deflationary correction is to be avoided and, in particular, if more growth is to be created again via cheap credit. In order to achieve the money growth the state authorities desire, they will have to take increasingly direct control of the entire money creation process, of lending and borrowing decisions in the economy, as these are no longer being undertaken by private entities to a sufficient degree. The state will increasingly be the borrower of last resort to the state central bank's lender of last resort. The system will move toward the nationalisation of money and credit.

Ideologically, these steps are a natural evolution of the present system. At the very heart of the state paper money system and modern central banking has always been the idea that, through the creation of money, interest rates could continuously be manipulated to levels below those that would prevail in an uninhibited market. In a state paper money system, the amount of available loans and the rates at which these loans are granted are determined by the state's monetary policy rather than the preferences and valuations of the individuals who spontaneously interact on markets, and who would determine loan volumes and rates in a commodity money system. The full nationalization of money and credit is simply the system's logical end point. Once the nominally private banking sector has been rendered immobile from the dead weight of previous credit creation, the state itself, via the central bank and via those formerly private institutions that had to be bailed out and nationalized, will have to take control of the money and credit expansion process and thereby, inevitably, also determine who will be the beneficiaries of further lending.

As misallocations of resources persist and accumulate, market forces point ever more toward the need for a cleansing correction while policy tries ever more vehemently to arrest this process and potentially reverse it. To protect the credit edifice against market forces, the printing of more money will be seconded by interventionist measures in other areas of state intervention, such as legislation, regulation, and taxation. Tax legislation and accounting rules will be changed in ways that are aimed at aiding certain asset classes, for example by lifting the need for mark-to-market accounting, allowing the owners of these assets to not declare investment losses. Via legislative and regulative intervention, the investment strategies of private pension funds will increasingly be influenced by state directive. Pension funds with insufficient ratios of current assets to claims will be bailed out by the state. This will be used as a precursor to more state-run pension schemes. Policy makers have already floated ideas regarding new taxes on financial transactions. This will be the first step on the path to outright capital controls, the introduction or reintroduction of which appears a question of time only. Private citizens will increasingly face hurdles when taking control of their own financial assets and, in particular, when moving assets abroad.

A free market in capital is impossible in an advanced state fiat money system. As long as the state considers the provision of cheap credit and the avoidance of a deflationary correction at all cost its policy goals, it cannot allow market forces to intervene with its efforts. Free capital markets, and thus free markets in general, are ultimately incompatible with state fiat money.

The Monetization of Debt

Transferring solvency risk from the private sector to the public sector and thereby socializing the fallout from excessive borrowing can suppress credit risk premiums only for as long as the public does not question the solvency of the state itself. Although the state is the only entity that can legally expropriate private wealth holders and market income earners via taxation, this privilege does not mean that the state can accumulate unlimited amounts of debt. Those who lend to the state will begin to doubt the willingness of future taxpayers to provide the funds to pay the state's lenders or, which is essentially the same, the willingness of future governments to impose the burdensome tax rates that would be required to repay the debt, or even just to continue to pay interest on it. The state's lenders will ask for compensation for this risk in the form of higher interest rates, which is exactly what the present system cannot cope with and what the policy establishment must prevent by any means available. At this point, the state will have to accelerate the process of direct monetization of its debt via the central bank. Ultimately, government spending will have to rely on direct funding by the printing press. This development appears not only inevitable. In fact, it has already commenced.

In the United States and in Europe, a crucial step in this direction was taken in 2010 when the U.S. Federal Reserve and the European

Central Bank (ECB) started using the printing press with the explicit objective of propping up government bond prices and massaging interest rates on government debt to lower levels. The official explanation for these manipulations of market prices was that they were just temporary crisis measures to—in the case of the United States—lower long-term market rates to encourage extra lending and borrowing, or to—in the case of the European monetary union—maintain "liquid and orderly markets" in government bonds. The ECB felt compelled to buy Greek, Portuguese, and Irish government bonds in particular as investors sold these securities heavily out of fear of sovereign insolvency. The reason for the central bank's intervention was to avoid a spreading of the sovereign debt crisis to other and bigger members of the monetary union, none of which are fiscally sound. In the United States, where the government is running record budget deficits, the central bank has, with its second round of so-called quantitative easing, become the biggest marginal buyer of U.S. government bonds and will soon be the largest holder.

The central bankers make every effort to portray these market interventions as only temporary. They are supposed to appear as creative stimulus measures or as short-term maneuvers that guarantee stability and liquidity. In fact, our analysis has shown that these policies are the inevitable next steps in the deterioration of the paper money system and that we should expect them to be continued and indeed expanded. What was unconventional policy last year will be normal next year.

It is difficult to imagine a scenario in which public finances will not, on trend, deteriorate further, even in the absence of activist fiscal policy. The welfare state in all highly industrialized democratic societies has assumed commitments that have, even in times of better growth and when the demographic backdrop was more favorable, routinely required outlays in excess of tax receipts. To run budget deficits has become a normal state of affairs for most states, and a monetary system of elastic state paper money has supported and encouraged such a policy.[7] As it becomes increasingly difficult to extend the money-induced boom, the gap will keep widening between government outlays on the one side, which are, as a rule, predominantly nondiscretionary social transfers that get larger at times of weak growth, and tax income on the other side, which declines at times of weak growth. Even if new Keynesian-style deficit spending is avoided, regular welfare state spending alone will cause most governments to run growing deficits. To avoid this and to run balanced budgets, governments would have to curtail established social transfers meaningfully. This is not only politically difficult in societies in which large sections of the electorate have become dependent on state transfers, but it also stands in sharp contrast to the contemporary political culture. By contrast, the funding of the state by ongoing money production from the central bank is simply a logical extension of the ideas behind the present monetary system. Indeed, it has historically been the very reason for introducing state paper money in the first place.

All of this is the logical and inevitable end point of the established monetary order. An elastic money system must, over time, create a capital and price structure that can only be maintained with an ever more extensive money production. This money production has to come increasingly from the central bank. The central bank will have to support the high prices and low yields of an ever wider range of assets in order to stabilize an overextended credit infrastructure, which means to maintain it and grow it against market forces. Just as the outright nationalization of banks and financial institutions is the logical consequence of a system of state-supported fractional-reserve banking, the manipulation of the prices of potentially every asset via the printing press is the inevitable consequence of a system of limitless state fiat money. It is the declared aim of such a monetary system to never allow price declines and deleveraging on an extended scale.

Within the accepted logic of the present system, the next steps must involve the use of the printing press for the funding of state spending but also corporate spending and, ultimately, consumer spending. Printing just enough money to keep the system suspended in an uncomfortable position of arrested collapse will not be seen as sufficient. Frustration will grow among politicians over the meek results in terms of new growth considering the aggressively expansionary stance of monetary policy. Of course, most of the impact of easy money is increasingly taken up by the maintenance of the overextended credit structure erected in the past. In order to generate new activity, the central banks will ultimately decide to bypass the private financial sector

entirely and, under the declared goal of avoiding deflation and supporting a stable economy, begin to buy corporate and consumer debt as a
precursor to lending directly to corporations and consumers. Finally,
the central banks will have entered the retail banking business. Purchases
of credit card loans, auto loans, and other consumer loans by the central
banks will be followed by direct funding of retail lending, such as by
lending to credit card users.[8]

This development, which is inevitable if economic policy continues
to pursue the present goals, leads to ever-larger sections of society
depending on the direct provision of new money from the central bank.
This has two consequences.

First, the risk of broad-based rises in prices grows considerably. It
has been shown that the more transparent money injections are and the
more even they are across the economy, the more they will lead to
price effects and the less they will lead to shifts in resource allocation
and incomes. The great money expansion of the past 30 years was
focused more narrowly. It was channeled via the financial industry into
specific sectors and benefited disproportionately the owners of equity
claims, debt claims, and real estate, and those who work in related areas,
in particular the financial industry. This money expansion created illusions of wealth, generated shifts in control over resources and in relative
prices, and, thereby, generated a lengthy artificial boom at the cost of
considerable misallocations of resources and gigantic levels of debt.
However, outside of certain asset classes, overall prices did not rise as
steeply as could be feared in a paper money system. Certainly, the
monetary unit continued to lose purchasing power but not at an alarm-
ing pace. This is bound to change as the channels through which money
is injected broaden, and as more sectors become recipients of the central
banks' flow of money, either by directly receiving money from the
central bank or by receiving central bank funded state transfers. The
response of broader price level indices to this money printing will be
more in accordance with what standard economic theory predicts: there
will be rises in standard inflation measures. For some time inflationary
policy may appear like "pushing on a string," but there will be a point
at which it will gain traction. The decline in money's purchasing power
will accelerate when the public realizes to what extent income streams,
asset prices, and the solvency of the banks and state institutions rest on

the ongoing printing of money. The rush out of paper money will then accelerate dramatically.

Second, as ever-larger sections of the economy depend on low rates and ongoing money creation it will be politically ever more difficult for the central bank to change policy, to slow the flow of money or even stop it entirely.

Inflationary Meltdown

Fiat money systems have historically always led to high inflation, ending usually in total currency collapse. Mainstream economists tell us that this time will be different. The present paper money system is built to last. Why? One can only assume that the reasons must be that we know more about economics today and, in particular, about how inflation is generated, than previous paper money producers did, and that those in charge of the printing presses today know what to do when inflationary pressures begin to build. This is certainly a view that appeals to many economists as it stresses the importance of their theories and their roles as policy advisors. But even on purely historical evidence this view appears naïve. It implies that those who were in charge of paper money systems were always completely unaware of the effects of ongoing money creation and that they pursued their disastrous course of action only because of their ignorance of economics. They are made to appear like a group of villagers of earlier times who, not being able to conceive of microbes as transmitters of diseases, kept using water from an infested well. However, we have reason to believe that the governments in many historic incidences of inflation and currency collapse were aware of the dangers of printing too much money or did became aware of them during money's decline. Many paper money systems were introduced with official commitments to strict and self-imposed limits on money creation, which were usually obeyed for some time but were then lifted at a later stage. As early as the eleventh century, the Southern Song Dynasty in China issued government paper money under a fixed annual quota and with the commitment to redeem old notes when new ones were issued. However, after a while new issues were enlarged and redemptions missed. Inflation naturally followed.[9] This appears to be a common pattern.

A much more realistic view of the problem appears to be the following: Over time ongoing injections of money change the structure of the economy and also the size and structure of the state apparatus to such a degree that the immediate consequences of turning off the monetary tab are considered to be so damaging that the monetary authorities feel compelled to continue printing money, and indeed printing it ever faster. Historically, it has almost always been the fear of the imminent consequences of an end to inflationist policies that persuaded those who controlled the money supply to continue. Obviously, this made matters only worse and the ultimate and inevitable disaster even bigger. Yet, those in power must have hoped that, given time, some other, less painful remedy than stopping the printing presses might be discovered. It is one thing to know that a painful end to a development is unavoidable; it is quite another to be the one to bring that end about.

The same problem will present itself to those in charge of the money franchise today. When inflationary pressures materialize, can policy makers change their policies quickly enough to save the currency? Will they have the courage and resolve to do it and face the consequences of these policies, which means allowing the very economic forces that they have desperately fought for so long to unfold?

Nobody maintains that rising inflation is the outcome that policy makers want. But when their inflationary policies finally overcome the deflationary forces of the accumulated dislocations of the past, policies will have to be changed quickly and radically in order to save the paper currency. After having worked persistently to weaken the purchasing power of the monetary unit, policy makers will have to suddenly switch to doing everything in their power to sustain it. They will have to subordinate every goal of economic policy, in particular goals such as the avoidance of bank collapses, supporting the overstretched credit edifice, and maintaining the liquidity or solvency of state institutions, to that of protecting the established fiat money. Saving the paper money unit will certainly require high real interest rates, with all that that entails. The policy establishment will finally have to accept that the credit structure must correct and that a deflationary recession is necessary to cleanse the economy of the misallocations of capital and the mispricing of assets. Market forces will win in the end. The only question is if this happens before money is destroyed or after money is destroyed. In stopping money injections and allowing interest rates to rise in order to save the paper currency, state authorities will have to pull the rug from underneath much of the financial industry that they worked so hard and so long to protect against market forces. The overwhelming danger for the paper money system is that the point in time when this switch in policy is still possible will be missed or that the courage and determination needed to make this switch will be lacking. Those who bet on the survival of the paper money system in the face of the present dislocations apparently do so in the belief of almost superhuman judgment and fortitude on the part of a few decision makers in politics.

Finding Perspective

It can be argued that the paper money system was saved once before. At the end of the 1970s, concerns over ever-rising inflation and doubts about the survival of a complete paper money system were at a peak. Under then-chairman Paul Volcker, the U.S. Federal Reserve tightened liquidity drastically and allowed high real interest rates to put the brakes on further monetary expansion. Inflation and inflation expectations were crushed, the economy was put through the most severe recession at the time since the 1930s, and confidence in the paper dollar was restored. Paper money was given another lease of life, but monetary aggregates were soon allowed to expand again and indeed expand quite healthily. After all, nobody wanted to really return to a system of hard money.

Over the subsequent two and a half decades, ongoing money creation predominantly lifted the prices of equities, bonds, and real estate, which was conveniently interpreted as a sign of economic health, while consumer price inflation was less pronounced, thus projecting a false image of monetary stability. As this book has shown, economic dislocations still accumulated and they have now reached proportions that dwarf anything the system had to deal with at the end of the 1970s.

Debt levels and overall financial leverage are multiples of what they were in 1979. When confidence in paper money begins to erode seriously this time around, it will be an infinitely more herculean task to restore it, while the political will to take the necessary pain of large-scale deleveraging, of high real interest rates, of defaults and deflation, is not only smaller than in 1979, but it also appears to be all but non-existent. The events surrounding the collapse of Lehman in 2008 have exposed not only the fragility of a financial system that has grown, thanks to a 30-year diet of new fiat money and cheap credit, to unmanageable proportions, but also the unwillingness to accept its radical downsizing through market forces. From today's vantage point, Volcker's policy was a short-term aberration on the paper money system's innate course toward ultimate collapse. It has postponed the inevitable, but it won't prevent it.

Future Considerations

Whenever confidence in paper money erodes, the public takes measures to protect itself from the fallout as well as possible. This process has already commenced but will probably intensify in coming years. We should see a persistent trend toward investment in more tangible assets, in assets the supply of which cannot be expanded easily, such as hard and soft commodities, certain forms of real estate, forestry, and arable land. But of particular interest will undoubtedly be the precious metals, gold and silver, which are the most essential self-defense assets in any paper money crisis. At the same time the public will try to reduce economic exposure to the government and to the banking sector, both of which have in the decades of the paper money–induced credit boom become the dominant issuers in fixed income markets, and to which insurance companies, pension funds, and other investors consequently have substantial exposure. Government bonds and bank bonds are going to come under pressure. The public will also reduce bank deposits, and try to minimize their holdings of paper money. This will, of course, undermine the financial position of states and banks even further. As we have seen, the system cannot cope with higher real rates or wider risk premiums. This in turn will provoke additional money creation by the central banks (quantitative easing) in order to provide funding for banks and state, and to sustain the image of solvency. However, this will necessarily only intensify the public's concerns about the loss in purchasing power of the monetary unit.

In all paper money crises, the public returned to the eternal forms of money—to gold and silver, and in particular to gold. It will not be any different in this crisis. At the time of writing, gold has already been in a 10-year bull market, although on an inflation-adjusted basis it is still below its previous high reached in 1980 and this despite the fact that a policy of paper money stabilization, as we just concluded, would today be much more challenging than it was 30 years ago. The remonetization of gold should continue.

It is sometimes maintained that holding gold is not a sensible investment strategy because gold does not offer a steady return. It does not pay interest or dividends. Indeed holding gold is a "negative carry trade," because the investor in gold has to pay for storage and insurance. But this is entirely beside the point. Gold is not an investment good; it is money. It is the oldest and most consistently used form of money throughout human civilization. As we have seen, there are good reasons for this, and they are as valid today as they were a thousand years ago.

People often struggle to understand how something can be a monetary asset if it is not being used presently by the public for everyday transactions. It is true that even at an advanced stage of paper money decline and at elevated inflation rates, the public often continues to use the established paper money. Only at a later stage of paper money collapse will it be replaced for these purposes with something else, usually commodity money. But even before that happens, gold already is a monetary asset. It is such not by governmental decree, of course, but—and this is much more important—by the voluntary and spontaneous use as such by the public.

We have seen early in this investigation that we have demand for a monetary asset in order to hold some of our wealth in the form of readily exercisable purchasing power. When paper money loses its purchasing power, it may retain its "instant exercizability" for whatever purchasing power it still has as it may still be accepted widely when trading goods and services, but as it does not keep its purchasing power, the public has increasing demand for other monetary assets in addition to the established paper money. These cannot be investment goods, such as equities or debt claims, and they must be monetary assets that can still be turned fairly easily into spendable cash but that importantly retain their spending power better than paper money does. These monetary assets are gold and silver, with gold still the preferred choice. Gold is a purer monetary asset. It is also an industrial commodity but less so than silver. It is also scarcer and has historically been more important as money. When confidence in paper money erodes, when inflation rises and more and more paper money is being injected, getting hold of paper cash for everyday transactions is not a challenge. Paper money is literally "a dime a dozen." But having a proper monetary asset, something that—unlike a stock or a bond or a bank deposit—is not simultaneously somebody else's liability and something that—unlike paper money—cannot be created by the state at the stroke of a pen, will be urgently desired by a growing number of people.

Here is another way of looking at this. At any moment, all our personal wealth can be divided into three categories: consumption goods, investment goods, and money. In a stable economic environment, our demand for money may be fairly low, and we may use our portfolio of investment goods to retain spending power for the future. This situation changes at the end of an artificial, paper money–induced credit boom when the prices of most investment goods have been lifted to levels that are difficult to justify with economic fundamentals. The money producers accelerate money production further in an attempt to avoid, or at least postpone, the inevitable correction but, as we have seen, this strategy will deliver quickly diminishing returns. The public will increasingly be concerned about the sustainability of high asset prices and artificially low yields as well as the survival of many banks. In such an environment it makes sense to remain on the sidelines and keep exposure to investment goods fairly low, in particular to debt claims, and to hold the monetary asset instead, as this gives one the flexibility to reenter the investment goods market at a more opportune time. However, as more and more paper money is being printed in order to avoid a correction of current economic structures and prices, this demand for money does not go into paper money but into money proper—gold.

It should be stressed again that gold is not a monetary asset because the state or the economists recommend it as a monetary asset. Quite

to the contrary, governments and most economists today are advocates
of paper money. Gold is money because it is uniquely qualified as a
monetary asset, and because it has a long history as money. These are
the reasons why people again and again—freely, voluntarily, and spontaneously—choose it as money. Gold is the least corrosive of all metals.
It does not decay. It is indestructible. It is perfectly divisible. Its value
is easily ascertainable. It is sufficiently scarce without being too rare. It
has an unparalleled history as money. It is global. It is cosmopolitan.
It is apolitical. And as we have seen, its almost fixed supply makes it
an ideal form of money.

Could mankind at some stage come across a better form of money?
Theoretically, yes, but no alternative is in sight. And paper money is
certainly not it.

Summary

At this point, we conclude our excursion into the future of the present
system. It has not been the main goal of this book to provide investment recommendations or detailed forecasts about current events but
to explain, on a fundamental and conceptual level, why the present
monetary system is not only suboptimal but unsustainable. When the
present crisis morphs into a full paper money crisis, many people will
ask how this could have happened. Many will try to identify specific
policy mistakes or turning points at which things went wrong. This is
a superfluous exercise.

As we have shown conceptually, paper money systems are inherently unstable. They must, over time, progressively destabilize the
economy and ultimately lead to economic disintegration and chaos.
Even if some policy intervention, such as the one by the Federal
Reserve under chairman Volcker in 1979, should extend the life of the
present system once more—something I consider exceedingly unlikely
as just explained—it would only mean that the inevitable demise of the
system had been postponed. An even bigger crisis could safely be
expected in the not too distant future.

But, as has been shown, there are no valid reasons to artificially
prolong this system's lifespan. We have seen that paper money is not

only not inevitable or necessary, it has no advantages over inflexible commodity money. It has, however, many disadvantages. All the reasons frequently cited for why a paper money system can be made to be superior to commodity money have been exposed as fallacies.

A collapse of the paper money system will, of course, be a momentous event. It will create many losers and a few winners. A transfer in wealth of historic proportions will occur. However, paper money collapse does not mean the end of capitalism. Quite to the contrary, capitalism, properly understood as a system built entirely on private property and voluntary, nonaggressive exchange between independent property owners, requires for its smooth operation apolitical and hard commodity money. The money of the free market has always been gold or silver. As we have seen, a complete paper money system is never the outcome of the market but always the result of politics. A paper money system is a system of continuous market intervention, in which interest rates and credit availability are the result of administrative decisions, not of market forces, and in which the banks and large parts of the financial industry cannot be free enterprises but must end up under the tutelage of the state. The wealth-enhancing powers of the free market will be set free to spectacular effect once territorial monopoly money issued under the control of state agencies—a striking anachronism in today's world of an increasingly global division of labor—is replaced with international, apolitical, and hard commodity money. The sooner we transition—even if in a painful process—to this new system, the better.

Neither does a collapse of the paper money system mean the end of civilization as we know it. Decades of constant paper money injections, of artificially low rates and high asset prices, have created an illusion of prosperity, but that does not mean that all our wealth is illusionary. Great advances have been made in the efficient use of resources, technological progress has been phenomenal, and the international division of labor has expanded and intensified. Real prosperity and economic progress will always be the result of entrepreneurial initiative, of innovation and creativity, of voluntary saving and capital accumulation, all guided by unimpeded price formation in uninhibited markets, and not by paper money creation, artificially low interest rates, and artificially high asset prices.

Epilogue

A Return to Commodity Money

E verywhere we look, signs point toward the inevitability of a complete currency disaster. While this outcome is extremely likely, it is not, in the strict sense of the word, inevitable. In the history of the U.S. dollar and British pound, the authorities have returned their respective currency repeatedly from being "off gold" back to commodity money. There is no practical reason why this couldn't be done today. The obstacles are mainly ideological, not factual.

One sometimes hears the view that there is not enough gold around to resurrect the gold standard. This statement has no basis in fact. It has been shown that, within reasonable limits, any amount of gold is sufficient to function as money. No economy operates better or worse because of the available amount of money. The notional amount of currency that is to be backed by gold and the quantity of gold held by the financial authorities or the public at large naturally determine what the new exchange-relationship between the two should be. It is true that if gold were chosen today as the monetary asset of the United States, the gold price would have to be adjusted upward, or the purchasing power of the dollar in terms of gold downward. This, however, is simply a single administrative act, a currency reform that establishes a new relationship between dollar and gold. How much gold one U.S. dollar represents is immaterial. The important point is that the dollar would again be a form of commodity money and that its supply would be inflexible.[1]

It also appears possible that not all forms of fiat money and money substitutes that have been issued in recent decades would instantly be backed by gold. Many existing bank deposits might continue as uncovered fiduciary media. They would persist for some time as a legacy of the previous system. But reserve money and physical cash would again be backed by an inflexible commodity. This would already severely restrict the banks' ability to conduct further fractional-reserve banking. It is then a question of the specific design of the new monetary order to what extent ongoing fractional-reserve banking would be allowed. There can be no doubt that the most stable system would be a 100 percent gold standard, in which banks cannot create fiduciary media at all and in which all forms of money represent claims to gold. Even if this were the ultimate goal of the currency reform, some bank deposits from previous periods could still be allowed to remain uncovered while banks would be prohibited from issuing new uncovered deposits. If such a restriction on fractional-reserve banking were not to be enacted, then the state should in any case abandon all measures by which it supports and encourages these banking practices and socializes their risks. The disastrous and misguided idea of state-sponsored "cheap credit" has to be abandoned completely. The state has to exit, once and for all, the sphere of money and banking. Personally, this would be my preferred solution. I do not think that fractional-reserve banking should be outlawed by the state. The practice can correctly be called a Ponzi scheme, but in a free society people should still be allowed to join such schemes. As long as the fallout from this practice is not being socialized through central banking and other support mechanisms by the state, we should trust voluntary cooperation on free markets to properly guide and restrict this activity. But whatever the specific features of the new monetary order are going to be, the allegation that a return to commodity money is impossible because we lack sufficient supply of a suitable commodity is nonsense.

The probability that monetary authorities will take this route at any time in the near future is minuscule. The state derives substantial benefits from the money franchise, and so does the financial industry. Deflating the bloated credit structure will also be seen as politically too risky. But more importantly, large sections of the public today embrace a strong and interventionist state. They consider the government a magic cure-all and the answer to everything. Given the theoretical analysis in this book and the consistently devastating historical record of state paper money, it is remarkable that those who advocate commodity money today are either marginalized as slightly eccentric or made to extensively explain their strange and atavistic-sounding proposals while the public readily accepts a system of book entry money in which the state can create money without limit. The global financial crisis that commenced in 2007 offers a case in point. The crisis constitutes a thorough and illustrative indictment of the alliance of state and financial industry, of a system of expanding state paper money and government-supported fractional-reserve banking. Yet, the political class and the media managed to put the blame on capitalism and on greedy bankers. The result has been and will continue to be yet more money printing, more debt, more privileged treatment of banks and more government intervention in the economy. Given the interests of the political establishment, the views of the mainstream media, the vested interests of the financial industry, and the statist zeitgeist, a timely return to hard money can almost be ruled out. Sadly, the monetary breakdown seems inevitable.

But what will come after the paper money collapse? Nobody knows what will follow immediately but at some point mankind must and will return to inflexible commodity money. My hope is not so much that the policy establishment will suddenly see the light and embrace a gold standard. I think this is in any case unlikely. I also do not think we should wish for the soft solution of some gold-linked monetary system administered and managed again by the state bureaucracy. I don't think we should wish for the resurrection of the Classical Gold Standard that collapsed in 1914. Although this system was the relatively best international monetary system we have had since the Industrial Revolution, it was still a government-managed, gold-anchored system. My hope is rather that from the ashes of the collapsed paper money system a monetary order arises that is, once again, based on the market's choice of a monetary medium and that is regulated entirely by market forces, by the free, voluntary, and spontaneous interaction of the trading public and not by government dictate. In this system, financial services will be offered by true entrepreneurs, by fully capitalist enterprises, and the state will be completely removed from society's financial sphere. My very strong conviction is that this system will again be based on gold, given gold's unique qualification and its unparalleled standing as the world's eternal money. Over the past 10 years, the market has already begun to remonetize gold. I believe that this will continue. The public has accepted the state's inferior fiat money long enough. Withdrawal of that support and a shift to gold as international money and apolitical money has already commenced. I think it will continue to be the big story in markets and in politics going forward.

Division of labor is crucial for the advance of civilization. An extended division of labor requires decentralized organization via markets. Human cooperation via market exchange in turn requires the existence of private property and a medium of exchange. This medium of exchange must itself be a commodity. For the reasons elaborated here, human society will have demand for a monetary asset of essentially inelastic supply. People will again demand a monetary asset that:

- Is not simultaneously somebody else's liability
- Cannot be created out of thin air by privileged banks to enhance their profits from exaggerated lending activity
- Cannot be created in unlimited quantities by the state in order to generate an artificial economic boom, or to buy votes via debt-financed welfare spending, or to fund wars
- Is not a tool for a "determined government" to create whatever it deems to be the desired level of aggregate spending and overall inflation

- Is not a tool of ongoing economic manipulation and a source of expanding state power

They will once again need a monetary asset that is a tool for exchange on markets, for spontaneous, free, and voluntary interaction of individuals, for human cooperation beyond political borders and for an ever-growing wealth-enhancing division of labor.

Notes

Prologue

1. Ben Bernanke, Remarks before the National Economics Club, Washington, DC, Nov. 21, 2002, http://www.federalreserve.gov/boarddocs/speeches/2002/20021121/default.htm

2. Carmen M. Reinhart, Kenneth S. Rogoff, *This Time Is Different: Eight Centuries of Financial Folly* (Princeton and Oxford: Princeton University Press, 2009), pp. 204–207.

3. Board of Governors of the Federal Reserve System, http://www.federalreserve.gov/releases/h8/Current/

4. Federal Reserve Statistical Release H.6 Money Stock Measures, http://www.federalreserve.gov/releases/h6/hist/

5. Federal Reserve Bank of St. Louis, http://fraser.stlouisfed.org/publications/ERP/page/7254/download/46604/7254_ERP.pdf

6. Carmen M. Reinhart, Kenneth S. Rogoff, *This Time Is Different: Eight Centuries of Financial Folly*, p. 207.

7. Federal Reserve Bank of St. Louis, *St. Louis Adjusted Monetary Base*, http://research.stlouisfed.org/fred2/data/AMBNS.txt

8. Ludwig von Mises, *Human Action: A Treatise on Economics*, 4th rev. ed. (Irvington-on-Hudson, NY: Foundation for Economic Education, 1998), p. 572.

9. Gordon Tullock, "Paper Money: A Cycle in Cathay." *The Economic History Review*, Vol. *9*, No. 3 (1957), pp. 393–407; Peter Bernholz. *Monetary Regimes and Inflation, History, Economics and Political Relationships* (Cheltenham: Edward Elgar, 2003), pp. 52–63.

10. Peter Bernholz, *Monetary Regimes and Inflation*, p. 8. Bernholz' list does not include Zimbabwe, which made the list with its hyperinflation in 2007–2008. Steve H. Hanke, Alex K. F. Kwok, "On the Measurement of Zimbabwe's Hyperinflation." *Cato Journal*, Vol. *29*, No. 2 (Spring/Summer 2009).

Chapter 1

1. On this point and on much that follows, see Ludwig von Mises, *Theorie des Geldes und der Umlaufsmittel*, 2nd, improved ed. (Munich and Leipzig: von Duncker and Humblot, 1924), pp. 1–3.

2. Hans-Hermann Hoppe, *A Theory of Socialism and Capitalism* (Auburn, AL: Ludwig von Mises Institute, 2007), p. 2.

3. Carl Menger, *Grundsaetze der Volkswirtschaftslehre* (Vienna: Wilhelm Braumueller, 1871), pp. 250–260.

4. Hans-Hermann Hoppe, "Banking, Nation States, and International Politics: A Sociological Reconstruction of the Present Economic Order" in idem., *The Economics and Ethics of Private Property: Studies in Political Economy and Philosophy*, 2nd ed. (Auburn, AL: Ludwig von Mises Institute, 2006), pp. 77–78.

5. The first economist, to my knowledge, who elaborates this point clearly was Carl Menger, an Austrian economist and founder of the Austrian School of Economics, in his 1871 book, *Grundsaetze der Volkswirtschaftslehre*. See in particular pp. 253–255.

6. Joerg Guido Huelsmann, *The Ethics of Money Production* (Auburn, AL: Ludwig von Mises Institute; 2008), pp. 29–33.

7. Menger, *Grundsaetze der Volkswirtschaftslehre*, pp. 250–260.

8. Murray N. Rothbard, "The Case for a 100 Per Cent Gold Dollar" in Leland B. Yeager (ed.), *In Search of a Monetary Constitution* (Cambridge, MA: Harvard University Press, 1962), p. 99.

9. Ludwig von Mises, *Human Action*, p. 421.

10. Ibid.

11. Those who are hostile to the concept of commodity money sometimes try to undermine it by constructing extreme examples. What if there were only one gram of gold in the world? Would that also constitute the optimal quantity? The answer is, of course, no, it would not. A commodity that is that rare is not suitable as money. If gold had been this scarce, no society would have used it as monetary asset. But this is hypothetical. Gold is not that rare. What if gold could suddenly be produced in laboratories and its supply therefore easily expanded? In that case, gold would lose its unique qualification as money. The public would then probably choose a different commodity. But if a commodity is neither extremely scarce nor extremely abundant, and if its physical qualities make it suitable as a medium of exchange, such as durability, homogeneity, and divisibility, once this commodity has been chosen as a medium of exchange, any quantity of it can deliver all the services that money ever can deliver. A society derives no advantage or disadvantage from whether its supply of gold is such that the price of good "p" comes to 1/5th of an ounce of gold, 1/10th of an ounce of gold, or 1/20th of an ounce of gold. The benefit of using gold as a medium of exchange is the same in each scenario. This is what the statement that any amount of the monetary asset is optimal means.

12. Ludwig von Mises, *Human Action,* pp. 246–250.

13. See Chapter 5.

14. See Chapter 6.

15. Ludwig von Mises, *Human Action,* pp. 433–435.

16. Friedrich August von Hayek, *Denationalisation of Money: The Argument Refined* (London: Institute of Economic Affairs, 1990 (1976)).

17. Idem., *Geldtheorie und Konjunkturtheorie* (Vienna/Leipzig: Hoelder-Pichler-Tempsky AG, 1929).

18. Idem., *Prices and Production* (first published 1931; reprint. New York: Augustus M. Kelley, 1967).

19. Guilio M. Gallarotti, *The Anatomy of an International Monetary Regime: The Classical Gold Standard, 1880–1914* (New York and Oxford: Oxford University Press; 1995). For a good and concise description of the Classical Gold Standard, see John Laughland, *The Tainted Source: The Undemocratic Origins of the European Idea* (London: Warner Books, 1998; previously published by Little, Brown and Company, 1997), pp. 225–231.

20. Ibid., p. 236

21. Friedrich August von Hayek, *Denationalisation of Money,* pp. 109 and 130–131.

22. For a critique of Hayek's proposal from a Misesian point of view, see Murray N. Rothbard, "The Case for a Genuine Gold Dollar," idem., *The Logic of*

Action: One (London: Edward Elgar, 1997), pp. 366–370 (reprinted from Llewellyn H. Rockwell, Jr., ed. *The Gold Standard: An Austrian Perspective,* Lexington, MA: D.C. Heath, 1985); Bettina Bien Greaves and Percy L. Greaves Jr., "On Private Paper Money," Letter to the Editor of the *Wall Street Journal,* August 23, 1977, reprinted in Percy L. Greaves, ed., *On the Manipulation of Money and Credit* (New York: Free Market Books, 1978), pp. 275–279.

Chapter 2

1. Federal Reserve Statistical Release G.17 Industrial Production and Capacity Utilization, http://www.federalreserve.gov/RELEASES/g17/table1_2.htm

2. Federal Reserve Statistical Release H.6 Money Stock Measure, http://www.federalreserve.gov/releases/h6/hist/

3. Ibid.

4. The U.S. Consumer Price Index is calculated by the Bureau of Labor Statistics and is based on a 1982 base of 100. http://www.bls.gov/cpi/ For easy access to the BLS' historical data, see

   http://inflationdata.com/inflation/Consumer_Price_Index/HistoricalCPI.aspx

   Or you can use the following CPI calculator:

   http://www.usinflationcalculator.com

5. For a detailed description of the money creation process through fractional-reserve banking, see Jesus Huerta de Soto, *Money, Bank Credit and Economic Cycles* (Auburn, AL: Ludwig von Mises Institute, 2006), pp. 167–263.

6. Ludwig von Mises, *Human Action,* p. 433.

7. For a property rights discussion of fractional reserve banking, see Hans-Hermann Hoppe, Joerg Guido Huelsmann, Walter Block, "Against Fiduciary Media," reprinted in Hans-Hermann Hoppe, *The Economics and Ethics of Private Property,* 2nd ed., pp. 205–254.

8. Ellis T. Powell, *The Evolution of the Money Market 1385–1915* (London: Frank Cass & Co., 1966), p. 60.

9. http://www.uniset.ca/other/css/9ER1002.html; also quoted by Murray N. Rothbard *The Mystery of Banking* (Auburn, AL: Ludwig von Mises Institute, 2008), p. 92, and Ellis T. Powell, *The Evolution of the Money Market 1385–1915,* p. 73, footnote 2. To this day Lord Cottenham's ruling exasperates critics of fractional-reserve banking as the extent of the discretionary powers it bestows on the banker appears to them to be extensive. However, Lord Cottenham's specific conclusion that ownership of money changes hands is for the economist the inevitable consequence of the fact that interest is being paid.

10. I am grateful to David Goldstone for pointing this out.

11. Joerg Guido Huelsmann, *The Ethics of Money Production*, p. 30.

12. Tim Congdon, *Central Banking in a Free Society* (London: Institute of Economic Affairs, 2009), pp. 180–181.

13. Vera C. Smith, *The Rationale of Central Banking and the Free Banking Alternative*, Reprint. (Indianapolis: Liberty Press, 1990), pp. 11–12.

14. Murray N. Rothbard, *Classical Economics: An Austrian Perspective on the History of Economic Thought, Volume II* (Cheltenham, UK: Edward Elgar, 1995, reprinted 1999), p. 159.

15. Richard Cantillon, *Essay on the Nature of Commerce in General/Essai sur la Nature du Commerce en General* (New Brunswick, NJ: Transaction Publishers; 2001), translated by Henry Higgs, pp. 5–130.

16. Friedrich August von Hayek, "Richard Cantillon (c. 1680–1734)" in idem., *The Trend of Economic Thinking*, Volume 3 of The Collected Works of F. A. Hayek, edited by W. W. Bartley III and Stephen Kresge (London: Routledge, 1991), pp. 245–294; Murray N. Rothbard, *Economic Thought before Adam Smith* (Cheltenham, UK: Edward Elgar, 1995), pp. 343–362.

17. Niall Ferguson, *The Ascent of Money: A Financial History of the World* (London: Penguin Books, 2009), p. 139.

18. Mark Skousen, *The 100 Percent Gold Standard: Economics of a Pure Money Commodity* (Lanham, MD: University Press of America, 1980), p. 45.

19. Murray N. Rothbard, *A History of Money and Banking in the United States: The Colonial Era to World War II* (Auburn, AL: Ludwig von Mises Institute, 2005), pp. 51–56; Peter Bernholz, *Monetary Regimes and Inflation*, pp. 45–47.

20. M. Rothbard, *A History of Money and Banking in United States*, pp. 59–62.

21. Quoted from Lester J. Cappon (Ed.), *The Adams-Jefferson Letters* (Chapel Hill, NC, and London: The University of North Carolina Press, 1959, 1987), pp. 538–539.

22. Mark Skousen, *The 100 Percent Gold Standard*, pp. 42–50.

23. Murray N. Rothbard, *Classical Economics*, pp. 157–274.

24. Ludwig von Mises, *Theorie des Geldes und der Umlaufsmittel*.

25. Idem., *Geldwertstabilisierung und Konjunkturpolitik* (Jena: Verlag von Gustav Fischer, 1928), translated in Percy L. Greaves, ed., Ludwig von Mises, *On the Manipulation of Money and Credit* (New York: Free Market Books, 1978).

26. Roger W. Garrison, "The Austrian Theory: A Summary" in Richard M. Ebeling (ed.), *The Austrian Theory of the Trade Cycle and Other Essays* (Auburn, AL: The Ludwig von Mises Institute, 1996), p. 112.

27. Quoted from Elgin Groseclose, *America's Money Machine: The Story of the Federal Reserve* (Auburn, AL: Ludwig von Mises Institute, 2009), p. 59.

28. Ibid.

29. Ibid.

30. Milton Friedman/Anna Jacobson Schwartz, *A Monetary History of the United States, 1867–1960* (Princeton: University Press, 1963; ninth paperback printing, 1993), p. 192.

31. Ibid.

32. Ibid., p. 191

33. For further background on the history of the U.S. Federal Reserve System, see Murray N. Rothbard, *The Case against the Fed* (Auburn, AL: Ludwig von Mises Institute, 1994), pp. 70–145.

34. Milton Friedman/Anna Jacobson Schwartz, *A Monetary History of the United States, 1867–1960*, p. 16.

35. Murray N. Rothbard, *America's Great Depression*, 5th ed. (Auburn, AL: Ludwig von Mises Institute, 2000).

36. F.A. Hayek published his first English book, *Prices and Production,* in 1931, and Hayek's colleague at the London School of Economics, Professor Lionel Robbins, published his book *The Great Depression* (London: Macmillan & Co., 1934) in 1934.

37. Peter Bernholz, *Monetary Regimes and Inflation*, pp. 21–24.

38. Tim Congdon, *Central Banking in a Free Society*, p. 143.

39. Federal Reserve Statistical Release H.6 Money Stock Measures, http://www.federalreserve.gov/releases/h6/hist/h6hist1.htm

40. Ben Bernanke, Remarks before the National Economics Club, Washington, DC, Nov. 21, 2002, http://www.federalreserve.gov/boarddocs/speeches/2002/20021121/default.htm

Chapter 3

1. David Hume, "Of Interest"; Stephen Copley, Andrew Edgar (eds.), *Selected Essays* (Oxford: University Press, 2008), p. 177 –188, in particular p. 181.

Chapter 4

1. Ludwig von Mises, *Human Action*, pp. 259–264, 490–493.

2. Ibid., p. 524.

3. George Reisman, *Capitalism: A Treatise on Economics* (Laguna Hills, CA: TJS Books, 1998), p. 55.

4. Ibid., pp. 483–490; Mises improves the important theory on interest developed by Eugen von Boehm-Bawerk; see Eugen von Boehm-Bawerk *Positive*

Theories des Kapitales (3rd ed., Innsbruck: Verlag der Wagnerschen Universitaets-Buchhandlung, 1909), pp. 426–453; for a short and excellent summary of these theories, see also Joerg Guido Huelsmann *Mises: The Last Knight of Liberalism* (Auburn, AL: Mises Institute, 2007), pp. 773–779; also: George Reisman, *Capitalism,* pp. 55–56.

5. Ludwig von Mises, *Human Action,* p. 526.

6. Ibid., pp. 526–537.

7. It would be more correct to say that low interest rates indicate that the public is happy to see resources allocated to uses where they are at greater distance to immediate consumption. This way, the statement includes investments in long lasting consumption goods, that only expend their use-value over a longer period. The obvious example is houses. Low interest rates encourage investment in productive capacity and in long lasting consumption goods. For ease of presentation, the analysis will focus on productive investment only. The results are, for the purposes of this investigation, the same if we included real estate.

8. Carl Menger, *Grundsaetze der Volkswirtschaftslehre.*

9. Eugen von Boehm-Bawerk, *Positive Theories des Kapitales.*

10. Ludwig von Mises, *Theorie des Geldes und der Umlaufsmittel.* Further elaborations on Mises' business cycle theory include: Ludwig von Mises, *Human Action: A Treatise on Economics,* pp. 538–586; idem., *Geldwertstabilisierung und Konjunkturpolitik;* and Murray N. Rothbard, *America's Great Depression,* pp. 3–36. Friedrich August von Hayek further elaborated on and expanded the theory. Friedrich August von Hayek *Geldtheorie und Konjunkturtheorie;* idem., *Prices and Production.* For a detailed modern restatement see Jesus Huerta de Soto, *Money, Bank Credit, and Economic Cycles,* chapter 5 and 6.

11. Ben Bernanke: Remarks before the National Economics Club, Washington, DC, Nov. 21, 2002, http://www.federalreserve.gov/boarddocs/speeches/2002/20021121/default.htm

Chapter 5

1. Peter Bernholz, *Monetary Regimes and Inflation,* pp. 3–5.

2. Ibid., p. 8.

3. Roy W. Jastram, *The Golden Constant: The English and American Experience 1560–2007,* with additional material by Jill Leyland (Cheltenham, UK: Edward Elgar, 2009), pp. 221–222.

4. Ibid.

5. Howard S. Katz, *The Paper Aristocracy* (New York: Books in Focus, 1976), p. 24; Roy W. Jastram, *The Golden Constant,* pp. 143–149.

6. Murray N. Rothbard, *Classical Economics*, pp. 159–161; Vera C. Smith, *The Rationale of Central Banking and the Free Banking Alternative*, pp. 14–18.

7. Roy W. Jastram, *The Golden Constant*, p. 112.

8. Peter Bernholz, *Monetary Regimes and Inflation*, pp. 21–30.

9. Milton Friedman/Anna Jacobson Schwartz, *A Monetary History of the United States, 1867–1960*, p. 93.

10. Statistics Bureau of Japan, http://www.rateinflation.com/consumer-price-index/japan-historical-cpi.php?form=jpncpi

11. Milton Friedman/Anna Jacobson Schwartz, *A Monetary History of the United States, 1867–1960*, p. 15; see also: Jesus Huerta de Soto, *Money, Bank Credit and Economic Cycles*, p. 341.

12. Milton Friedman/Anna Jacobson Schwartz, *A Monetary History of the United States, 1867–1960*, p. 91.

13. Hans-Hermann Hoppe, "Theory of Employment, Money, Interest, and the Capitalist Process: The Misesian Case Against Keynes" in idem., *The Economics and Ethics of Private Property: Studies in Political Economy and Philosophy*, pp. 145–146.

Chapter 6

1. On this point and on much that follows in this paragraph, see Ludwig von Mises, *Geldwertstabilisierung und Konjunkturpolitik*, in particular chapters 1 and 4, pp. 18–23; translated in Percy L. Greaves, ed., Ludwig von Mises, *On the Manipulation of Money and Credit*, pp. 83–107.

Chapter 7

1. Joerg Guido Huelsmann, *The Ethics of Money Production*, pp. 29–33.

2. For this entire paragraph, see Gordon Tullock, "Paper Money: A Cycle in Cathay," pp. 393–407; Tullock uses different Westernized names for the Chinese dynasties from the ones we decided to use. He uses Southern Sung for Southern Song and Chin for Jin, and he calls the Yuan Dynasty the Mongols.

3. Ibid.

4. Murray N. Rothbard, *A History of Money and Banking in the United States*, pp. 51–56; Peter Bernholz, *Monetary Regimes and Inflation*, pp. 45–47.

5. Murray N. Rothbard, *A History of Money and Banking in the United States*, p. 54.

6. Vera C. Smith, *The Rationale of Central Banking*, pp. 11–12.

7. Murray N. Rothbard, *Classical Economics*, p. 159.

8. Niall Ferguson, *The Ascent of Money*, p. 139.

9. Ibid., pp. 139–158; see also Friedrich August von Hayek, "First Paper Money in Eighteenth-Century France," *The Trend of Economic Thinking*, pp. 155–163.

10. M. Rothbard, *A History of Money and Banking in United States*, pp. 59–62.

11. The paper notes carried the inscriptions "The law punishes the counterfeiter by death" and "The nation rewards the denunciator." John Laughland, *The Tainted Source*, p. 212; Vera C. Smith, *The Rationale of Central Banking and the Free Banking Alternative*, pp. 28–29.

12. Peter Bernholz, *Monetary Regimes and Inflation*, p. 8; Steve H. Hanke, Alex K. F. Kwok, *On the Measurement of Zimbabwe's Hyperinflation*.

13. Murray N. Rothbard, *Classical Economics*, pp. 159–161; Vera C. Smith, *The Rationale of Central Banking and the Free Banking Alternative*, pp. 14–18.

14. Vera C. Smith, *The Rationale of Central Banking and the Free Banking Alternative*, pp. 44–45; M. Rothbard, *A History of Money and Banking in United States*, pp. 72–90.

15. M. Rothbard, *A History of Money and Banking in United States*, pp. 122–159.

16. Ibid., pp. 151–159.

17. Roy W. Jastram, *The Golden Constant*, p. 17; see also Gulio M. Gallarotti, *The Anatomy of an International Monetary Regime: The Classical Gold Standard, 1880–1914*.

18. For a historian's account of these events, see Adam Ferguson, *When Money Dies* (London: Old Street Publishing, 2010/1975).

19. Peter Bernholz, *Monetary Regimes and Inflation*, p. 8.

20. Carmen M. Reinhart, Kenneth S. Rogoff, *This Time Is Different: Eight Centuries of Financial Folly*, p. 112.

21. Milton Friedman/Anna Jacobson Schwartz, *A Monetary History of the United States, 1867–1960*, pp. 461–493.

22. Quoted from John Laughland, *The Tainted Source*, p. 41.

23. Carmen M. Reinhart, Kenneth S. Rogoff, *This Time Is Different: Eight Centuries of Financial Folly*, pp. 204–206.

Chapter 8

1. Hans-Hermann Hoppe, *Democracy—The God That Failed: The Economics and Politics of Monarchy, Democracy and Natural Order* (New Brunswick, NJ: Transaction Publishers, 2005), p. 45.

2. Ibid., pp. 55–60.

3. Ludwig von Mises, *Human Action*, pp. 224–228.

4. United States Department of Labor, Bureau of Labor Statistics; National Employment Matrix; Occupation Report, http://data.bls.gov:8080/oep/servlet/oep.nioem.servlet.ActionServlet

Chapter 9

1. Ludwig von Mises, *The Ultimate Foundation of Economic Science: An Essay on Method* (Princeton, NJ: D. van Nostrand Co.; 1962), pp. 80–83.

2. Ludwig von Mises, *Human Action*, pp. 198–199.

3. Murray N. Rothbard, *America's Great Depression*, pp. 8–19.

4. Ludwig von Mises, *The Ultimate Foundation of Economic Science: An Essay on Method*, p. 83.

5. Friedrich August von Hayek, *The Counter-Revolution of Science: Studies on the Abuse of Reason*, 2nd ed. (Indianapolis: Liberty Press, 1979), in particular chapter 6, pp. 93–110.

6. Quoted from Henry Hazlitt, *The Failure of the "New Economics,"* reprinted (Auburn, AL: Ludwig von Mises Institute; 2007), p. 277.

7. We have implicitly dealt with all the key theoretical arguments of Monetarism already in our theoretical analysis here and have refuted all of them, including Friedman's reasoning for the state's supposedly preferable role in supplying a medium of exchange. In particular in: Milton Friedman, *A Program for Monetary Stability* (New York: Fordham University Press, 1992), pp. 4–9. There is no reason to dwell on them here.

8. Quoted from Roger W. Garrison, "Is Milton Friedman a Keynesian?" in Mark Skousen (ed.), *Dissent on Keynes* (New York, Westport, London: Praeger, 1992), p. 132.

9. Ibid., p. 145 (note 2).

10. "Sound money . . . was devised as an instrument for the protection of civil liberties against despotic inroads on the part of governments. Ideologically it belongs in the same class with political constitutions and bills of rights" (Ludwig von Mises), quoted from John Laughland, *The Tainted Source*, p. 214.

11. Milton Friedman, *A Program for Monetary Stability*, pp. 66–76.

12. Irving Fisher, *100% Money* (New York: Adelphi, 1935).

13. Milton Friedman/Anna Jacobson Schwartz, *A Monetary History of the United States, 1867–1960*, pp. 299–419.

14. See Ben Bernanke's speech in honor of Milton Friedman on the occasion of his ninetieth birthday, http://www.federalreserve.gov/BOARDDOCS/SPEECHES/2002/20021108/default.htm

15. "Between 1996 and 2006 (the year when prices peaked), the cumulative real price increase [in U.S. house prices] was about 92 percent—more than three times the 27 percent cumulative increase from 1890 to 1996!" Carmen M. Reinhart, Kenneth S. Rogoff, *This Time Is Different*, p. 207.

16. Friedrich August von Hayek, "The Paradox of Saving," *Economica*, vol. *11*, May 1931, reprinted in *The Collected Works of F. A. Hayek*, Volume 9 (London: Routledge: 1995), pp. 74–120.

17. Ludwig von Mises, *Geldwertstabilisierung und Konjunkturpolitik*, p. 1.

18. Ben S. Bernanke, *The Global Savings Glut and the US Current Account Deficit* (Federal Reserve Board, Washington DC, March 2005), http://www .federalreserve.gov/boarddocs/speeches/2005/200503102/

19. For example: Martin Wolf, *Fixing Global Finance: How to Curb Financial Crises in the 21st Century* (New Haven and London: Yale University Press, 2009).

20. Ludwig von Mises, *Human Action*, p. 435 (n.), p. 450.

Chapter 10

1. Ibid., p. 572.

2. Federal Reserve Statistical Release G.17 Industrial Production and Capacity Utilization, http://www.federalreserve.gov/RELEASES/g17/table1_2.htm

3. Milton Friedman/Anna Jacobson Schwartz, *A Monetary History of the United States, 1867–1960*, p. 4, chart 1; Federal Reserve Statistical Release H.6 Money Stock Measures, http://www.federalreserve.gov/releases/h6/hist/

4. Milton Friedman/Anna Jacobson Schwartz, *A Monetary History of the United States, 1867–1960*, p. 4, chart 1; Federal Reserve Statistical Release H.6 Money Stock Measures, http://www.federalreserve.gov/releases/h6/hist/

5. Federal Reserve Bank of St. Louis, *St. Louis Adjusted Monetary Base*, http:// research.stlouisfed.org/fred2/data/AMBNS.txt

6. Bud Conrad, *Profiting from the World's Economic Crisis* (Hoboken, NJ: John Wiley and Sons; 2010), p. 118.

7. From 1970 to 2009, the U.S. government absorbed on average 18 percent of the country's GDP in revenue while, on average, producing outlays of close to 21 percent. Congress of the United States, Congressional Budget Office, *The Budget and Economic Outlook: Fiscal Years 2010–2020*, January 2010, p. XIII, www.cob.gov, http://www.cbo.gov/ftpdocs/108xx/doc10871/ BudgetOutlook2010_Jan.cfm

8. Investor, writer, and entrepreneur Doug Casey has contemplated the possibility of the Fed entering the retail banking business. As a libertarian, Mr.

Casey comes to an equally devastating assessment of this process as the present study.

9. Gordon Tullock, "Paper Money: A Cycle in Cathay," p. 397–398.

Epilogue

1. For proposals for an "organized" return to a gold standard see Murray N. Rothbard *The Mystery of Banking*, pp. 261–268; Jesus Huerta de Soto *Money, Bank Credit, and Economic Cycles*, chapter 9.

About the Author

Detlev S. Schlichter is a writer and Austrian School economist. He had a 19-year career in international financial markets as a trader and investment manager. He worked at J. P. Morgan, Merrill Lynch, and Western Asset Management. He resigned from a senior position as portfolio manager in 2009 to focus exclusively on his first book, *Paper Money Collapse*. Detlev lives with his wife and three children in Hampstead, London.

Index